DATE		

BAKER & TAYLOR BOOKS

Even the Birds Don't Sound the Same Here

American University Studies

Series XI
Anthropology and Sociology

Vol. 28

PETER LANG
New York • Bern • Frankfurt am Main • Paris

Robert Proudfoot

Even the Birds Don't Sound the Same Here

The Laotian Refugees' Search for Heart in American Culture

PETER LANG
New York · Bern · Frankfurt am Main · Paris

Library of Congress Cataloging-in-Publication Data

Proudfoot, Robert.
  Even the birds don't sound the same here : the
Laotian refugees' search for heart in American culture /
Robert Proudfoot.
    p. cm. — (American university studies. Series XI,
Anthropology and sociology ; vol. 28)
      Bibliography: p.
      1. Laotian Americans—Cultural assimilation.
2. Refugees—United States. 3. United States—
Emigration and immigration. 4. Laos-Emigration and
immigration. I. Title. II. Series: American university
studies. Series XI. Anthropology/sociology ; vol. 28.
E184.L25P76   1990   305.8'9591—dc20   88-39607
ISBN 0-8204-0841-7   CIP
ISSN 0740-0497

CIP-Titelaufnahme der Deutschen Bibliothek

Proudfoot, Robert:
Even the birds don't sound the same here : the
Laotian refugees' search for heart in American
culture / Robert Proudfoot. — New York; Bern;
Frankfurt am Main; Paris: Lang, 1990.
  (American University Studies: Ser. 11,
  Anthropology and Sociology; Vol. 28)
  ISBN 0-8204-0841-7

NE: American University Studies / 11

© Peter Lang Publishing, Inc., New York 1990

Printed by Weihert-Druck GmbH, Darmstadt, West Germany

TO :

Maria, in fulfillment of a promise; Steven, Richard, Peter and Barbara, for their unqualified friendship and support; and the Laotians who became my teachers and friends.

Table of Contents

PREFACE

Wishing both to create a buffer zone between
Thailand and Vietnam and to cut the supply
lines between North and South Vietnam, the
American airmen, like the Thai generals of the
nineteenth century, are systematically de-
stroying the capacity of a large part of Laos to
support human life. It remains to be seen if a
scorched earth policy of this sort can continue to
be implemented by a democratic nation such as
the United States, even under the cover of a
'hidden war.' The Thai war destruction of Laos
in 1827-1832 is more than a black spot in Asian
history; the image of Thailand has been stained
by it forever. When the facts come to light and
become more widely known, the Laotian case,
1945-1970, will probably become, along with
the war in Vietnam, one of the most appalling
'success stories' of Western enterprise in Asia--
something a 'silent majority', feeling guilty of
complicity and cowardice, will certainly not like
to discuss.[1]

There has been a rapid influx of Laotian refugees into the
United States of America since 1978. According to the United
States Department of Immigration Report to Congress (1981),
in the years immediately following 1975, the Southeast Asian
population that entered the United States was over ninety
percent Vietnamese.[2] Much of our initial data, many of our

language and vocational education theories, our cultural response, and most of our informal social awareness of and relationships with the refugee population are based upon experience with the Vietnamese. The major body of immediately available information is the direct result of a carefully orchestrated governmental and media portrait cultivated throughout the duration of the Southeast Asian War.[3]

More recently, large groups of refugees have arrived from Laos and Kampuchea. The origins of these peoples are found in distinctly different cultural traditions than the Vietnamese, though they have shared a similar historical relationship with the United States. In particular, they hold in common the American Southeast Asian War, 1945-1975. In the period since 1978, about three hundred and fifty thousand Laotian refugees have been admitted to the United States. The principal categories of refugees from Laos are the Lao Lum (lowland Lao), or ethnic Lao which include farmers, rural villagers from the lowlands, former government bureaucrats, soldiers of the Lao faction that supported the United States, and Lao Sung (the Hmong and Mien tribespeople) from the highlands. Some ethnic Chinese and Vietnamese traders have left the urban areas of Laos and applied for refugee status.[4] The majority of the Laotian refugees arrived between 1977 and 1981. As of December 1983, the United States Department of State officially estimated that forty-four thousand Laotian refugees had residence in the Pacific Northwest and California.[5]

Both the refugee population and its new host country (the United States of America) were active participants in the Southeast Asian War. The arrival of refugees, first the Vietnamese in large numbers and then the Laotians and Kampucheans, has been the source of a number of perceptual and cultural adjustments and problems for the Asian and American populations alike. Among the difficulties the Laotian population has encountered include:

-overcoming and coping with loss of culture, status and
support groups;
-adjusting to a new culture, language, and values system;
-understanding that Vietnamese, Laotians, and
Kampucheans speak different languages and, for
the most part, cannot translate or interpret for each
other or each other's experiences;
-discovering and then accepting the fact that the American
population was deceived by four different Presidents
concerning the nature and extent of the "hidden war" in
Laos;
-recognizing and acting upon the racism present in North
American society and as it is expressed through
institutional and individual interaction;
-providing adequate funding, realistic and meaningful
educational opportunities for the Laotians during the
period of economic recession and inflation; and
-developing an understanding of the experiences of the
returning veterans who fought in the Southeast Asian
War.

. . .They are here, we know very little about
them...we are bumbling in the dark in an attempt to
understand them and then to reach them as they deal
with the seemingly insurmountable problems they
face when they arrive here.   There's alot of
unproductive fear, mistrust, frustration aimed at the
Laotians by Americans who perceive them as the
enemy, as Vietnamese, as lazy, as stupid. . .[6]

Fieldwork Interview, Refugee Health Service
Provider, 1982

. . .I don't like having to teach gooks, wherever they came from. Hell, I spent thirteen months in Nam. I want to forget it. I don't want to look at those ugly faces in class every day. I've cleaned that experience over there from my mind.[7]

Fieldwork Interview, Community College Teacher of
Refugees, 1982

We passed through our fifth long year of struggle against the U.S. aggressors, and we have scored a certain number of successes. We rely on ourselves and have the support of the progressive peoples of the world, including those of the United States. . . We have had lots of trouble and difficulty but despite our long struggle, little is known about our situation outside of Laos. . .[8]

Interview of Phao Phimphachanh, Laotian Leader,
by Noam Chomsky, 1970

. . .to speak to each other as human beings...the reaching out of the hand is important...this is what my people need the most. . . Once they know they are welcome then they will have the strength to face whatever else. . .[9]

Fieldwork Interview, Laotian Refugee Community
Leader, 1982

To date, no comprehensive study exists that records the initial stages of acculturation of the Laotian refugees. Nevertheless, more than 350,000 Laotian refugees are now residing in the United States as a direct result of American involvement in Southeast Asia from 1954-1975. In light of this influx of refugees, the year 1980 witnessed the passage of the historic Refugee Act, designed by Congress to meet the needs of arriving refugees and to establish support systems for complete cultural integration. This legislation established the broad legal basis for refugee admission into the United States. Up to three years of basic economic subsidy, provisions for learning English and obtaining extensive vocational training were guaranteed by this document.

With the change of governments in 1980, a reassessment of the 1980 Refugee Act was initiated by the Reagan Administration. This resulted in new national policies in regard to refugees that initially cut benefits in half and limited funding to eighteen months from date-of-entry. The focus changed from the learning of English and North American cultural orientation to the new priorities of job preparedness, learning the language of the "work place," and rapid assimilation into the work force. May of 1982 signalled the advent of these new policies as programs and services were cut back even more and as new systems initiated by the Reagan Administration were implemented. The "hope" that most Laotians expressed for uniting families, finding a home, and reconstructing their lives post-war would soon turn into a nightmare of serving hamburgers at fast food joints, washing dishes and cleaning the homes of the upper classes.

Due to a deep economic recession in the United States, accompanied by escalating inflation, funding cuts for all public service projects were executed on regional and local levels. On the regional level, it was demonstrated that the severity of funding reductions had a tremendous impact on all aspects of the acculturation experience.[10] This factor, combined with Reagan Administration changes in public policies, was one of the key elements which may determine whether long term acculturation is probable or possible. In addition, the changing economic situation created new pressures for the American public, thus weakening its relationship with and acceptance of the refugee population.[11] These developments have contributed to additional stress on the community level and generated additional hostilities toward the refugees by frustrated Americans.

Numerous educators and anthropologists have observed that public education as employed in the past often alienates immigrant and minority peoples from their own cultures. This has often created attitudes among minorities that are not conducive to rapid acculturation (Hezel, 1975; Ramauri, 1973; Freire, 1976; Kozol, 1976; Spaulding, 1976; Zeigler, 1980).

The American public has had little or no preparation for the influx of Laotian refugees. The war on Laos and the extent of American involvement was a well-kept secret from the American people.[12] It has come to be identified as the "hidden war" (Chomsky and Zinn, 1972; Ellsberg, 1972; Burchett, 1970; Branfman, 1973). Few Americans have studied Laotian culture and there is much confusion as citizens attempt to understand where the Laotian refugees have come from and how to relate to them.

Americans have only recently begun to look beyond the confusion and disillusionment of the post-Southeast Asian war period. People have begun to raise questions concerning the government's attempt to manage information as opposed to the Congress' and the public's right to know. They have also raised questions related to the issue of whether a war need be declared by Congress for it to be recognized as a war.[13] Simultaneously, apologists have begun to rewrite the factual history of the Southeast Asian war in favor of the U.S. Government. Most recently, these issues have been brought to the forefront of the media and juxtaposed with new and similar involvement throughout Latin America by the Reagan and Bush Administrations.

CHAPTER I

Ravaged Lands, Ravaged Cultures

If there is any one country that may be described as the geographic heart of Southeast Asia, it is Laos. Laos has common frontiers with virtually every country in the area...even if we were not interested in the fate of the Lao people, the defense of Laos would be a strategic necessity because ultimately, the fate of all Southeast Asia, and our own security may hinge on it...[1]

Senator Thomas J. Dodd, May 1962

I want to make it clear to the American people and to the world, that all we want in Laos is peace, not war-- a truly neutral government, not a Cold War pawn... the test of a truly neutral country is whether one side or another dominates it and uses it. . . [2]

President J. F. Kennedy, March 1962

We desire nothing more in Laos than to see a return to the Geneva Agreements and the withdrawal of North Vietnamese troops, leaving the Lao to settle their own differences in a peaceful manner. . .[3]

President Richard Nixon, March 1970

2

> In the eyes of United States imperialism, Laos is to
> serve the American plans for the encirclement of, and
> attack on the socialist camp, the D.R.V.N. and China
> in the first place, and for checking and sabotaging the
> national liberation movements in Indochina and
> Southeast Asia. From D. Eisenhower and J. F.
> Dulles to J. F. Kennedy and Lyndon B. Johnson, the
> American leaders have always considered Laos a key
> position in U.S. global strategy. . .4
>
> Phoumi Vongvichit, Laotian Historian,
> 1969

For the greater part of the last thirty years, the United States
has conducted a bitter campaign against the civilian population
of Laos, first by war and then by economic isolation.5 The tiny
country of Laos, bounded on the east by Vietnam, on the south
by Kampuchea, on the southeast and southwest by Thailand, on
the northwest by Burma, and on the north by the province of
Yunnan, China, occupies a strategic position in Southeast Asia
and in global dynamics. Since the end of World War II, this
arena has been a focus of American manipulation and
interference which has ultimately led to the widespread
devastation of the social, environmental, political, and
economic structures.6

The question of United States involvement in Laos is well
documented. The role and the official interpretation of the
record of American involvement raises many unanswered
questions. According to the Committee of Concerned Asian
Scholars, in each case of the series of Indochinese crises, the
President of the United States consistently refused to relate to
the American public the full truth concerning American
involvement.7 According to Mirsky and Stonefield in
America's Asia: Dissenting Essays on Asian-American

Relations, "O.S.S. operatives made initial contact with the anti-Japanese resistance movement in 1945" and activity increased until 1968 when "American planes destroyed every village in parts of Sam Neua province." In addition, from the period 1946 to 1963, Laos was the recipient of more American dollars per capita than any other country in Southeast Asia.[8] Eventually the pro-American faction, represented by the Royal Lao Army, would be the only foreign army totally supported by American taxpayers. The conclusion of the Committee of Concerned Asian Scholars was that "...the result, time and time again, has been the distortion of reality, the escalation of rhetoric, intensification of secrecy, circumvention of Congress, manipulation of the press, and hoodwinking of the public [by American Presidents]..."[9]

After the debacle, it has come to light that for over a decade, the United States Central Intelligence Agency (C.I.A.) waged a secret war with a secret army in Laos. The operation was so clandestine that American operatives in Laos kept much of their activity a secret from even the pro-American faction. The same cloud of secrecy had initially extended to communications between the President and Congress, as was revealed when Senator Symington testified during congressional hearings on the hidden war, saying "...not only was it without approval of Congress, but literally without its knowledge, including me, on a sub-committee supposed to be the regulating committee."[10] That it ceased to be a secret war was due ultimately to its size and its failure to accomplish its goals.

Like many Third World peoples during World War II, the Laotians developed a resistance movement to free themselves from colonialism. In this case it was against the French, an ally of the United States. The French had been in complete control of Laos since late 1893 when the Scott-Pavie talks between the colonial powers, Britain and France, established mutual boundaries for their Southeast Asian colonies. The French imposed a colonial administration on Laos and collected heavy taxes, including a capitation tax. French was taught as the official language in the few schools that existed. According to Vongvichit (1969), during the nearly ninety years of French domination over Laos, more than ninety-five percent of the people remained illiterate, and there were no books or newspapers published in the national language. For the whole of Laos the people had "no freedom of assembly, no right to stage demonstrations, or hold political gatherings."11 In addition, there were no elections and no voting rights. Vongvichit cites over twenty different instances of rebellion by Laotians that were suppressed during the French occupation. On October 12, 1945, a coalition of Laotian groups proclaimed their independence and adopted a constitution. Mirsky and Stonefield indicate that Prince Souphanouvong, leader of one of the factions, appealed to the United States for assistance with achieving independence. Purportedly O.S.S. agents admonished the French while reminding them of Roosevelt's anti-colonial sentiments. At the same time, Souphanouvong elicited support from the newly proclaimed Vietnamese Republic headed by Ho Chi Minh. This period signalled the birth of the Pathet Lao (Lao National Movement).12 The Provisional Lao Government denounced all treaties with France, deposed the King, and began to unite the whole of Laos which had historically been ruled by regional governments with loose and shifting alignments.

The French returned in force after the withdrawal of the Japanese after October 1945. The Lao Issara (Lao Provisional Government) fled to Bangkok where they set up a government in exile.13 The King of Vientiane and Luang Prabang, siding with the French, merged with the royalty of the kingdom of the south and the French recognized them as a constitutional monarchy and included them in the French Union. Thus, the northern aristocrats, educated and trained by the French, secured power. This set the stage for American involvement and further support for the French. By 1953, with the help of (then) Cambodian and Vietnamese liberation movements, the Pathet Lao under Souphanouvong claimed to be the only government representing the Lao people. The United States government without much difficulty, convinced the French to withdraw and to recognize the Vientiane faction as the legitimate leader of the Lao.[14] Bitter civil war ensued between internal groups and the faction supported by the French and the United States. According to Vongvichit, the United States had supplied the French with almost twenty-five million dollars worth of military aid between 1950 and 1953 to consolidate the French position and defeat the Pathet Lao. The French were unable to suppress the Lao Independence Movement. By 1954, the Pathet Lao were invited to the Geneva Agreement Conferences, which recognized the sovereignty and independence of Laos and that sanctioned the establishment of a neutral government of National Union.[15] History would prove this neutral position to be short-lived.

> Geneva 1954 was a lost opportunity for peace as far as Laos was concerned. American determination to maintain in its eyes a stable, well-armed, "non-communist" regime outfitted with foreign advisers, together with the resolution that no political considerations should be allowed to endanger this regime, precluded neutralization of the country and national recognition of the Pathet Lao. . .[16]

The American presence in Laos in the 1950's must be examined as a part of a larger framework of events which includes the Cold War, the policy of "containment," and the "Asia Doctrine." The years immediately following World War II were characterized by mutual hostility and suspicion between the United States and the Soviet Union. After the communist victory in 1949, official relations between the United States and China were similarly strained. American policy generally viewed China as a puppet of the Soviet Union. This same narrow status was extended to communist or socialist movements in Southeast Asia. American fears of a universal threat posed by communist subversion and aggression led to the policy of containment, which sought to restrict the activities of communist nations to spheres of influence already stabilized. The fears of a growing communist block were instrumental in creating an enormous intelligence network to counter the perceived threat. As Allen Dulles noted in 1958, "the National Security Act of 1947 has given Intelligence a more influential position in our government than Intelligence enjoys in any other government of the world."[17]

The policy of containment as espoused by the United States clearly dictated that communist incursions into either neutral or pro-West areas were to be firmly resisted, the means to achieve this were to include covert operations, political and economic sanctions, military aid to friendly third parties, commitment of American troops, and even nuclear "brinkmanship." Within this context, the Asia Doctrine was developed. This doctrine placed America in the role of international policeman of and economic provider and controller for all of "non-communist" Asia. It was based on what has proven to be the erroneous assumption that all of the communist nations were unified in their purposes in opposition to the United States. This role was further complicated by post-war Asian nationalism which struggled against European colonialism. President Franklin D. Roosevelt, commenting on France's activities as a colonial power, observed in 1944, "France has milked it [Indochina] for one hundred years. The people of Indochina are entitled to something better than that."[18]

The insurgent Asian nationalism was often socialist or communist in nature, which put the United States in a awkward position as the post-war superpower. The United States consistently refused to recognize the ideological and functional diversity as well as the political divisions across the spectrum of the communist or socialist nations. In fact, there is still no universally agreed upon definition as to what constitutes a communist or socialist nation. The central question for America became which to support: Asian nationalism, which appeared to be communist or socialist by American definition, or European colonialism? By the time of the Truman Administration, the United States chose the latter, with the justification being opposition to the spread of communist influence. The United States chose to view the various Southeast Asian nationalist movements as puppets of the Soviet Union or China, rather than as the legitimate expression of the Indochinese peoples to be free from foreign oppressors. Self-determination, neutralism, or a moderate stance became impossible for the Laotians as long as the United States maintained this hardline perspective.

Thus the United States embarked on the long road of escalating intervention in Laos by economically supporting a moribund French presence from 1950 until 1954, when the decisive defeat at Dien Bien Phu ousted the French from Indochina, despite a last minute attempt by the United States to save the garrison there. American officials then made the decision to move forward to achieve its objectives in Southeast Asia alone. These objectives, enumerated by the Assistant Secretary of State under President Eisenhower, were "to assist the Lao:

1. in keeping the communists from taking over Laos;

2. in strengthening their association with the "free world"; and

3. in developing and maintaining a stable and independent government willing and able to resist communist aggression and subversion. . ."[19]

8

Control of American efforts to achieve those objectives were secretly assigned to the C.I.A., as the United States was careful to keep a low profile with its involvement in Laos. The C.I.A. soon coordinated the functions of tribal guerrillas, Thai, Royal Lao, Philippine, Korean and South Vietnamese military forces, the United States Agency for International Development (U.S.A.I.D.), American Air Force and Army military missions in Laos, Thailand, and South Vietnam, American embassies in the region, and even the International Voluntary Services Agency (I.V.S.), an organization whose "roots. . . lie in the pacifist religious sects of heartland America."20 In a Metromedia Radio News interview conducted by Dan Blackburn in June 1970, Dr. John H. Hannah, Director of the United States Agency for International Development made the following comments:

> Dan Blackburn: Doctor, how do you respond to complaints that the A.I.D. program is being used as a cover for C.I.A. operations in Laos?

> Dr. Hannah: Well, I have to admit that this is true. This was a decision made back in 1962 and by administrations from then until now. . . I don't like the way that C.I.A. cover, but we have had people that have been associated with the C.I.A. and doing things in Laos that were believed to be in the national interest, but not routine A.I.D. operations. . .21

According to Vongvichit, after signing the Geneva Agreements on Laos, "the U.S. combined its military advisors" P.E.O. [Program Evaluation Office], M.A.A.G. [Military Assistance Advisory Group], P.A.G. [Police Advisory Group], U.S.O.M. [United States Operations Mission]--all under the cloak of the U.S.A.I.D. In turn, the U.S.A.I.D. and the

U.S.I.S. [United States Information Service] worked under the American Embassy. Through these groups, the United States set "a camouflaged apparatus. . ." for control of the administrative, economic, cultural, and military aspects of the Lao government."22 An article in the Revue de Paris, December 1959, stated: "The Americans behave in Laos as in a conquered territory and that the veritable government in Laos is the U.S. Embassy. . ."23 Despite the complexity and the strength of this sophisticated network, the desired objectives were never forthcoming.

During the first decade of American intervention in Laos, it is evident that the United States fully intended to disregard its tacit approval of the Geneva Agreements, and had long range plans to prevent a neutral Lao stance in Southeast Asia. As early as 1954, Richard Nixon, then Vice-President under Eisenhower, called for the United States "to take the risk now by putting our boys in . . ."24 Marek Thee, in Notes of a Witness, refers to the "secret Western understanding" worked out in a seven-point Anglo-American paper in Washington D.C. during 1954 and then signed at a tripartite Anglo-Franco-American conference at the American Embassy in Paris. At that secret conference, Dulles, Mendes-France, and Eden concluded that any Indochinese agreement must:

A. preserve at least the southern part of Vietnam. . . and be unwilling to see the line of responsibility drawn further south than Dong Hoi [near the Eighteenth parallel];

B. not impose on Laos, Cambodia, or retained Vietnam any restrictions materially impairing their capacity to maintain stable non-communist regimes; and especially restrictions impairing their right to maintain adequate forces for their internal security to import arms and to employ foreign advisors;

C. not to contain political provisions which would risk loss of the retained area to communist control.[25]

In addition, S.E.A.T.O. (Southeast Asian Treaty Organization) was instructed to provide the police force for the imposition and enforcement of the provisions the three Western nations agree upon in Paris. Thee concludes that the Paris Agreements were contrary to the provisions agreed upon in Geneva in these areas:

1. The Geneva Agreements provide for a political solution with specific dates for free elections. The secret Paris document stands against any elections that might risk the loss of 'retained areas' to communist control.

2. The secret Paris Agreement leaves unmentioned the necessity of consulting the will of the people of Indochina. Instead, it persists on maintaining a "bridgehead" in Vietnam.

3. Unlike the Geneva Agreements which proposed to neutralize Southeast Asia, the secret Paris Agreements are specifically aimed at converting Southeast Asia into an anticommunist block with "adequate military forces, supplied arms, and free foreign advisors."[26]

In the final analysis, it is apparent that the secret Paris Agreements, not the Geneva Convention Accords of 1954, became the blueprint for American involvement in Laos. Quietly the French withdrew, transferring all of the agencies' functions to the American Mission.

Specifically, under the 1954 Geneva stipulations for Laos, there was to be a general cease-fire, removal of the Viet Minh (North Vietnamese) and most of the French troops, the regrouping of the indigenous Pathet Lao forces to the two

11

northern provinces of Sam Neua and Phong Saly pending a political settlement, and prohibition against the introduction of foreign military personnel or advisers.27 These provisions were intended to protect Laos from the wider Indochinese conflict by insuring its neutrality through the formation of a coalition government free from foreign interference. This last provision, however, presented enormous problems for the attainment of American objectives. Circumvention of the prohibition on foreign advisers was accomplished by the C.I.A. As the former Under-Secretary of State U. Alexis Johnson explained, "Under the Geneva Agreements, we were prohibited from having American personnel in Laos. . .[the] C.I.A... is really the only other instrumentality we have. . ."28

As previously cited, Intelligence had been given the highest priority by the Truman Administration under the National Security Act of 1947, and by the 1950's the C.I.A. was read for operations in Laos. The nature of Laos itself facilitated these covert operations. Few Americans had a clear understanding of its place in Southeast Asian dynamics. It was small, poor, mountainous, and largely inhabited by tribal groups with few ties to the outside world. The comments of an American official in Vientiane, the capitol, provide this evaluation in 1961; "This is the end of nowhere. We can do anything we want here because Washington doesn't seem to know it exists..."29

In post-war Laos, there were three significant political factions: a small group of rightists, supported by urban elites and increasingly by the C.I.A, led by General Phoumi Nosavan, the spectrum of leftists supported by large segments of the rural population and the Viet Minh and led by Prince Souphanouvong; and the neutralists, supported by the Geneva Accords and ostensibly by the United States and led by Prince Souvanna Phouma. Depending upon shifting political alliances, the Soviets and the Chinese would on occasion lend support to the neutralists or the leftists. However, with few exceptions, that aid was minimal in comparison with American aid and involvement.

In accordance with the 1954 Geneva Accords, the neutralist Souvanna Phouma was assured the post of Prime Minister. His primary task was to form a coalition government composed of the three factions. Within ninety days after the 1954 Geneva Convention, he resigned, citing increased foreign intervention as the cause.[30] His attempts to integrate the Pathet Lao into the new government so that it would be representative of the entire Lao population were opposed by the United States. The formation of a neutral, representative government in Laos remained a target for American dollars and American intervention "By merely withholding the monthly payment to the troops," Roger Hillsman remarked, "the United States could create the conditions for toppling any Lao government whose policies it opposed."[31]

For the next several years, with the United States opposed in both policy and objective to a neutral government, the power shifted back and forth from the center to the right, with Souvanna resigning due to rightist opposition to his negotiations with all three factions representative of the Lao population, or with the rightists gaining control and then failing to muster enough support from the Laotian government or from the population to maintain control. This instability was entirely supported by American taxpayer dollars and orchestrated by Americans in defiance of the Geneva Accords. C.I.A. activity in Laos was conducted with the knowledge of successive American Presidents and kept a secret from key members of Congress as well as from the people of the United States.

By 1956, the United States became more blatant in its violation of the Geneva Agreements and established a military mission in Laos under the euphemism of a Program Evaluation Office. This deception was far from covert, as only a year later the State Department listed Laos as a country where "M.A.A.G. personnel are stationed."[32] In 1956, through another shift in alliances, Souvanna Phouma regained power, negotiating once more with the Pathet Lao. Despite interruptions, by 1957 he was able to work out a series of agreements with the Pathet Lao, known as the Vientiane Agreements. With the upcoming elections of 1958 to include the Pathet Lao, American officials became worried about a possible Pathet Lao electoral victory, and hastily developed a crash program named Operation Booster Shot.[33]

This program entailed the implementation of massive social welfare projects designed to sway the opinion of Lao voters. Despite these efforts, a coalition of the Pathet Lao and the moderates won a majority of seats in the National Assembly. Much to the disappointment of American officials, Prince Souphanouvong was elected Chairman of that assembly. Needless to say, the large infusion of dollars had been a total failure. The Lao people's preferences were contrary to American plans for that country. The C.I.A. subsequently organized an opposition group, the Committee for the Defense of National Interests.[34] The United States then cut off aid to the duly elected government which expressed the will of the Lao people. Within two months of the 1958 elections, the government fell. American interests and American plans for that country took precedence, over the will of the Lao people.

At this point, the C.I.A. put all of its energy into the support of General Phoumi Nosavan, but failed to get him appointed Prime Minister.[35] Nosavan remained in the powerful post of Minister of Defense and Veteran Affairs until he was able, with the help of a massive infusion of American dollars and C.I.A. manipulations, to influence the elections of 1960. Contrary to the Geneva Accords, the rules were revised to exclude the Pathet Lao supporters and Souphanouvong, winner of the 1956 elections, was held in "house custody" and disqualified from participating in the 1960 election. As one author pointedly noted:

14

C.I.A. agents clearly participated in the election rigging, with our without the authority of the Ambassador. A foreign service officer flatly told one observer. . . that, prior to the voting, he had seen the C.I.A. distribute bags full of money to village headmen; the inescapable conclusion was that the U.S. had bought votes.36

The C.I.A. further expanded its involvement and influence by supervising the Green Beret teams that conducted the covert training of the Hmong tribespeople in 1959 as the core of the secret army.37 Hmong means "free people" and is the name by which they identify themselves. Because the Hmong were considered intruders by the Lao, having migrated from China in the late eighteenth century, they were ideally suited for the purposes of the C.I.A., whose objective was to create internal divisions within the population. By setting Lao against Lao, American forces could theoretically be kept to the "advisory" level. Through the process of capitalizing on traditional Lao antagonisms, a secret army was formed. This generated a split among the Hmong tribespeople as well, as many of them supported the Pathet Lao. A C.I.A. Chief in Laos declared:

. . .even if the Pathet Lao seize power, which is difficult for it to achieve, the United States of America will remain in Laos, for Meo [Hmong] forces could be used in a lasting way. . .38

General Nosavan, with C.I.A. backing, finally gained power through fraudulent elections. His high style of living, based in part on his monopoly of imports of gold, wines, and spirits, as well as ownership of the biggest opium parlor in Vientiane,39 generated hostility and resentment in a nation whose annual per capita income was one of the lowest in the world: estimated at only sixty-six American dollars.40 One Lao historian commented on the influx of American dollars which saturated the Lao economy and which were controlled by a chosen, pro-American elite:

> The Lao economy is rotten, a victim of a sham prosperity brought about by foreign [American] aid. It has turned Laos into a market for U.S. unsalable goods. It has limited the importation of means of production so as to put a brake on national production and increased the importation of consumer goods, especially luxury articles. . . It has spawned a stratum of valets of the Americans, who together with their masters hold the monopoly of trade. . .[41]

Corruption was widespread, reaching a point in 1961 where the Royal Lao Government bought two million dollars worth of gold with "their" savings: that is savings from the American cash grant program. The government engaged in the re-exporting of petroleum, cement, and other items to Cambodia and Thailand in order to make a profit. Almost no records were kept, and U.S.A.I.D. never audited, indeed did not have audit rights on the use of American taxpayer monies.[42]

The Pathet Lao, on the other hand, were known among the people as generally honest. They had a long record of opposition to colonial exploitation and to French rule. The Pathet Lao organized schools and study groups for the rural peoples, trained medical assistants, introduced improved agricultural practices and promoted Lao culture, and introduced the first adult education programs for minorities in the country's history.[43] Additional reasons for strong Pathet Lao sentiment were based on the fact that Nosavan's corruption greatly inflated prices on the black market, a vital source of goods in Laos. Rural people nevertheless, disliked being forced into hard labor as porters for the Pathet Lao, and some resented the Viet Minh presence in northern Laos. However, the Lao people perceived the Pathet Lao as Lao, not outsiders, as a group that had their general interests at heart. Other groups were often identified with outsiders--the rightists with the Americans and the neutralists with the former French elite.

In the early 1960s, a combination of the previously mentioned points as well as mounting pressures for a neutralist stance within large segments of the army led to a growing crisis for General Nosavan. the Second Battalion, the finest unit in the Royal Lao Army, was thrust into direct conflict with Nosavan. Kong-le, the neutralist commander of the Second Battalion, was slighted when his troops were assigned to "rest" in a series of old shacks on a mud flat outside of Vientiane. Having borne the brunt of the heaviest fighting, Kong-le demanded better treatment and more suitable quarters for his men. Nosavan promised better conditions but never followed through. Expressing utter lack of confidence in General Novasan's leadership, Kong-le carried out a well-planned coup d'etat by seizing Vientiane in a pre-dawn strike while Nosavan and his Cabinet were out of the city.[44] As a neutralist, he called upon Souvanna Phouma to head the government and pursue a course in alignment with the Geneva Accords. Souvanna invited Nosavan to join in a coalition government. The United States formally recognized the coalition upon the recommendation of the American Ambassador.[45]

Parallel to these events, the C.I.A. and the American military missions secretly gave General Nosavan substantial moral and material aid at his base at Savannakhet. This course of action was contrary to the official public posture assumed by the Ambassador. Nosavan's support in Thailand, under pressure from the United States, closed the border, hence preventing the flow of vital commodities into Vientiane. Nosavan, through covert advice from the C.I.A., held off joining the new coalition as he built up his forces and supplies with the intent of retaking control. In furtherance of that objective, the C.I.A. diverted large amounts of supplies meant for Vientiane to Nosavan's camp at Savannakhet.[46]

With blatant disregard for international agreements, Assistant Secretary of State for Far Eastern Affairs Parsons demanded that the coalition government cut off all ties with the Pathet Lao. This demand, clearly contrary to the Geneva Accords which placed great emphasis on a neutral coalition government that included all three factions, again frustrated Lao attempts to solve their problems from within. Souvanna Phouma refused to exclude the Pathet Lao.[47] The Thai-Nosavan blockade of basic supplies, including food, was continued. At that time, when the attempts to conform to the Geneva Accords were thwarted by the United States, Souvanna turned to the Soviets for aid. Not to bypass a golden opportunity, the Soviets responded by air-lifting supplies by way of Hanoi on December 11, 1960.[48]

Only a couple of days later, "with plans drawn up by American advisers," Nosavan moved on Vientiane with his forces.[49] As a result of the battle that followed, hundreds of Lao civilians were killed and Kong-le was forced to retreat. Kong-le had been supported by the police force, segments of the Army, and by urban and rural people constituting a broad coalition of Lao nationalist elements. As he left the Vientiane area, he distributed over ten thousand American-made rifles to the Pathet Lao.[50] Souvanna Phouma expressed his bitterness over the American efforts to destroy the neutral coalition in the following statement: "What I will never forgive the United States for. . . is the fact that they betrayed me and my government. . ."[51] In a thinly masked attempt to cover up its activities in Laos, the United States found another scapegoat when it charged that ". . .the responsibility for the current strife in Laos [rests] squarely upon the U.S.S.R. and its agents."[52]

Ultimately, this activity on the part of the United States pushed the neutralists into a strong partnership with the Pathet Lao, and within months the Pathet Lao took control of the strategic Plain of Jars in the north. In 1961, Nosavan's troops were soundly beaten and the recently elected President Kennedy responded by increasing the ranks of the secret army, which had long been in action. According to General Lansdale, an American counter-insurgency expert, by July 1961,

> About 9,000 Meo [Hmong] tribesmen have been equipped for guerilla operations, which they are now conducting with considerable effectiveness in Communist dominated territory in Laos. . . command control of Meo operations is exercised by the Chief C.I.A. Vientiane with the Advice of Chief M.A.A.G. Laos. The same C.I.A. paramilitary and U.S. military teamwork is in existence for advisory activities. . . and aerial resupply.[53]

The Hmong general, Van Pao, directed the secret army for American advisers. His involvement with the United States ultimately led to a diaspora of Hmong people across the globe.

By 1962, events in Laos took a disastrous turn for the United States and its rightist forces. President Kennedy approved an increase in the secret army from two thousand to eleven thousand.[54] At this time, an additional force composed of Thai, Philippine, Korean, Taiwanese, and Vietnamese mercenaries was combined with the eleven thousand Hmong to allow aggressive undertakings by the United States without committing actual American troops to the secret war. Regardless of this support, Nosavan suffered severe defeats in 1962 which compelled Kennedy to order several thousand American troops, stationed in Thailand, on alert. The Pathet Lao were close to taking control of their own country. Ironically, the extreme reluctance of American allies to support direct intervention, the Congress' fears of escalation of activity, poor leadership, the ineffectiveness of Nosavan's American-supported and American-armed troops, and the ultimate possibility of a Society-American confrontation forced Kennedy to seek a negotiated settlement at the Geneva Conference of 1962.[55]

Marek Thee, as a member of the I.C.C. (International Control Commission), recalls that taking into consideration the distrust among the various parties across the Lao political spectrum during close to twenty years of warfare, "it was astonishing that agreement to form a coalition government was reached so quickly."[56] The Pathet Lao, according to Burchett (1970), were extremely modest in accepting a "parity" role with the rightists in the government. This acceptance of a cease-fire and a new coalition government by the neutralists and the left was the only reason that Nosavan's forces were not subject to complete destruction, a course of action which would have been easier for the Pathet Lao. President Kennedy and the American Embassy supported the neutral coalition only because it saved the remainder of the pro-American forces. Ironically, such a government could have been formed anytime during the preceding years of warfare except for the consistent intervention on the part of the United States. Like the previous Geneva Accords, the period of calm was to be short-lived. Hillsman, in To Move A Nation, quotes Averell Harriman as saying at that time,

We must be sure the break comes between the communists and the neutralists, rather than having the two of them teamed up as they were before. . .[57]

Again, as during the period after the 1954 Geneva Accords, the United States had a hidden agenda. Nothing had changed except the emerging global awareness of the extent of American involvement in the Laotian civil war and its relationship to activities in Vietnam and Kampuchea.

The coalition government, however, never even got off the ground. Nosavan and his troops were in control of the

Vientiane area and ". . .from the very first day it [the new coalition government] was a prisoner of Nosavan's troops and police. . . Nosavan's policemen staffed the ministries. . . to have broken Nosavan's grip on Vientiane at this time would have meant restarting the civil war. . . "58 Souvanna Phouma, involved in class interests, was pleased to see the progressives held in check by the American-backed reaction. Thus, the stage was set for weaning the neutralists away from the Pathet Lao, a fulfillment of Harriman's stated purpose.59 Burchett states that Nosavan's secret instructions to his civil servants staffing the ministries included warnings to obey ". . .only orders from his old administration, on pain of severe punishment if they disobeyed."60

President Kennedy used this period as an opportunity to build up forces in Thailand, escalate involvement with the secret army, and to refinance Nosavan. McCloskey (1972) states that during this period the Congress had the "annual responsibility to provide for the common defense and to fund the standing army." The failure on the part of the President and the C.I.A. to provide pertinent information to the Congress subverted the balance of power between the branches of the federal government as embodied in the American Constitution.61 Furthermore, he states that as a member of Congress,

> I was in Congress for almost two years (from December 1967 until November 1969) before learning that my votes for the various defense appropriation bills included over one billion a year to conduct a war in Laos. How can Congress meet its constitutional responsibilities when most of its members don't know and can't know what they are voting for. . .? 62

The period between the Geneva Accords of 1962 and the American defeat in 1975 was characterized by growing resentment on the part of the Congress with the failure of the President to provide necessary information for a clear understanding of the extent of American involvement, by increasingly large numbers of American citizens swelling the ranks of the anti-war movement, by opposition to the exorbitant costs of this and other ventures in the region, and finally by the C.I.A. acting more and more as an entirely independent agency with few external controls. Recent CIA involvement in Latin America, including some of the same players that were involved in Southeast Asia, lead us to believe that the American public learned very little from the Southeast Asia War while the American Government has only refined strategies and policies first applied during that war.

Pertinent to Laos in this period were the events concerning American involvement in Vietnam. The relative calm in Laos after the 1962 Accords gradually evaporated while the secret war intensified. This intensification was directly related to American interests in and plans for the entire region. Though of course the two were integrally entwined, Laotian internal interests took a back seat to the regional conflict. Any kind of cease-fire in Laos would have hampered American interception efforts along the newly formed Ho Chi Minh Trail that passed through Laos on its way south, supplying Vietnamese resistance forces, and interfering with the American military operations in Vietnamese. Continued support of destabilizing activities in Laos was critical to the success of the United States in the region.[63]

On August 11, 1964, William Bundy of the Kennedy Administration stated that:

> if despite our best efforts, Souvanna on his own, or in response to third country pressures, started to move rapidly toward a conference, we would have a very difficult problem.[64]

Continued economic and military pressures by the United States precluded the possibility of any successful peace talks among the internal factions in Laos. Covert interdiction of the Ho Chi Minh Trail and covert air strikes over the Plain of Jars continued. Noam Chomsky castigates the American press for waiting so long to break these stories, commenting that:

> The media have often feigned a touching regard for lovely little Laos and its 'gentle' folk, even while they were suppressing the abundant evidence of the murderous United States attack on the land and its people. . .[65]

Regarding an article on the war in Laos in the New York Times, Chomsky proceeds to remark that:

> the history is very well sanitized as benefits America's newspaper of record. The U.S. role [in Laos] is completely ignored apart from a few marginal and misleading references. As late as 1975, the New York Times is still pretending the U.S. bombers were striking only North Vietnamese supply trials. . .[66]

As awareness of the American-sponsored destruction of Laos surfaced, the press began first to focus on the refugees and only later on the secret army. Meanwhile, the Van Pao and Nosavan forces, coupled with the United States Air Force, systematically destroyed bridges, factories, hospitals, and civilian population centers. McCloskey quotes a Life Magazine article of April 30, 1970 as stating ". . .from all reports, the wholesale bombing of Pathet Lao areas goes beyond anything the North Vietnamese have experienced."[67] Twenty-one I.V.S. volunteers are cited as having written to President Nixon that

. . .the extensive bombing of civilian areas is particularly vicious. . . refugees told of being forced to live in holes and caves, of having to farm at night, of systematic destruction by U.S. war planes of the human basis for a society. . .[68]

The State Department, however, continued to deny any knowledge of the bombings.

McCloskey further develops the following points concerning the refugee situation in Laos:

1. Reports were in the possession of the U.S. Embassy showing the bombing was clearly the most compelling reason for the refugees leaving their home. . .

2. Some of the refugees had moved because of the direct orders of the Royal Lao Government [rightists], not voluntarily; and transportation was provided by U.S. aircraft. . .

3. It is apparent that cluster bombs and white phosphorous were used against the civilian population of a country against whom the United States had not declared a war. . .the bombing was done under the direction and control of the U.S. Air Force. . .

4. Both the extent of the bombing and the impact on the civilian population of Laos were deliberately concealed by the State Department. . .[69]

A quote by Los Angeles Times reporter Arthur T. Dommen sums up the situation:

There were many reasons for this policy [of secrecy imposed on Laos operations by the Executive branch]. Among them was certainly the desire to avoid possible congressional inquiries into what was going on, and thus possible restrictions on the operations.[70]

Bernard Lassiter, writing in the International Herald Tribune, October 20, 1969, testified to reports that every operation mounted in Laos by Royal Lao forces was directed and controlled by the American establishment there. He stated that ". . .the U.S. flies up to 300 sorties a day against the Pathet Lao. . ."[71] Congressman McCloskey further maintained that

> . . .in July 1969, U.S. planes intensified their attacks against the towns and villages in and around the Plain of Jars, reducing every building down to the humblest bamboo hut to ashes... Incidentally, the code name for this air offensive in Laotian was "Ke-Kheu"-- [Revenge] . . .[72]

The original C.I.A. operatives in Laos who commanded the secret army were an unorthodox breed. Known as "true believers," these staunch Cold Warriors had seen action in World War II, the Korean War, or both. Symbolic of the "true believers" was Tony Poe, who was known to have bribed his Hmong troops to bring in enemy ears at a dollar each. He hung a large plastic bag on his porch and the ears were collected there. Poe also paid ten dollars for a severed head if accompanied by a Pathet Lao Army cap. He was supposed to have stopped these practices when he found out his troops were killing people needlessly for the bounty, but Poe still kept the heads of his most hated foes pickled in jars that lined his bedroom wall.[73] A former American agent in Laos said of Poe, "He's a great guy, who I really respect. But I'm not sure how he can justify the slaughter of the Meo tribe and love them as much as he does."[74]

A 1971 Senate Staff report noted that "these irregular forces have become the cutting edge of the military, leaving the Royal Lao Army as a force primarily devoted to static defense."[75] This same report continued, "the brunt of irregular losses has fallen heavily upon tribal groups such as the Meo, which is one of the reasons why Thai irregulars have been brought in. . ."[76] The secret army was also supplemented by ethnic Lao, Lao Theung, and Mien peoples.

Hmong losses mentioned above were described in 1968 by an I.V.S. volunteer, "Pop" Buell, who was the man most responsible for providing relief supplies to the Hmong warriors and their families, who often became refugees:

> A few days ago I was with Van Pao's officers when they rounded up three hundred fresh Meo recruits. Thirty percent of the kids were fourteen years old or less, and about a dozen were only ten years old. Another thirty percent were between fifteen and sixteen. The rest were thirty-five or older. Where were all the ones in between? I will tell you, they are all dead. . . these little kids. . . looked real neat. . . they were eager. . . they wanted to play Indian themselves. But Vang Pao and I know better. They are too young, and are not trained. In a few weeks ninety percent of them will be killed.[77]

By 1971, thirty-five percent of the Hmong were dead. Many of the casualties were civilians who were forced to leave their homes, largely due to daily American bombing.[78]

The Senate staff report above notes that Thai irregulars were being introduced to cover Hmong losses. In 1970, it was revealed that the C.I.A. was paying five to ten thousand Thai troops in Laos, so Congress passed a law against that. The C.I.A. ignored Congress and kept the Thais on the payroll, with the rationale that they could be considered volunteers in the Royal Lao Army.[79] This was a catalyst for Senator Fulbright, Chairman of the Senate Foreign Relations Committee, to remark:

> This seems to me to be a very low state of affairs for the United States to come to, fighting our wars with [mercenaries]. . . and then giving the impression all over the world that those people are so devoted to our welfare. . . that they [donor nations] have voluntarily sent these people to fight.[80]

Despite such misgivings, 1970 was a low point for the secret army, and more mercenaries were needed due to intense pressure by the Pathet Lao. In one northern village, Long Pot, previous losses of their youth led village elders to refuse American request for more recruits. Air America, the C.I.A. airline that handled guerilla deployment and support, refugee (Hmong family) evacuation from combat zones, as well as other tasks, warned the elders that if no recruits were forthcoming, rice drops might be stopped. None were sent, "so they stopped dropping rice to us."[81] For most tribal groups in Royal Lao or disputed territory, and especially for those groups whose men fought in the secret army, rice drops were often their only means of survival. The relocations of populations due to the war interrupted the planting and harvesting of rice, and for the Hmong, priority had always been given to the growing of opium anyway, as opium is their traditional cash crop. Laos, in the heart of the Golden Triangle, is well known for its high grade heroin.

From several sources it is clear that Air America and hence the C.I.A. was deeply involved in the drug trade in spite of former C.I.A. Director William Colby's assertion that "resolutely refusing to permit Air America aircraft to carry drugs, C.I.A. kept free of contact with the trade. . . "[82] Air

America pilots are recorded as offering different versions. As one admitted,

> We knew we handled a lot of dope, although we didn't do it intentionally. . . some damned Lao general would be the customer. . ., and you had to carry what he wanted you to carry.[83]

It is also well known that Air America aircraft were exempt from the customary border checks other aircraft were subject to, since Thailand and South Vietnam were both American client states, If the Hmong's opium was not marketed, they would have faced financial ruin, an unthinkable prospect for an ally making the secret war so cost effective. Long Cheng, the C.I.A.'s northern Laos covert operations base and Vang Pao's secret army headquarters reportedly sheltered a heroin refinery. Vang Pao was known to have been involved in major international drug deals.[84] In 1970, one author concluded that there

> . . .can be little question that the de facto policy in Laos is to wink, at the very least, at the transportation of opium locally by American quasi-governmental employees. There is further evidence that designated opium shipments are cleared and monitored by the C.I.A... [which would indicate] a major contradiction of American's stated policy on narcotics, as well as a violation of international conventions to which we are party.[85]

In Laos, the secret army, civilian refugees, communication and transportation systems depended almost entirely on air power. As a mountainous, underdeveloped nation, Laos had few roads, and even those were mostly dirt strips that were virtually useless in the rainy season. Any sort of large scale operation, such as the secret war, required massive air support to function. The C.I.A. saw to this vital need by employing the Taiwan-based Air America, Inc. The New York Times described Air America as ". . .an enterprise that is shadowy and vague even by Laotian standards."[86] Most of the flying was done by helicopter or small plane, due to the rugged terrain. The tasks of the pilots usually included food and medicine (soft rice) drops, or weapons, explosives, and ammunition (hard rice) drops, or ferrying American officials and agents from base to base; more dangerous tasks included searching for bands of refugees from allied tribes in combat zones, and picking up or dropping off guerilla counterinsurgent or reconnaissance teams behind enemy lines.[87] Bombing raids also played a part in Air America's diverse activities, though they were normally carried out in conjunction with American Air Force, Navy, and Marine squadrons based in Thailand, South Vietnam, or on the Seventh Fleet.

From 1964 on, bombing played an increasingly large role in American war strategy in Indochina. As has been cited, more American bombs were dropped on Laos from 1965 until 1975 than on the Axis powers in World War II, or more tonnage per capita than any other nation in the history of warfare. Eighty-two percent of that total was dropped between November 1969 and March 1973, and are known collectively as the "Nixon bombings."[88] Bombing on such a scale went far beyond the considerable abilities of Air America, so the C.I.A. co-ordinated Air Force, Navy, and Marine bombing sorties over Laos that reached a peak of some seven hundred sorties a day.[89]

From June 1964 until March 1970, the United States would only admit to flights of "armed reconnaissance" over Laos.[90] The official definition of "armed reconnaissance" is "an attack sortie flown in search of targets of opportunity"; however, in case of a downed plane, American officials felt it best to "continue to insist that we were merely escorting reconnaissance flights. . . "91 American officials claimed to adhere strictly to rules preventing the bombing of civilian villages, but pilots were rewarded for structural damage inflicted, not for sparing civilians.92 At the height of the Nixon bombings in 1969, eighty percent of the ordnance (bombs) at the regional air base at Udorn, Thailand, that was to be used in Laos, was anti-personnel ordnance.93 These bombs and other types of ordnance (mines) are designed to kill and maim people indiscriminately.

One brief description of such ordnance serves to illustrate the damage that was intended by the American government to be visited upon the people of Laos:

> The anti-personnel bombs include the pineapple, which has 250 steel ball bearing pellets into which shoot out horizontally. One planeload carries 1,000 such bombs, which means that one sortie sends 250,000 steel pellets shooting out horizontally over an area the size of four football fields; the guava is an improvement over the pineapple in that it is smaller and its pellets shoot out diagonally; one planeload of guave bombs shoots out 300,000 to 400,000 pellets diagonally so that they will go into holes where the peasants are hiding; the plastic bomb, which breaks into thousands of slivers one-eighth of an inch by one-sixteenth of an inch, will not show up on an x-ray; the fragmentation anti-personnel bombs. . . which break into dozens of jagged fragments, are larger and calculated to do far more damage than the steel ball-bearing pellets. Similarly, flechettes are tiny steel arrows with larger fins on one end which peel off the outer flesh as they enter the body, enlarge the wound, and shred the internal organs. . . Anti-personnel mines differ from the bombs in that they are not dropped with a specific target in mind.

Rather, they are part of an officially designated "area denial" program. Under the Nixon Administration, hundreds of square miles [were] flooded with hundreds of thousands of such tiny mines as the Gravel, Dragontooth, and Button bomblets, in an attempt to make areas under attack uninhabitable for human life. . . Air Force representatives testified that the area denial program had been instituted in [an area inhabited by] over 200,000 people. These mines are camouflaged to look like leaves and animal droppings. . .94

The effects of this bombing on civilians was studied in a report by the United States Information Service in 1970. In one survey, two hundred and fifteen refugees from various parts of the Plain of Jars were interviewed. From those refugees, which represented a cross-section of the hundreds of thousands of refugees in Laos, it was found that ninety-seven percent said they had seen a bombing attack; ninety-five percent said their villages had been bombed; eighty percent of the casualties were civilian, twenty percent were Pathet Lao; seventy-one percent said the United States was responsible for the bombing, seventeen percent said it was the Royal Lao Government; and forty-nine percent said that fear of bombing was the reason they left their homes to become refugees, with only twenty percent giving dislike of the Pathet Lao as the cause.95 However, even after the Untied States had dropped over two million tons of bombs on Laos, the Pathet Lao controlled more territory than they had before the bombing.96

In 1971, the American Embassy in Laos printed a book that stated that the refuges were fleeing from the Pathet Lao, and this was eight months after the above survey was made, a survey that concluded that "the bombing is clearly the most compelling reason for moving."97 The fact is that anti-personnel devices were used against the civilian population of a country with whom the United States was not at war. This led to charges that the bombing was a deliberate policy to destroy the "civilian infrastructure" of the Pathet Lao (i.e., the tribal groups in the areas of conflict).[98] American officials could hardly admit that such was their policy, and as one author reasoned, something else must have been the cause for the enormous number of refugees, because

> Policy says that the United States does not bomb civilians. Policy is true. Therefore refugees could not have been moved on account of the bombing. Because they were not bombed. Because policy says they were not bombed. . .[99]

The historical record clearly indicates that the C.I.A. managed a massive secret war in Laos, that Congressional regulatory bodies were evaded and deceived by the C.I.A., that American Presidents lied to the general public and Congress to cover up C.I.A. activity, and as a result it was the people of Laos that suffered the consequences of the C.I.A.'s murderous policies. By 1973, American involvement in Laos was sharply reduced as yet another coalition government was formed in response to plans for withdrawal of the American military presence in Indochina. The United States shifted its focus to shore up the deteriorating situation in South Vietnam. In December 1975, after the fall of Saigon, the Lao coalition was dissolved, with power going to the new Lao People's Democratic Republic, a socialist government that supported a mixed economy allowing for some private enterprise.[100] To this day some American companies remain in Laos as well as an Embassy staff maintaining "normal" relations.

In the final analysis, the policy the United States pursued was a tragic failure. Despite the fact that seven hundred thousand of the one million people estimated to have inhabited Pathet Lao-occupied sections of Laos became refugees during the war years, the United States did not defeat the resistance. Despite the fact that their life styles were entirely devastated by American bombing, the Laotian people have endured. Branfman notes that great portions of the urban population of Laos were "left relatively unscathed"; rather, "it is the ninety percent who earn their livelihoods by tilling the soil and raising livestock who are the corpses, the soldiers, the refugees..."[101] Ironically, with the exception of the segment of the Hmong who fought in the secret army, a clear majority of those people remained at home to rebuild. They had barely survived the policy of "Let's bomb 'em back to the Stone Age" as advocated by General Curtis Lemay.[102] Most Americans have little or no idea of the horrors that were rained upon the Lao people by the armed forces of the United States of America.

The period from 1975 to 1979, the time after the American withdrawal from Southeast Asia, marks the historical exodus of thousands of Laotians. For the new Lao government, there were the momentous tasks of rebuilding a nation whose ecology, cultures, and economy were decimated as a result of decades of war, and of fostering the developing of a national consciousness and a common language among it's more than sixty-eight ethnic groups. These problems were exacerbated by the fact that over sixty percent of the population was pre-literate; the average annual income per capita was less than sixty-six American dollars; there were unresolved differences of an ideological nature between the former supporters of both the Pathet Lao and those who had sided with the Americans' and there were roving bands of armed, unaligned Hmong guerillas to contend with. Hundreds of thousands of displaced persons became either internal or external refugees.[103]

According to Chomsky, with the withdrawal of the Americans, the survivors of the various hill tribesmen who had worked for the C.I.A. to fight the Lao people were abandoned, as they were no longer of any service to the United States.[104] John Everingham, an Australian journalist, noted that "the incredible bombing had turned more than half of the total area of Laos into a land of charred runs where the people fear the sky..."[105] In 1977, Norman Peagam of the New York Times wrote that on the surface, little seems to have changed in the daily life of Vientiane, though the economy was down, "partly as a result of the total halt in U.S. aid in 1975 and the blockade imposed by neighboring Thailand."[106] He noted further than "crime, drug addiction, and prostitution have been greatly reduced..."[107]

Nayan Chanda, writing for the Far Eastern Economic Review in 1977, reported that Thailand had blocked food, supplies, and even medicine from the International Red Cross from entering Laos.[108] Chanda further explained that the Thai blockade, combined with structural problems resulting from American imperialism and the false Lao economy that was dependent upon it and the American dollar, wrought havoc on the traditional Lao subsistence economy.[109] Chomsky quotes Lao Vice-Foreign Minister Khamphay Boupha as saying:

> The United States has dropped three million tons of bombs--one ton per head- forced 700,000 peasants to abandon their fields; thousands of people were killed and maimed; the unexploded ordnance continues to take its toll. Surely the United States does not show humanitarian concern by refusing to help heal the wounds of war.[110]

In addition, Chomsky noted that the United States has forced Thailand to close the border with Laos.[111]

Chomsky, in Laos: War and Revolution, concludes that by the time the information concerning American involvement in Laos reaches the public, it will be of little help to the "peasants of Laos, rotting in refugee camps, huddling in their caves...[112] Furthermore, the war in Laos has been expensive for Americans only in dollars, and not in American lives, land, or environment. Despite the enormous investment of dollars, military equipment, and the tragic number of civilian casualties, the Pentagon could not record any progress by the end of the war.[113]

The problems of the shortage of essential equipment and money to reconstruct, interference by the United States with attempts by the new government to recover from the war, a huge and unstable internal refugee population, the aforementioned destruction of the ecology and regional infrastructures, massive starvation and disease due to destroyed cropland, the widespread drought of 1977-78 that made food scarce, the Thai blockade of international war relief efforts, and the out-migration of the small professional class prompted thousands of people to leave Laos for other areas where stability might be found. Refugees left for economic, political, ideological, and/or personal reasons. Among those leaving Laos were the members of the present Laotian communities in the State of Oregon. It is their story and their journey I hoped to document and to understand as I departed for my fieldwork in November 1981.

Events related to fieldwork in the United States and Southeast Asia are recorded in the following chapters. In addition, the latter months of 1982 and subsequent trips provided the opportunity to journey to Thailand and Laos as an educational and cross-cultural consultant to provide educational and cultural workshops for personnel working in the Southeast Asian refugee camps. These experiences aided in placing the refugee process in context as I retraced the Lao's journey from their homelands through the various experiential stages involved with resettlement in the United States of America.

The Thai Refugee Camps, 1982

Any analysis of the refugee camp experience is as complex as it is disconcerting. Thailand was the first country of asylum for almost all of the Laotian refugees. Some refugees flew to Paris or London prior to 1975 and requested asylum there. These were mostly diplomats or students, and they compromised only a small percentage of the three to five hundred thousand refugees that eventually left Laos. In context, it is important to consider that while attempting to deal with Laotian refugees streaming in from the north and northeast, simultaneously the Royal Thai government had Vietnamese and Kampuchean refugees crossing its borders in the southeast. Camps sprung up all along the Thai borders with Laos and Kampuchea. In 1975 alone, almost two hundred thousand people entered Thailand seeking asylum.[114] This escalated over the years and Thailand, out of economic and political necessity, reached out to the international community for assistance. It is also important to remember that Thailand was and is a client state of the U.S.A. This has had tremendous bearing on its interactions with Laos and the Lao refugees.

Officially, the Thai Ministry of the Interior was responsible for administering official camps such as Ubon, Nongkhai, Ban Vinay, Hovei Yot, Sob Trang, Chieng Khan, and others.[115] Each of the Lao camps in Thailand was characterized by its own special conditions including population, size, ethnic distribution, and relationship with international agencies. Basic services such as food and shelter, when available, were initially provided by the Thai government.

With the dramatic increase in the refugee population in 1975, the United Nations High Commissioner for Refugees took financial responsibility for the official camps.[116] Additional aid and services were provided by international voluntary agencies. Numbers of other camps, however, were administered by the Thai military and were subject to erratic and questionable administration. The Thai regard refugees as displaced persons with no rights under the law. The United Nations regards them as "refugees" and hence falling under the protection of the Geneva Convention on Refugees of 1967. For the Lao refugees, getting to a United Nations-administered camp was a high priority. The kinds of abuses they were subject to without this protection are clearly defined in the narratives in Chapter II.

During my visit to Thailand, interviews and conversations with refugee camp personnel, administrators, and refugees shed light on the information I had already accumulated during my fieldwork in the United States. A sample of narratives freely given by these individuals are arranged in the following order: Excerpts from interviews with American, Philippine and Thai teachers in the camps, conversations with United Nations High Commission on Refugees and State Department personnel, Thai teachers in Northwest Thailand, and Thai citizens.

Narrative 1

This American teacher/supervisor is a Vietnam veteran in his early thirties. He originated from the Midwest, and after the war became involved with refugee services at home. Later he "signed on" with a voluntary agency, which led to his experience in the refugee camps in Hong Kong and then Thailand.

> The bureaucrats here are full of shit. They lead a comfortable life and that cushions them from reality. Money. . . homes. . . women. . . power. . ., Christ, who wouldn't lose sight of reality! These guys live high, so what's the fate of a few refugees in relation to all that lies in waiting for these guys. They turn their heads. . . they rationalize, they pop another pill and hell. . . they manage to sleep easy between the silk sheets and the brown thighs. I hate to think of what will happen if they ever have to face the reality of what has happened here. . . their part in the process and what continues to happen here. It may certainly plunge them into a bummer they might not

be able to recover from. I fought in Nam, I came back hoping to contribute in some small way to the repairs. . . Well, now I know. . . I don't sleep well. . . but at least I'm not going to wake up somewhere down the line and face it all again. I'm doing that now. . . it isn't easy. I guess that's the price I have to pay for being naive in the first place. Hell, I was eighteen. . . death, war, Vietnam, army, they were all words. I didn't understand their meaning. . . I just wanted to win. Isn't that what we always strove for? Now I understand, but who the hell listens anyway? I'm just another crazy vet.

Narrative 2

This Philippine national was a teacher in her own country and has obtained a Master's degree from an American university. She was involved with the Peace Corps training before her tenure with the international voluntary agencies. In her own words, ". . .partially to avoid the growing domestic problems in the Philippines and partly to gain additional international experience. . ." she accepted a job as a teacher trainer with the Save the Children Federation which, along with the Experiment in International Living, are involved in the refugee camp education process in Thailand. She perceived this as a "career ladder" to a Ph.D. program at a "good American University."

We are here to help these refugees. They couldn't do it alone. When I was in the Peace Corps, I always reminded people to keep a positive attitude. What does it matter now about the "war" as you call it? That's over. Forget it. Most people have forgotten it. . . right now we have to help these people in the camps. That's what we're here for. You can do a lot with your education. . . why focus on the unpleasant? Lift them up. . . you won't do that by raising all of

those unpleasant questions. When they get to your
country they will be OK. . . free again like before
they were refugees, free to be what they want. I
wouldn't have made it so far in life if the United
States had not helped my country. It still helps. . .
that's why we tolerate the refugee camps. They
[refugees] have caused us much trouble. Be
positive... then the refugees will feel positive also.
Anyway, isn't it better to be American than anything
else. . .?

Narrative 3

This interview was conducted with a twenty-two year old
American teacher of English as a Second Language in the
refugee camp at Nong Khai. Hired by a church-sponsored
voluntary agency right after her graduation from college, she
worked three months in the United States before her recruitment
as an "expert" to teach in a refugee program in Thailand which
was struggling to define its role and purpose.

I have a degree and I was an honors student in
college. I also worked in community organization
before and after college. We had a number of
refugees in our community. . . nobody seemed to be
able to deal with the many problems associated with
their being there. I worked indirectly with them; I
wanted to find out just what was the origin of their
adjustment problems. The courts, the welfare
agencies, the schools seemed totally perplexed with
the myriad of problems and had few or no strategies
at all for dealing with the uniqueness of those
problems. The entire refugee scene appeared to be in
utter chaos. . . applying band-aids here and there, but
never touching on the real crux of these problems. I
applied for a job here in the camps and I got it. . .
they figured that because I worked in/with various

aspects of the community that I was prepared or qualified to teach cultural orientation. In all honesty, I, too, thought I was qualified. After all, I am American, I am a fairly sensitive and aware person, and I do have a degree. After being here for a while, I realize that I was not adequately prepared to teach cultural orientation. . . I was not prepared to teach, I hadn't had experience in either areas. When I began to question just what I was doing and what that meant to the well-being of the people we are supposed to be "teaching," I began to freak out. More so, when I went to the supervisors I realized they weren't prepared. A lot of them have come through the Experiment. . . middle class student types who come to the camps to do their fieldwork for international management experience. In a number of cases I found I was more prepared than the individuals who were supposed to be training me. I had at least seen the refugees in the community and was aware of their problems. A lot of these guys have spent their time on campus with "foreign" students. We all know that's a far cry from working with refugees. I don't mean that in a derogatory manner. So, they come over here and associate with middle and upper class Thais. . . barely touching on the refugee experience. In addition, the Consortium doesn't give us much in the way of training. It is truly amazing how few of the people over here are prepared to teach. . . there is a real need for time planning, management, and basic teaching methodology. It really makes you think of how arrogant we are. Now that I am here I can see the camp experience creates a number of problems, additional ones, for the refugee to deal with. I have some real questions about just how much we are doing to help create a sense of dignity and independence for these people. One thing I do know.

. . we are not preparing them to deal with the realities of American life. We are told we can't mention welfare. . . that's totally unrealistic. So, we end up creating artificial situations that don't relate to the past experience of the refugees and may very well be situations that these individuals will never experience in the States. In the long run, its a sort of cultural imperialism. . . we do things in a manner that predisposes the refugee to act and to think in a manner that is convenient for our society. . . regardless of the cost to the human being. Then there is the situation related to the Thai teachers. Even though many of them have been to the States as students, they are not teachers. . . and they sure are not the people who should be teaching <u>American</u> culture. A good number of the Thai teachers really try. . . yet they are faced with a task that is impossible for them to achieve. Try discussing American culture with the Thai, or a great many of the Americans, for a matter of more than five minutes. . . the whole situation works out to this equation: teachers who have not been trained to teach teachers, or in some cases who have never taught and, who have never been schooled in the teaching of American culture, are training Thai teachers who have never taught, who are teaching in a second language a complex process they don't understand to a third group of people who are learning in a second language of experiences very different from their own cultural perceptions. Let me ask you, how valuable do you think this is for the refugees? What is going on? A lot of us work hard here, long days, little pay. I just don't understand why the focus isn't on getting these people out of here... I thought about breaking my contract but I'll finish it. I'm learning a lot. . . maybe I can apply it back in the States. . . whatever. . . It just doesn't

seem like we make a dent in the misery over here. . .
it's really disillusioning. . . certainly not what I
expected. I think a lot about the fact that we seem to
be failing the refugees here and are probably setting
them up for failure in the States.

Narrative 4
The following presentation is an excerpt from a longer
interview which this twenty-three year old Thai teacher asked
me not to put into print in its totality. The concerns of this
man, like most of his Thai peers, focused on the administration
and on teaching as opposed to some of the broader political and
social implications of the refugee process raised by some of his
American peers.

We are trying to find a way to let the administration
here [Panat Nikom] know that we are dissatisfied with
our wages and benefits. There is no job security
here. . . only one cycle at a time. We get an
orientation, but very little on-going training. We
have many needs. . . most of us have never taught
before. I was a university student in the United States
for a year. . . that really doesn't make me an expert
on the U.S., especially since my field of study was
quite different. . . in the sciences. I needed a job. . .
they hired me on the fact that I had lived in the U.S.
and can speak English. This is my first job. I
couldn't work in the U.S. as a student. . . my parents
paid for everything. We now know the Indonesian
teachers are paid more than us, and have more
benefits. Work in the camp isn't easy. . . it can be
depressing. . . I'm very tired at the end of the week.
Some of the teachers here [Thai and American]
thought we should raise a lot of noise over these
issues. However, I think we should carefully write
them down, get everyone to agree, and then present

them as adults. My father has warned me <u>not</u> to disgrace him by causing any trouble with the Americans here. . . he's very sensitive to that. Also, his business could suffer if the wrong people got news of any trouble on my part. . . I have to be cautious, we all have much to think about. American teachers don't seem to understand that we can't act as freely as they do... we have to consider many other people and the family name each time we get involved. It isn't easy. . .

Narrative 5

Characterizing herself as a "late sixties idealist," this thirty year old American woman was involved with the refugee camp programs in Thailand, Hong Kong, and Indonesia since 1978. As a teacher, teacher trainer and, when I met her, a camp monitor for the United Nations High Commission for Refugees-related teaching programs, she has an extensive background in camp-related stages of the refugee process.

We've been over here [Thailand] three years or so. I've seen a great many different types of people. . . both American and Thai. . . this isn't the first time I've been through this discussion. . . the question is where to begin. At first I was really aghast at what I was seeing, experiencing, witnessing all around me. If you think Panat Nikom is bad now, you should have seen it a few years ago. There have been a lot of changes here. . . almost entirely in the physical realm, though, the camp remains the camp. The Vietnamese incarcerated across the road. . . separated from everyone else... had and still have it the worst! Many of the Americans here are so ugly, in the lowest sense of the word. They play tennis after work with the middle class Thai students. . . they live in that "suburban" housing separated from the Thai community, you know, ovens and flush toilets and toll house cookies. . . a little American enclave in the middle of Panat. The Thais that live there are either married to Americans or they have been to the States and identify with the States more than they do with their own country. They dream of going back there... are one step removed from their own people. . . many steps removed from the refugees. . . and not quite "Americans." From the number of Thai teachers I have spoken to, worked with. . . they are much more aware of their situation here than most of the Americans. I need to explain that. A goodly proportion of the American teachers (remind me to comment later on their teaching experience) have come out of the Experiment or other "schools" like that, and they truly don't have a grasp on what's going on over here. Yes, they're schooled in cross-cultural awareness but hell, what does that mean when its all developed from the American perspective?. . .by Americans, for Americans. . . they've never questioned what's going on. . . the political and economic aspects. . . the repression of what's happening over here. . . and what's happening to all of these human beings. They've been trained in the mainline American perspective. . . America is good, the communists are bad. . . the U.S.A. is "saving" these people. . . we're all do-gooders! They believe that. More so, they've never stopped to question why and what they as individuals are doing here. . . they assume what they are doing is right. They have the degrees, they are getting the experience abroad. . . they will be the beneficiaries in the long run. They have to believe what they're doing is right. . . to face the truth would shatter them, most of them. it's easy to fall into the "American Abroad" routine. . . knowing what's right for the refugees, being the interpreters of American culture (only one perspective), being so sure. . . at least from nine till five. The rest of the time is spent in Bangkok whorehouses, living high, collective lucrative per diem expenses, travelling, having hand-made clothes, career-building, playing tennis, playing American abroad. They know so little about themselves. . . their own country, the history and depth of U.S. involvement in Southeast Asia, the economic and political motivations behind that movement. It's a comfortable system for certain Thais and for the Americans abroad. Ironically, most of them have forgotten that this is all a realty of war. Teaching is another question, separate from the fact that I don't find the cultural orientation program realistic or meaningful for the refugee. . . the fact is that most of these people never taught. A great deal has been said about schools of education and teachers but, in the final analysis, there is methodology that is useful. . . effective. . . and can be meaningful, especially for adults. Hell, the refugees are treated like children. . . or not complete adults. . . or culturally inferior. . . whichever way you want to look at it. What's the anthropological term?. . .[ethnocentric]. . . yes, ethnocentric. We know more, we're better, do it our way. . . the right way, "you inferior, primitive people." Hell, it makes me angry. From the top to the bottom that mentality prevails. I now the refugees feel that. It may sound strange, but they do have the full range of human emotions. There is a tremendous need for some sort of teacher training over here. . . real training. . . not how to put together bulletin boards. . . rather, how to make people think, how to stimulate discussion, how to share with the refugees about extremely difficult cultural idiosyncrasies. . . and then work together to make them meaningful as

these humans strive to integrate this knowledge with
their own experience. The system, the way it is set
up, is an obstacle to this process. Inadequate
classrooms, inadequate teachers, young people not
yet adults. . . not yet aware of the problems and
dimensions to adulthood. . . not having worked out
their own life process. . . directing, pressuring adults
to "learn" in a most uncompromising manner. I guess
I could go on for days. . . I hope you are
understanding me. It's only fair to say there are some
good people here... it doesn't seem they last very
long. . . they burn out, burn up. . . get tired of
fighting an inadequate system. . . the lethargy of the
process. . . tired of absorbing the agony of human
beings caught in this camp life. . . tired of being
undermined by the do-gooders. . .lacking a support
system. After a while,. . . for your own sanity. . .
people come and go. . . like lightening bugs in the
night. . . a brief spark of light, a moment of hope.
Things are disrupted a bit, but in the long run, this
process. . . like the darkness. . . prevails. The
system sluggishly moves ahead, even before the spark
has diminished. . . been absorbed. . . forgetting that
moment of uncomfortableness. We are left with few
good teachers.

Narrative 6

At twenty-eight years old, this Thai woman has had
extensive university training as well as political experience in
Thailand. She describes herself as "always having been
opposed to U.S. intervention in Southeast Asia." When I
interviewed her, she was working as a translator/teacher for Lao
refugees in English as a Second Language program in a refugee
camp. As Thai Issan, her immediate ancestors were Laotians
living on the Thai side of the Mekong River.

The story of what has happened in my country and in other Asian countries goes way back. . . before our lifetime and before those our grandparents. . . back to early French and British colonization. It's a long story. . . and volumes could be written about what they labeled Southeast Asia. Our histories do not refer to the Thai, Lao, Vietnamese, Kampucheans, etc., as one big block of states. . . This is a Western concept through which farangs [a derogatory term for Western whites] have misrepresented all of us and done great damage to our cultural identities. I don't need to cover the whole of the colonial period with you. Needless to say, we were all exploited, pitted against each other, drained of resources, and given nothing in return. You must remember that we have seen many generations of this. The West found traitors among our peoples. . . willing to sacrifice identity for money, for position, for power, despite their skin coloring and heritage. They became Westerners in mind, philosophy, and in desire. They often covered that with the trappings of the military or with official positions, using empty words of "saving the people" from one thing or another. Who was to save us from them? It took a long time for many people to realize that we were the only ones who could save ourselves. . . and what was left of our lives and our futures. The last military campaign in Southeast Asia, one basically fought against American imperialism but born in colonialism. . . had a tremendous impact on all of us. The consequences of the physical damage that the American war machines wrought on our lands and our populations were the darkest moments of our recorded histories. I find it difficult to believe that the American people understand the extent of the damage. We have many questions concerning the sanity of a government supposedly "of the people and for the people" that would allow the carnage we were exposed to. I try to believe some form of socialist democracy is preferable to all other systems of government and economics, but we have concluded that either the U.S. has a democratic system and the populace willingly endorsed the horrors of the war or the U.S. doesn't have a democratic system and only a minority create the decisions that determine policy. It is difficult for us to believe in the former because many of us can't accept that so many Americans could be so ignorant of reality. Many of us conclude the latter and that prospect makes the U.S. more dangerous than we might have believed. Many peoples believe that the U.S. is willing supporters of democracy and self-determination. We believed that also. We now know that democracy and self-determination are secondary to the world capitalist profits, not unlike the U.S.S.R., no? We were encouraged by the dissent in the late sixties and seventies, but we are not hearing those voices any longer. From our conversation, I know I have no need to barrage you with statistics... you seem to know the numbers as well as I do. However terrible those numbers reflecting death and destruction may indicate, there is much more... Of course, during the war across Southeast Asia, we were faced daily with the physical confrontation and all that entails. Simultaneously, the U.S. waged a devious war on us. . . one that divided our peoples and pitted them against each other, one that splintered our culture into fragments, one that destroyed our religions. . . our very meaning in life. Even if the United States was willing to help with the reconstruction, which it hasn't, things would never be the same. Today, our farmers still lose legs or lives because of your saturation bombs in the fields; today

our forests and rivers are ruined, today or peoples are
still divided; today the U.S. still imposed economic
sanctions, political oppression, and constant
harassment of our government. All in the name of
fighting communism. So powerful a legislative body
still doesn't understand the difference between
economic and political systems. They seem to view
the world as American and other.

Narrative 7
   A friend and co-worker of the woman in Narrative 6, this
twenty-four year old male was working as a teacher of "cultural
orientation" in the refugee camp at Nong Khai.

My friend has been speaking and has covered many
points I would make. I would be inclined to state
things differently. . . simply because I no longer feel
the hate I felt earlier. There isn't time in our world
for hate. . . it takes away much of the constructive
energy we need to survive. That, however, does not
absolve the United States in my mind, from the
responsibility for the destruction it created.
Certainly, one point that seems to have been given
little attention is the nature of war. You have a very
powerful war-creating mechanism structure that we
are powerless to deal with. It consists not only of the
actual technology. . . the machines of war. . . then,
too, the control of the international banks and a great
deal of the press. In addition, people throughout the
world have been educated through the Westernization
of their sensibilities to believe the U.S. is for self-
determination. Thus you make war in the name of
peace-making? It is difficult to understand why the
Americans do not seem to realize what they do to
other peoples, other lands, other cultures. Your
people brag about your diversity, your freedoms, your

institutions. . . yet you deny others the opportunity to create their own meaningful institutions. In effect. . . you enjoy what you enjoy at the expense of the rest of humanity. I do not hate you personally for this. . . but I will fight against your country's way as long as I live. All humans deserve those freedoms... on their own terms, not on terms dictated by the U.S.A. or by the U.S.S.R. either. You can keep both of those systems as far as I am concerned. Both have created enormous suffering and problems for the world. As mean, as oppressive as the U.S.S.R. is, it does far less to contribute to the misery of Third World people than the U.S. The U.S. has much more power, many more resources, and it is ironfisted. You are free to come here and talk to us. . . but we could never come to your country and state our views. You know that. Many of the intellectuals here suspect there isn't as free an exchange of debate in the U.S.A. . . despite what your Radio Free American broadcasts. If you were to listen to U.S. and to Russian propaganda. . . all you'd have to do is scramble the names here and there and you'd find them both saying about the same thing. We aren't fooled by either of you. We know we are pawns in a much larger game. We want something better than either of you have to offer... and we want a part in the creation of it. Otherwise it will have no meaning to us. Both the U.S. and Russia were born of the West. . . you know very little about us. You view us as inferior human beings... you make war on us for your own selfish reasons. We will survive. . . even if you don't think so. The time may come when you may need us. I hope our people respond with more generosity than you have treated us. I nope they remember that for all of the inhuman treatment you have given other peoples. . . you are still to be considered as human beings. It may be quite the difficult proposition to keep that viewpoint alive. We have suffered too much through your hands to have us believe otherwise.

Narrative 8

This woman, now working for the United States State Department, had along history as a Peach Corps volunteer and then later as a supervisor for Peace Corps volunteers in Thailand. She was candid during her interview and was one of the few State Department people willing to invest some time in the discussion of the refugee situation in Thailand.

> Well, we've experimented a lot with cultural orientation over the past few years... but, I think we're heading in the right direction now. . . people are teaching more realistic things. . . the importance of a job, the way to fill out applications, etc. This way the refugees know how to begin to access the system. I haven't been back in the States for any length of time in the past several years. . . I understand things have changed a bit. . . but when you think about it, a large country like the U.S. have always responded to the plight of the needy. . . with the President's emphasis on volunteerism that has been heightened and brought to international focus. The refugees have to understand they are going to an entirely different world. . . they can't act the way they did in their respective countries. . . in the U.S.A. there are more complex laws, different expectations of the citizens, stricter rules relating to sanitation, far more involved than what most of the refugees are used to. . . let's face it, our technology has created a lifestyle that is more advanced than most Asians experience. . . it's our job to see to it that these unfortunate people are prepared to make the transition from almost primitive conditions and lifestyles to the

most advanced technological societies on the planet. That's a difficult task. . . I'm very proud to be one of the Americans doing my small part in this process... it isn't easy being away from the cultural surroundings you are familiar with. However, it's worth the sacrifice. . . in a few years many of these people, particularly the young, will be like any other American. . . you won't be able to pick them out of a crowd and say, "there's a refugee". . . isn't that great... they have a lot of potentiality and many of them will make it successfully in the U.S. . . granted, they may have to take a job they don't like in the beginning. . . however, that isn't any different from what other refugees have had to experience. . . it's almost a part of American tradition that they go through these stages. . . haven't studies indicated that by the second and third generation all this is forgotten. . . they are already into the mainstream by then. That's what happened to the Italians, the Blacks, Germans and others. . . in the long run, they all enjoy the benefits of being American. I try to get them really psyched up. . . you know, really positive about going to a better, safe, cleaner world. . . no more camps, enough to eat, prospects for their children. They really respond to that. I relate to them on the human level. . . I think they appreciate that kind of involvement.

Narrative 9

A brief conversation with another State Department official, a white male in his late fifties, produced the following statement. He has lived in Thailand or Vietnam for over fifteen years.

We've learned a great deal from the process and the experiment in Southeast Asia. . . it has been a long,

52

difficult road. . . initially we weren't prepared to deal
with the sheer numbers of refugees that crossed into
free Thailand, free Malaysia, and free Indonesia...the
good, positive aspect of this is that we've generated
models that we are beginning to use in Africa. . . and
possibly soon on a limited basis in the Caribbean.
This is extremely difficult work, complex, with
constantly shifting needs, personnel, and political
conditions. I believe we've done a fairly good job
given the circumstances we've had to deal with. One
has to be objective. . . not judgmental and certainly
not political when assessing our role over here.

Narrative 10
This is a part of a conversation with a Thai merchant in
northwest Thailand. Ethnic Chinese in origin, he owns a hotel
and another small business in Chiang Mai.

Oh, we didn't have any war here in Thailand. Many
refugees came here because there was no war here.
We are a peaceful country. We work hard. The U.S.
favors us because of this. We are a country to trust.
The communists would take away my property. We
work hard for this property. No war came here
because of the U.S. Those other countries made bad
mistakes. Our little Lao brothers did not listen to us.
Now they have nothing. They are refugees. Tell me,
what does a refugee have? My sons are alive. They
are healthy, they go to school. I will have
grandchildren some day. This is why I work so hard.
This is why I believe in the U.S.A. The others will
not have this. They were foolish. They listened to
the intellectuals. No one is free. All people are
bound by some things. Birth, then sickness, life
problems, and then one and all die. Is it not better to
be alive than to be dead? The smart stay alive the

best way they can. This is why we call the Lao "little brother". . . they are like children sometimes. They can't see the way we see. . . we help them by giving them work now that they have lost everything, but we can't help them all. This is too bad. You listen to me. I know. If you don't believe me look at my house, my restaurant, my animals. Who has this if they are communist? Do not believe everything you hear. . . let your eyes tell you. You see, I am right. This is a better life. . . not so hard. It is my hope it stays this way for my family.

Narrative 11

A brief statement by a stewardess from Hong Kong who has worked on international flights carrying refugees to the United States follows.

I don't know much about these refugees. . . all I do know is they cause a lot of crime in our city [Hong Kong]. They are many problems. . . both Vietnamese groups are continually fighting each other. You know what they do. . . they "sell" their children to the merchants to work. . . isn't that awful?! Now the authorities are moving all of them away from the city center to a small island that used to be an army base. . . then we won't have to worry about them being around decent people.

Narrative 12

This stewardess had a different perspective than the previous woman. A British national, she was based with an airline in Bangkok. She had made three international flights from Thailand to the Philippines with large groups of refugees in the process of resettlement.

I've found most of the people to be very gentle, very
polite and respectful. I've seen many people get on to
the aircraft for the very first time. We try to relax
them, to make them feel comfortable. There is a
great tension before takeoff and on landing. . .
especially with the old people. You can seem many
of them very, very frightened. A smile or a gentle
touch on the shoulder is very reassuring for these
people. Other times it's really exciting to see people
experiment with new food, the bathrooms, or moving
the seats. On a flight of that nature I learn so much.
I watch faces and they tell me so much. These people
are very brave. They leave their whole world behind.
. . everything they know. . . everything they love. . .
Sometimes I can feel the great emotions they are
experiencing. Only once in a great while have e
really had a problem. Most of the time it's a result of
fear, confusion, or ignorance. As I said, I have
learned so much from these flights. A lot of
personnel won't work these flights. . .

Narrative 13

The following account was part of a series of conversations
with a Laotian refugee hoping to come to the United States
where some of his family and friends had already arrived in the
Seattle area.

I come from District Xieng Khouang. My family
were farmers. . . nice fields, beautiful fields. We had
two houses, one my sister and her husband lived in...
my grandfather built it. . . it was very old, mostly
wood darkened by age. We also grew vegetables and
fruits and we owned buffalo. the village had many
buffalo, ducks, and chickens. My father told us that
once our village was very peaceful. There were many
festivals. . . people were happy. We had rice to sell,

people were always clearing new land and people
prospered. A few years after I was born, I am told
that peaceful life ended. . . the airplanes and the guns
arrived. . . they could be heard from far away. . .
everyone was very frightened. We didn't know what
to do or what we had done to cause this. Many
airplanes flew across the sky. . . some alone. . .
many together. big ones and little ones... all kinds.
Later they bomb our village. . . almost everything
was burned or broken. . . even some airplanes shot
the buffalos. I don't know why they did that. . .
many people were dead. My sister was outside in the
rice field and her legs were blown away. She was a
good sister. . . she worked very hard, was generous
and kind. I take care of her children. . . her husband
is dead too, he was killed later when he was gathering
wood in the forest. Many of my friends came before
us... we stayed with them. I took a new wife. . . my
mother died and my baby brother, too. . . later we
came to Bon Venai and then to Panat Nikom. My
wife and cousins sell the things we sewed. . . we are
still here waiting. . . a long time. I am learning
English for when I come to your country. Maybe
then I can have a farm. . . we will have plenty of
food. . . and our children will grow healthy. See,
very skinny here. . . not enough food. Maybe I will
see you in your country. I want to go to Seattle. . .
there I have friends who say it is a much better life. I
hope for that day.

The preceding statements are a representative sample of
those I was privileged to gather in Thailand. As late as 1983,
with already almost three-quarters of a million Southeast Asian
refugees in the United States, and with greater numbers
dispersed throughout the world, no single individual--from
camp administrators to "cultural orientation" teachers--could

give me an adequate explanation of what was going on in the camps. Despite attempts by American and other international groups to bring some cohesiveness to the situation, each camp, and often individual programs within a given camp operated with a great deal of autonomy. "Experts" will tell you that there exist cohesive curriculums and integrated language and "cultural orientation" components. That is true, to some degree, if one is speaking of the paper process.

First-hand examination and evaluation of these curriculums, programs, and experiences as the refugees were exposed to them and as the Thai teachers attempted to teach Lao refugees about American culture in English (which is a second language for teacher and refugee alike) indicated to this writer/educator that this experience, at its very best, is most confusing for the refugee. It reduced the possibility of transferring anything but the most fundamental of human tasks as the refugee eventually dealt with the reality of living in the United States as opposed to the myths internalized before arrival. The disparity between the simulated "cultural" experience in the camps and the actuality in the United States created ludicrous, if not detrimental contextualizing experiences for the refugee. The situation was further aggravated by the use of poorly trained teachers. I recall sitting in on one classroom session where a Thai teacher, with the greatest sincerity, proceeded to explain that a correspondence school is a place where one learns to correspond--to write. A literal definition right out of Webster's. I witnessed Thai teachers hitting the hands of confused students or shouting an order at people who were unresponsive. I was appalled that Americans in charge of programs would turn their heads to abuses by Thai soldiers and police; "This is the way it is here," I was told. In addition, I saw Thai teachers asking refugees what kind of job they would like in the United States. A long list composed almost exclusively of professional occupations--doctor, lawyer, teacher, etc.--was far from the real experience that awaited the refugee in the United States. These kinds of expectations generated by foreign nationals and

Americans out of touch with the reality of being a refugee in the United States could never be fulfilled as the Lao resettled in American communities. Furthermore, it complicated the task that resettlement facilitators at home had to deal with. As of late 1982, articulation between refugee workers at home and those in the camps was virtually non-existent. More often than not, various stages of the refugee process were viewed by the individuals involved as separate and unrelated entities. A holistic perspective on the part of the administrators responsible for the educational experience in the refugee camps in Thailand appeared to be lacking, and was one of the greatest weakness of the system. Attempts during 1983 to develop articulation between camps and stateside workers came too late and were not extensive enough.

On a personal and experiential level, I was aghast at the environmental and sanitary conditions in the camps. Over crowded and often dangerous housing (when housing was available), inadequate diet, lack of competent medical care, absence of counseling for individuals arriving from war zones who were suffering cultural shock as well as from personal loss, and insensitivity compounded by ethnocentricity on the part of international workers contributed to bizarre and unhealthy situation for human beings. I have documented these aspects of the camp experience as part of the ethnographic film process contributing to a holistic pictorial record of the Laotian refugee's journey from homeland to resettlement.

A last note: as I had experienced in the American community working with Laotian refugees, I also encountered a fraction of the personnel in the camps who, beyond language and culture, and in a seemingly impossible situation, reached out as human beings to the refugee population. These individuals, like their American counterparts at home, were an inspiration to observe as they faced the almost impossible task of reassuring, comforting, supporting, and challenging a population that was highly stressed, often confused, painfully lonely, longing for their homeland and friends, and vulnerable beyond imagination. Unfortunately, these individuals were too few, burned out, or were closed out by other "professionals" in the camps. Besides having to deal with all of the complexities generated by the camp situation, they had to deal with roadblocks and resistance on the part of the American and Thai bureaucrats and administrators whose career investments in the refugee resettlement process took priority over the needs of the refugees.

Noam Chomsky, writing for the Indochina Chronicle (April 1976) articulates the way I responded to the evidence of my country's involvement in Southeast Asia:

> The American record in Indochina can be captured in three words: lawlessness, savagery, and stupidity, in that order. . . Intellectual apologists for state violence have begun to focus on the stupidity. . . translating that into bad policy. . .116

Beyond the stupidity lies the greater questions of lawlessness and savagery. As I witnessed the ravaged lands, the ravaged human beings, I asked myself just what is it that places the United States in a special category where it is not held responsible for the violence, destruction, and terror it perpetrated upon these human beings. It would seem, as Chomsky further elaborates, that ". . .as long as these doctrines hold sway, there is every reason to expect a re-enactment of the tragedy of Vietnam. . ."117

On the plane home I wondered if my countrypersons truly understood what role and to what extent their government played in the devastation in Southeast Asia. Could they possibly know the intensity to which hate for our government has grown among Third World countries? Do they know that by keeping silent they lend support and longevity to those perverted policies which have so drastically altered the lives of the Laotian people? By keeping silent, they in fact became the silent killers. The experiences in Southeast Asia changed my perspective on the land of my birth. The experience served as a mirror, a device through which I could obtain a different perspective on the manner in which North American culture spreads across the globe which we share with other cultures and humans. Simultaneously, we continue to systematically exploit and destroy those cultures and humans in order to sustain a system that has generated unconscionable greed and destruction.

CHAPTER II

NEW WORLD/OLD WORLD MEMORIES:

LAOTIAN-AMERICAN VOICES RECALL THE REFUGEE
EXPERIENCE

Even the birds sound different here; they sing in a
different language. . .

Lao refugee, 1983

Oh, that I could go home, now I know that can never
be. . .

Lao refugee, 1982

I am dead, and I am alive. . .those parts of me, Lao
and American have a hard time living together. . .

Lao refugee, 1983

There are two sections of this chapter; each reflects a
different facet of the refugee experience. In total, these
narratives are the result of an anthropological field study
conducted in Lao refugee communities in Oregon and the
Pacific Northwest. Beyond that they are gifts of trust in
friendship from Laotians. The rich narratives in Sections I and
II are expressions of refugee realities as perceived by those who
traveled the varied landscapes--social, psychological,
ideological and geographical. Eight Lao translators and scores
of human beings contributed to the compilation of these stories.

The individuals contributing did so with full consent. They are adults, respected by their family and friends, and they exhibited a clear grasp of the complexity of their experiences as they put forth their voices. They are justifiably proud of their past, of being Lao, and of their survival here. At the same time, many have reached the point in acculturation where they are questioning what has happened to them and what the future holds for their lives, their children, their dreams and aspirations.

Once the fundamental conditions of confidentiality and respect were clearly understood, Lao men and women, in the privacy of their own homes, among trusted friends, spoke as freely as possible, struggled with difficult questions, released anger, dealt with painful memories--as they reflected upon their experiences as refugees, on the harsh realities of adjusting to their place in American culture, and on the long range questions of survival in a foreign land. As always with humans from different cultural orientations, speaking through different perceptual structures and languages, accommodations had to be made.

My sole intent and role as ethnographer was to act as a recorder of their perceptions, as well as to attempt to understand. Rarely have we listened to what the refugees have had to say about their experiences. The media have generally portrayed refugees in a collective sense--as a faceless mass of statistics, a nameless sea of bodies descending the stairs of modern aircraft to enter their "new country," as recipients of American generosity to be counted among the waves of immigrants who have come to the United States of America and, lastly, as a testimonial to America's commitment to respond to the "needy" as they fled from the contrived myth of "rampant communism."

From what I understand of what the refugees have said, there is a wholly different perspective, that of the individual, the already complete adult human being having to deal with the additional dimensions to existence that war creates. The condition of being a refugee is a reality the press, the academicians, the statisticians and others have barely touched on. Refugees left Laos for a multitude of complex reasons. Most of those reasons have not been fully explored by the academicians or the media. As media coverage has shifted elsewhere, Americans appear to have forgotten... or are unwilling to deal with... the fact that these individuals are refugees from a war experience. Their presence here is a direct result of over thirty-five years of a ruthless military and economic devastation of the social, political, environmental, and economic structures of Laos. The role of the United States in that process is well documented. Responsibility for those actions as well as continued American economic and trade restrictions on Laos through client states have yet to be acknowledged by the United States government.

These histories touch upon the complexity of the refugee experience: the problems of adjusting to a new culture while simultaneously coping with the loss of the primary culture, support groups, and status; the difficulties of trying to identify and then to accept a new set of values and a totally different lifestyle; struggling to survive during a period of adverse and fluctuating economic conditions in the United States; attempting to understand American expectations and perceptions of the Lao refugee; adjusting expectations of the new culture and society with the harsh and sometimes hostile realities of living here as a refugee; coming to grips with the ultimate probability of never going home, never fully being "Lao" again, and never being quite like "Americans"; and finally the loss of their children to a new way of life that often separates them.

As a matter of obligation, out of fundamental consideration and respect, the narratives in Section I appear unaltered as they were offered by the various speakers. Section II is a brief profile of an entire Lao refugee family. These unique and personal stories are the results of the combined efforts of translators, of informants, and of the researcher-friend. Over the course of time, through informal, open-ended interviews, individuals were requested to comment on three separate areas of the refugee experience: life in Laos prior to making the decision to leave, life and experiences in the refugee camps, and life as a newly arrived refugee in the United States. Every adult member of the community was interviewed as a part of the effort of developing accurate demographics. The following thirty-three biographies were constructed as a result of as few as one or as many as fifteen sessions with a given individual. As months grew into years, both the translators and informants became more comfortable with the shared experience. As time moved on, more and more adults began to build a repertoire of words in English as well as experiences in the United States. This growth was reflected in the quality of the interviews during the latter stages of fieldwork. One cannot forget that "translations" and interpretation, the working through from an oral tradition--where life is perceived and interpreted through interactions--to a linear and written tradition presents certain difficulties. It was difficult for the Lao to speak while recording, and many refused to do so. The more traditional the perspective, the more difficulty there seemed to be with separating words and events by paper, pen, and electronic devices. Often I was given information or clarification and then asked not to write it down. That was "for you only," was a common comment. In reflection, I am aware that my years with the Lao community only touched the tip of the iceberg. That is why what they have selected to say about their experiences as they suffered through a war, transited refugee camps and made initial contact with North American culture becomes all the more critical for us to listen to.

Narratives: Voices from the Laotian Community

Narrative 1

A thirty-four year old mother of five children, this Lao Lum woman originates from the province of Vientiane. Both she and her husband have maintained part-time work since arrival in the United States.

> We came as a family. . . my husband, daughter, and sons. . . we left our country because of the bombing... what could we do?. . . no schools. . . our farm broken. . . some relatives dead. . . everyone fighting. . . this is no way to live. . . we didn't want to leave. . . there was no other way... there was nothing left. . . one cousin said there was better opportunity in America. . . we thought about this. . . we saw many Americans in Laos. . . many things they did we didn't understand. . . they were all healthy and rich. . . they wore nice clothes. . . they had big cars. . . everyone treated them special. . . we took a chance. . . the new government wasn't bad but it made everyone work very hard. . . they promised us land once they dug up all the bombs. . . some of our friends waited. . . we left. . . the Thai soldier took our money and a little jewelry. . . we hid some and they didn't see it. . . we put it inside the diaper of the baby. . . this helped us in the camps. . . there wasn't enough water or food. . . we waited and waited. . . three years we waited. . . we couldn't go back. . . we were sorry we left. . . then we got sponsors and came to your country... they did not like us. . . we did not know many things about the American life. . . we were afraid. . . we were farmers. . . we know little about what to do here. . . some other people were nice. . . they talked and show us what to do. . . we are so ashamed to have the American see us do something the old way. . . we try hard to do everything like the American. . . We went to learn English. . . they show us many things. . . we laughed at some of our mistakes. . . now we know better. . . they were the best to us. . . even when we

couldn't talk they smiled. . . we weren't afraid of them. . . they were kind. . . we will never forget that... because of them we are learning. . . they show us that American can be kind. . . have a heart... you tell them that for us. . . you tell them because we can't... because we are only refugees. . . we have a small apartment now. . . my husband works part-time. . . our children go to school. . . we do not have much money. . . no car. . . we are glad to be here. . . our children have a new life. . . we tell them to study hard. . . speak the English. . . We want them to be American. . . there is the future. . . they do not remember Lao. . . that is o.k. . . . they will not be sad in their heart like we old one sometime. . .

Narrative 2.

This Lao Lum man, age twenty-four, has recently relocated to California because of layoffs on his job. Only a few days after the layoff, the "American" woman he married, who is the mother of his daughter, left him to live with another man. Discouraged and emotionally drained, he left with his daughter for a larger Laotian community in Stockton, California. There he has friends and has become part of an extended family where believes he has found a supportive environment to rear his daughter in the "Lao way." Before he left he stated that the "American" woman had robbed him of all the money he had saved, of the family life he loved and needed, and of his heart.

I don't know what to say to you. . . I have never done anything important. . . I lived in Laos all my life until I was eighteen. . . I didn't live in the capitol, but Savannakhet. I lived in many temples. . . I moved about. . . I left Lao at eighteen. . . I was two and one-half years in the camps. . . life was difficult. . . I

worked there. . . that way no one had to bother me...
and I didn't depend on anyone else... I am married.
I have a baby child. . . I left because of the war. . .
there wasn't any future. . . not enough food. . . no
gas. . . everything broken down. . . I want a home...
a family. . . peace of mind. . . my own garden. . . I
didn't want war and more death. . . that was what was
left of my Lao. . . What do I now of politics. . .
Communists, Americans. . . all of them. . . they had
a price for the little man like me to pay. . . what
happened in Lao is gone. . . I left that there. . . I saw
much. . . war has so many ugly faces. . . it is a new
life here. . . not easy. . . but I didn't expect that. . . I
have a job. . . a wife. . . and no one troubles me. . . I
trouble no one. . . what I can do for someone else. . .
I do. . . I learned this in the temples [Buddhist]. . .
this has worked well for me here. . . the one good
thing I have learned is how valuable friends and
family are. . . more than governments or money or
anything else. . . Despite all I am a wealthy man for
my friends and for my family. . . I have my health...
What more could I ask for? I don't have more to
say... talking too much can get you into a lot of
trouble. . . so can asking a lot of questions. . . I've
learned that. . . I am alive. . . for that most of all I
am lucky. . . I have a garden, too. . . you will stay
and eat with us, yes?

Narrative 3

Twenty-nine years old and originating from the area around
Vientiane, this Lao Lum man left his wife and two children in
Laos. In the time since he has been in the United States, he has
married another Lao woman and they have two children.
Despite persistent efforts to locate full-time employment, he has
been frustrated by finding only occasional part-time work.

I left Laos in 1978. . . I came with my mother, two younger brothers, one sister, and cousins. . . before leaving I was a motorcycle repairman. . . I went to school for seven years and then was in the army. . . there I learned mechanics. . . Our family owned several houses and we all had small businesses. While the Americans were there we made much money. . . things were good. . . my brother worked for the U.S. Embassy. . . we lived nearby. . . we thought we had a great future. . . when the Americans left we were forced to give away some of our land and the new government took all of our houses except the one we live in. . . actually,, some of our relatives took some of the houses. . . we couldn't get parts for the business. . . food and gasoline were hard to get... my brother was set to the country to work on a farm because the government said he had made money off the Lao people and was on the side of the Americans... we worked for what we had. . . we didn't believe that the farmers who lost their land in the war should get our land. . . some of the farmers went back to their old land and the government helped them. . . it was no fun. . . everyone was expected to do extra work to rebuild the country. . . lots of night clubs and other activities were stopped... what a plain life. . . we saw no future. . . we planned to leave. . . my grandmother and some cousins stayed in our house. . . we said we were going to visit relatives in the south. . . when we went there we kept on going. . . life in the camp was difficult. . . especially at night it was very dangerous. . . we tried to stay together. . . the Thailand guards were very mean. . . for no reason. . . there is much I could say but I won't that is gone. . . our family got broken up... some came to the U.S. and some went to the

Philippines. . . I have been here two years now... one
of my brothers, my sister, and my mother are here. . .
on the way we got separated from one brother and
some cousins. . . we hope they are in the U.S. and
that we find them. . . we worry much for them. . .
My life has changed. . . we are very poor. . . we try
hard. . . we belong to the Christian church. . . we do
not smoke or drink. . . I am worried for finding
work... a man should be able to support his family...
they tell us times are hard here right now. . . that
many Americans are out of work. . . we did not
expect this. . . we thought everyone in the U.S. had a
job. . . we did not expect to find the same problems
that we left in our country. . . Who would have
dreamed that? That's o.k. . . we believe everything
will get better. . . we have met many good people
here. . . our neighbors treat us well. . . they help us
when we don't understand something... they say we
are now Americans. . . this is a clean city. . . we
fish. . . we go to the park. . . I married a woman. . .
her husband died in the camp. . . our children are
learning English very good. . . somehow we will
make it. . . you know, the American people are
great... another thing. . . governments are the same
everywhere. . . wherever you are. . . it's the people
who count. . . once the American people were good
to us we had great hope that everything will be o.k...
governments. . . I have no use for them. . . they
always forget the people. . . well, what questions do
you have? [None, I'd rather have you tell me what
you think is important; it's your story]. . . well. . .
most important now is work. . . I want to work. . . I
want to have a house again. . . I want to bring my
family together. . . this is important for a man to have
his family around him. Do you know what I mean?
This is good this writing you will do. . . later we will

forget much of this. . . putting it in history will help us to remember. . . you remember. . . you promised to forget my name. . . this story is between us without my name. . . When you were here before you made me think of many things. . . my mind has been busy. . . some things I can't tell you. . . not so secret. . . instead, it hurts too much to remember. . . I am glad we talk. . . there is much inside I don't have the words for. . . now, I have to be very strong. . . I can't think of the past. . . when I do, I am sometimes confused. . . that is why I don't drink. . . my mind becomes confused and the thoughts hurt. . . my hope is to find work. . . any kind of work. . .

Narrative 4.

This Lao Lum man, in his late fifties, has recently found part-time janitorial employment as his first "American" job. He is presently attempting to cope with radical changes in roles and in the structure of his family as acculturation begins to take effect. He has had initial complications on the job as he has difficulty taking orders from young Americans who do not respect his age.

We like you. . . we like America. . . this is our new life. . . we don't talk too much about the past. . . Lao was our old country. . . it was far away. . . very different. . . hard to explain. . . I work for many years at the American Embassy. . . I sort mail. . . open the mail from the communist country. . . send to the supervisor. . . they paid good. . . I had a big house. . . we have many American friends. . . when they leave we leave too. . . we do not like the new government. . . we wait in the camp for many year... then we come to the United States. . . we have the big family. . . one son and his wife stay in Lao to

keep our house. . . the other are here. . . now I try to
learn English... very hard. . . We go to the church...
the people help us... they send clothes and food. . .
they help with the problems... I worry for the job. . .
we have many children... sometimes my wife is
sick... I will do any work. . . there is much to learn
here. . . I am not a young man. . . I try any job. . .
here I am the refugee. . . not like in my own country
where I am a man. . . here I am the refugee. . . this is
hard. . . I can not speak the English so good. . .I can
not say the words in my mind to you. . . I am like the
little child in English. . . we can not talk as the
man... I have not the words in your English. . .
maybe some other time later. . . when I speak more
English we can talk the politics. . . history. . .
religion. . . I know these things. . . I feel very
uncomfortable to use the translator. . . he is a good
man. . . a good friend. . . but we use different
words... he is very important here. . . he is our mouth
and ears. . . we trust him. . . I hope next year or
sometime I can talk to you as a man. . . I enjoy this
talk. . . I am very interested in the whole world. . . I
like to know very many things. . . In my country we
have many people to our house. . . we talk. . . my
wife cook good food. . . here we have people to our
house. . . I can not talk very too much... this is very
hard. . . I have something to say. . . I have the
questions. . . I have no way to say many thing. . . it
is much better now. . . when I first came I was almost
crazy... I am already a man and I could not talk for
myself... this was the very hard thing. . . I am very
sorry I did not learn the English at the Embassy. . .
they did not like us to speak the language. . . those
Americans were very different. . . my neighbors are
not the same. . . very friendly. . . very good to us. . .
very helpful. . . they come to our house to eat the Lao

food. . . they take us in the car... they explain for us when we can not speak the right answer. . . they are the very good friend. . . they are good with the children. . . their children come here. . . they do not have the bad racial feeling. . . we learn very much from them. . . we miss Lao too much sometimes. . . there we know what to do, what to say, where to go... we are lucky to be here. . . many die in the war... some die in the refugee camp. . . I hope for the good job soon. . . there are many in my family. . . the man must work for the food, the clothes, the rent, too many things. . . we are happy to be in your country. . . maybe soon I am lucky to find the very good job. . . because you are here my wife has made some special Lao food. . . we want you to try. . . this way you know a little more about our people. . . our ways. . . they are good, too. . . we Lao are good people. . . we will talk later. . . maybe my son will have something to say to you... He say he has to think more before he talks. . . after we eat or maybe next time, o.k.?

Narrative 5.

This forty-one year old Lao Lum man is currently attempting to learn English as he struggles by on part-time and seasonal landscape jobs. Because he has adult children in the United States, both he and his wife have escaped poverty. The supplementary income received from the family has given the parents a more comfortable living experience than many of the other Laotians in the community.

I had a small business outside Vientiane. . . we sold ice. . . we were never very rich. . . we were not poor... we owned a small farm that came from my uncle's family. . . Others worked the farm and we took part of the crop. . . we had a radio. . . please

excuse my bad English. . . I am ashamed. . . there is
no way to my many thoughts out of my head into
English. . . I speak Lao, Thai, Chinese, and some
French. . . now I am learning English. . . When I
can, I will answer in English. . . otherwise, my friend
here will help us both. . . I think your Lao is better
than my English. . . I have thought about your
questions and about my life in the time after I spoke
to you. . . First, let me describe my country. . . it
was beautiful. . . many flowers, good farms. . . there
were rich and poor. . . many big temples. . .
celebrations. . . we had our own way of living life. . .
it was different from the French or American way...
even the very rich [Lao] were Lao first when the
French were in power behind the king. . . the
Americans changed our nation. . . they brought with
them many discoveries. . . toasters. . . television. . .
and different ways for people to act. . . much
money... they were very powerful. . . you always
knew where they were. . . I cannot lie. . . I liked
much of their discoveries. . . I wanted both. . . to be
Lao and to have some of the American way. . . many
people said this was not possible. . . some in our
family wanted to stay out of the American war. . .
you know, the one in Vietnam. . . we were having
our own war. . . the Americans took sides and then it
seemed to be like everything was upside down. . .
everyone had to be on a side. . . I didn't want that. . .
I didn't want the communist way. . . Remember last
time you said all stories were private...? [Yes]
O.K., is that the rule now? [Yes] O.K., then I didn't
want the American way. . . we (my wife, too) wanted
some of the good things. . . but we wanted to stay
Lao. . . that was not for us to have. . . one side or the
other. . . so, we knew the Americans were bigger. . .
it wasn't so bad in Vientiane. . . the war in the North

and other parts of the country was awful. . . relatives told me of bombs everyday and sometimes at night... they had bombs that fell and then more bombs came out of their inside. . . this caused many deaths and much destruction to people and animals and the land... also there was fire and gas. . . the others weren't all communists. . . at first they wanted an independent Lao. . . you know, our own government... it almost went that way but we didn't quite make it. . . the Americans helped some people and they were big. . . the communists were there, too. . . the war went on and on. . . we got food and other things flown in by the Americans and then in the country people started to grow less food. . . How could they? It was war. . . everyone began taking sides and no one trusted anyone. . . it was a crazy life. . . we couldn't live that way. . . at first many refugees came in from the countryside. . . we never thought we'd be like them. . . By the end of the war twenty-seven people were living in our house. . . all relatives. . . their farms gone. . . then we heard the Americans were leaving. . . we couldn't believe it. . . What would we do?... we were on their side... we knew if they left things would be rough. . . they left... there was almost no food. . . little medicine. . . all kinds of problems. . . the new government couldn't repair all the war damage. . . it was too great. . . the Americans turned their back son Lao. . . they weren't interested any more. . . many people were angry. . . confused. . . now what?... every chicken had to be counted under the new government... we knew they had to do this because there wasn't enough food. . . much farmland was destroyed. . . we didn't want to live this way. . . we had to leave. . . I want my children to live. . . so, you see, I did leave. . . I would like to go back if

things change. . . right now I can't... this is now the
country of my children. . . I don't know if it will ever
be my country. . . I am a guest here. . . yes, a
refugee. . . my side lost. . . it is another story about
the camps. . . we escaped. . . we got out. . . another
day we can talk. . . now, let's drink some beer. . . I
want to show you photographs of my family. . .

Narrative 6.

Twenty-six and the mother of two children, a third having
died in the camps, this Lao Lum woman in illiterate in both her
native language and English. She depends entirely upon her
husband to provide for the family and to negotiate any business
with the American community. She said her world has become
very small since leaving her country. Her husband has worked
full-time since arrival as a dishwasher in a local restaurant.

My story isn't much. . . We lived outside o f
Vientiane in the country. . . I am here because of my
husband. . . he worked for the Americans. . . we
made much money. . . we owned land, we had a car
and a motorcycle. . . after the war the new
government said we had to share. . . we did not want
to do this. . . we left. . . While the Americans were
there we had a good time. . . many parties. . .
dancing. . . plenty of food. . . money to spend. . .
after the war my husband had to take a new job. . .
less money. . . not enough for gas. . . not enough
food. . . We thought the United States would be a
better place. . . We couldn't live in Lao anymore. . .
everything was a mess. . . we sold things and crossed
the river. . . we lived only a half-mile from the river
and came across at night. . . we had to be careful. . .
both the Thai and the new government might kill us if
we get caught. . . we were lucky. . . all of us made

it... we [were] surprised. . . we got to the town and
we have friends there. . . they take us to the camps...
now we are poor here. . . no job. . . no money. . .
many people in our apartment. . . the American don't
like us. . . What to do? There is no place for us. . .
in Lao. . . in America. . . this is sad. . . we try. . .
maybe things get much better. . . we work hard. . .
then the Americans can know we are a good people...
we hope they will let us try with a job. . .

Narrative 7.

This eighteen year-old "unaccompanied minor" is atypical of
the many young Laotian refugees who resettled in the United
States without family. More fortunate than many other males
in his peer group, he has a Laotian girlfriend and has become a
peripheral member of her parents' extended family. Continuing
with school and with part-time work, he is unsure as to his
plans for the future.

I don't know too much. . . I was too young. . . I am
only eighteen. . . I was thirteen when I left my
country. . . we were wanting a new life. . . my father
was not wanting to leave our country. . . he is the old
way. . . my brother and I came away for a better life.
.. there was no future for us... no chance for
education. . . the country was in bad shape... the war
messed it up. . . I miss my family. . . I'm here. . . I'm
doing o.k. . . I have a girlfriend. . . I work part-
time... I don't know what's best. . . When I was in
the camps I couldn't wait to get here. . . I had
dreams. . . it's not the same. . . it's not easy here. . .
sometimes I think I shouldn't have left. . . my father
wanted me to get ahead. . . I'm here. . . I'm not
always happy. . . I get confused. . . I worry I'm never
going to be a part of things. . . If I go back it could

be that things have changed and I won't be a part of
things there. . . who knows. . . I just hang in there...
I know my brother will go back. . . he is saving
now... he says he is too much Lao to become
American... If they won't take him back he'll stay in
Thailand. . . he hasn't learned much English. . . he is
very lonely. . . if he goes. . . I don't know what I can
do. . . Right now, I'm trying here. . . I learn many
things. . . I study. . . I am a man now. . .

Narrative 8.

This twenty year old Lao Lum male originates from the rural
area near Champassak in the south of Laos. Despite enormous
psychological battering, he has worked hard in school and on
his part-time job. An active member of the community, he is
"on hand" to help new families, to assist with translation, or to
play a "tough" game of soccer. By keeping busy, he says that
he has been able to escape the past.

I am seventeen. . . I have been here two and a half
years... I spent five years in the refugee camp. . . I
was about ten when we left our country. . . If you
want the truth I will tell you a hard story. . . My
mother and sister were killed by the Thai army. . . we
left our farm when the American bomb burn
everything. . . our buffalo, our chickens, and our
father were all burned. . . one other brother died later
from the burn. . . we traveled until they got us. . .
they were screaming. . . they took off my clothes and
used me for sex. . . I hurt and was bleeding. . . other
farmers came and took me to their house. . . later
they sold me to go to Bangkok. . . there for one year
they sent me to the hotel room of the many foreigner
for sex. . . one man bought me and took me with

him. . . I ran away and got to the camp... there I learned the English. . . no one knew about the other... then I got sent to the Philippines and then to San Francisco. . . I have the Mormon sponsor. . . they were good. . . no fun. . . it was hard for me to stay there. . . the mother want to sleep with me. . . I don't like the sex. . . it hurt too much when they sold me to Bangkok. . . when I run away I decide never again. . . I rather die first. . . many time they beat me. . . I have a girlfriend here. . . When I finish school we will marry. . . I want children the family... the happy life. . . I want to be the father. . . I study very hard. . . I have many friends. . . they like me... I am happy to live in this city. . . here I sleep without worry. . . you have said if I tell you my story you will not tell my name. . . I know you are true to your word. . . the refugee is a hard life. . . now it is over... this is my new country... there is no war here... there is plenty of food... people are happy. . . there are many schools. . . there is much to learn. . . most of the time I feel good. . . I am happy for life... I like the dance and the music. . . only sometimes I am sad. . . I remember my mother on the ground. . . I think of our buffalo all burn. . . I see the face of the fat foreign man and the hand on me. . . then I am sad. . . I do not tell my girlfriend of this. . . someday I will forget all this. . . I will be the father. . . I will have the family. . . then I will be very happy. . . now I have a job as a dishwasher. . . I have much to learn of my new country... I have a television and listen to English. . . I try to speak the English every chance... I go to school. . . I am very busy. . . that is very good. . . this is a good future for me... I think I will never be this happy when I wait in the camp... I save a little money. . . I want a car. . . this is very good... that is all. . . that is the story of me. . .

Narrative 9

A traditional Lao Lum woman in her late fifties, this person has refused to make any direct comments about her past. Over the years I have been a frequent guest in her home and have subsequently learned through informal "family" conversations much about her past life, family, and her growing u p experience in Laos. Over time, she has served as a valuable informant regarding the daily comings and goings of the Laotian community where she is known as an indefatigable gossip.

> Why do you ask of us? We know nothing. . . the
> American people do not need to know about Lao. . .
> it is a sad story... for me to tell would be bad for a
> new person here... what good to it? The Americans
> would think us bad. . . it is all dead. . . this is a new
> life. . . If you ask many questions you cause trouble
> for us. . . my husband says go away. . . we suffer
> much. . . in Lao. . . in the United States. . . we do
> not need more. . . you are a good man. . . I [am]
> surprised you ask me to remember pain. . . that is
> all... my mouth is shut about that. . . come and eat
> with us. . . next time. . . do not ask questions. . .let's
> talk about other things here in America. . . that is
> more interesting for me. . .

Narrative 10

In his late fifties, this Lao Lum man has been unable to find employment in the United States. Over the past two years, he has watched the gap widen between his traditional Laotian family perspective and the "American" perspective newly acquired by his children. Fortunately, his wife has maintained part-time employment as a motel maid. In her late fifties, the work is exhausting but serves as the only means of income and the stabilizing factor keeping the family together.

While I was still a young man, the Americans came... they brought many new ideas into my life. . . it would never be the same for me again. . . I was not satisfied with Lao as it was. . . I was determined to be like the Americans. . . they were on top. . . I like that. . . by working with them I got a good job. . . my children went to a good school. . . I wasn't rich, but I was very comfortable... living in Vientiane wasn't so bad. . . I was all on the American side. . . There were communists and there were nationalists as well. . . the Americans and who wanted to be neutral were called communists. . . this was not so. . . On the other hand, the nationalists were stupid to think they could remain neutral. . . I was for the Americans, they were my friends. . . they helped me... when the U.S. pulled out, we knew we had to leave. . . we disagreed with the new government. . . I don't believe in Socialism or Communism. . . to me, all people can never be equal. . . it is unnatural. . . Some are always more powerful than others. . . some have always been the top class. . . that is the natural law. . . We crossed the river... it was difficult then... we believed the Americans would be good to us. . . We took a lot of money with us. . . once in Thailand things changed. . . the soldiers took much of our money and my wife's jewelry. . . my oldest daughter was raped. . . then came hardship. . . we thought it would only be a short time before the Americans would come to help us out of the camps... this was not so. . . there was little food or water in the camps. . . we were kept under guard. . . One of my daughters got very sick. . . although she

recovered, she will be crippled for life. . . I almost
died with worry. . . they treated us like animals. . . it
was very hard. . . we could not understand why we
were treated like this. . . we were friends. . . we even
fought against our own government. . . for the first
time I thought maybe I should have stayed in my
country. . . later, we were sponsored by the
Mormons. . . they said no drinking, no smoking, no
coffee, no coca-cola. . . this was hard for us... they
laid down conditions. . . we had no choice. . .
America proved very different. . . we found out we
weren't really wanted here. . . I hardly speak the
language. . . they do not see me as a man. . . I mean
an important man. . . here I have become a common
laborer. . . I will do this. . . I need to feed my
family... I don't like the way many Americans feel
about us. . . Of course, I have no say. . . only to
you. . . what are words?... you know, you
intellectuals were the downfall of my country. . .
some of you were for socialism. . . others buried your
heads in the books. . . nothing practical. . . no
offense. . . but what power have you?... the same as
happened in my country could happen here. . . wise
as many of you seem, you have little experience in
the ways of the world. . . you are too comfortable. . .
there is much crime here. . . no police to control. . .
they worry more about the traffic ticket than the communists in the United States. . . [What did you
expect before you got here?]. . . Well, everyone to
be rich. . . you know, no hard work. . . houses for
everyone. . . no hunger and no poor. . . I have
learned this is not so. . . This was a great
disappointment. . . What is the difference for me?...
if I had stayed in my country, the new government
would have taken away much of my wealth. . . here,
I am considered too ignorant to get the kind of job

82

where I can improve myself. . . this is a great sadness. . . What is the word? [Disillusioned]. . . the journey has changed me. . . now, I just want safety... I want to grow old in peace. . . I don't care about much else. . . enough food, a place to live... no one to bother me. . . Again, I say, what good these words?... we have spent this time talking. . . What have we accomplished?... the words of a bitter man... How do you know I have even told you the truth? [I have no way of knowing]. . . and you will never know. . . write down that I live this new country. . . this is all anyone needs to know. . . this rainy place is good for a man like me. . . it is how I feel about life now. . . bitter tears. . . little sun. . . the frangipani will never bloom for me again... my children are becoming American. . . in time, they will not know me. . . already they are ashamed of my ignorance. . . This is what it means, this word, refugee. . . a dark spot that can never be washed away.

Narrative 11

A thirty-two year old Lao Lum originating from the province of Champassak, this woman works part-time as a clerk for a local store. Gregarious, well-liked by the people she works with and by the people of the Laotian community, she recently has acquired an American boyfriend. She is now talking of "adopting" children.

We lived on a big farm in the south. . . we went to Bangkok every year. . . my father was rich, we had many lands. . . I went to school. . . I was very lucky... not all women get the education I got. . . I speak French, Lao, Thai, and some English now. . . we had a big house. . . wooden and part over the water. . . it was beautiful. . . I miss that house. . . at

first we knew there was a war but it didn't hurt us too
much. . . we had plenty of food and my father
worked with the Americans. . . I was married four
months. . . then my husband was killed in a boat that
was bombed by the Americans. . . he was delivering
rice. . . that is hard to remember. . . we had great
plans for life. . . I wanted children. . . not long after
that our cousins came from the north. . . there was
much trouble. . . some of our people wanted to be
independent. . . Father said it was impossible to be
independent of the Americans. . . they were too big...
my other brother and some relatives left and fought
with those who wanted independence. . . life just
wasn't the same. . . everyone was worried. . . my
father said they could never come home. . . as time
went on the war got pretty bad. . . many airplanes in
the sky all day long. . . we couldn't plant. . .
sometimes we had to work the fields at night. . . then
Americans went crazy. . . they thought everyone was
a communist. . . they bombed and bombed and
bombed. . . then my father got mad, too. . . he began
to help those who were fighting all the outsiders. . .
the Americans didn't know this. . . he wasn't a
communist... he loved Lao. . . My father and brother
were both killed. . . one by bombs, the other by the
military police. . . they took our house and I fled with
other cousins... we crossed into Thailand. . . I had
some money and a little jewelry. . . we got caught by
the Thai police. . . one of my cousins was raped. . .
two were killed. . . I was raped and beaten and part
of my [breast] was cut off. . . now I can never have
children. . . other refugees found me and took care of
me. . . one caught T.B. and died in the camp. . . in
the camps we stayed together. . . it was hard... What
do I say?... most of those things you wouldn't want to
hear about or I won't tell you. . . it's hard to speak to

a man about many things. . . Finally, I got to San
Francisco, then another part of the country, then
here... At first my sponsor was very good, but after a
while I didn't want to stay home and clean their
house. . . I wanted to learn the language. . . I wanted
to be independent. . . maybe even marry again. . . I
am still young. . . they were angry with me and said I
should be ashamed of myself. . . they said they saved
my life and do so much for me. . . the woman said
more than the man. . . he always treated me like a
little girl. . . he liked to touch my hair. . . even
though I am a grown woman. . . coming here there
was much, and still is, I don't understand. . . Some
Americans have been very good friends. . . others not
so. . . even most of my American friends treat me as
not American. . . Often I am very lonely. . . I wish
for smells and sounds and things I have known all my
life. . . because there is much I do not know about
America. . . I am like the child. . . I work here. . . I
am going to school. . . I don't know what will come
of me. . . the life of a woman here is strange. . .
many live without family. . . this is hard for me. . .
so many people are dead. . . this is the hardest
thing... I am trying to be a Christian. . . they say this
helps. . . I wait. . . nothing has happened to now. . .
I wonder why I live. . . why me to live when so many
die. . . this is a little of my story. . . I am tired now...

Narrative 12

This Lao gentleman has asked me to be "careful" with the
identification of his comments. I worked and interacted with
him for over a year, and he shared an enormous amount of
material relating to Laotian history, customs, and cultural
idiosyncrasies. Obviously a member of the aristocracy in Laos,
he seemed to have adjusted to leaving that behind as he created

a new life in the United States. As I got to know him better, it became apparent he strove to function in two entirely different realms of perception.

You ask me to tell my life story. . . or whatever I wish to tell. . . I have been thinking about all of this since we spoke last. . . few of the Lao refugees will tell you the true story... there are many reasons for this. . . there are many kinds of Lao refugees. . . just like your own people, they all see and tell the story of their experience very different... this is not unusual... you must not be naive if you are to see and to feel the true story. . . the farmer, the craftsman, the diplomat, each will see the same thing but will tell a very different account. . . only when you put them all together will you see the threads that lead to some truth. . . be careful what you ask. . . you may get answers to your questions instead of the truth about what happened. . . let the people tell from their own experience. . . there are many things you know about our people. . . the first secret is always to put your hand out first. . . especially in the case where you are the most important man. . . this lets them know you care. . . do not forget this. . . you will have a very difficult time with this work you propose. . . it is my advice that you spend some time with our people before you ask the questions. . . they have to learn to trust you. . . to feel your honesty. . . to feel comfortable with you. . . probably at this time there is no reason in their minds for them to tell you any-thing. . . they probably will not see this project in terms of history. . . what meaning does history have for the farmer?... more likely he is concerned with the weather. . . the women may be more difficult than the men... they are not so used to telling about their

private life to foreigners. . . Here we are guests. . .
the good guest will keep his mouth shut and be
respectful. . . this is our way... to get to the truth you
will have to be very patient. . . you knew before you
asked that my story would be different. . . because I
came from a very important family, because I have
been a leader, my experience and perspective are
different. . . again this is just my experience. . . I will
tell you some things. . . these you cannot write down
for I am easily identified through them. . . when I am
finished I will tell you a few more general things you
can write down. . . there is much to say. . . maybe
we can speak of governments. . . not a specific
government, just the idea... I have seen many. . . at
the heart of a good government is the heart. . .
remembering to do whatever your job is with the
human in mind. . . I believe there are many ways to
do this. . . it would seem through the study of history
that we often forget this. . . there is much discussion
about what is good for human beings and further who
will decide what is good and bad. . . still, I believe
that if one truly listens to the heart and is honest about
what he hears, there are things that all human beings
know without having to be told. . . there is no excuse
in this world for hunger, lack of medicine, illiteracy,
and many other such basic human needs and rights. .
. most governments, the communist to the democratic
have failed to address these concerns. . . communism
and socialism have never appealed to me. . . We are
allowed in our country to study all things. . . I prefer
the integrated economy mixed with the basic
democracy. . . if given the time to think, one can
dream up many kinds of governments that might
satisfactorily include these and be quite successful. . .
We get caught up in systems and forget that systems
should be used to improve the quality of our

existence, not to tie us down. . . the philosophical question of whether we as humans purposely set ourselves up for failure by not choosing to remember past experience and mistakes has been intriguing for me for many years. . . a lifetime is very difficult to relate.... I am no longer a young man. . . what I've seen, the things I have learned, the things I have thought of and wondered over would fill many books... over time I have come to think that if the cover to this experience which I call my own were to be stripped away, one would find the ordinary questions, problems, dilemmas that we all share in common as the human being. . . closer to the end of the path for this life I find I have barely moved along the path of awareness... having to be the refugee has reminded me of this fact. . . things change. . . if we get too caught up in the moment we can forget that there is a tomorrow. . . maybe tomorrow will catch up with us before we remember it is coming. . . it is not the guest. . . it comes to stay and changes life. . . sometimes it is good or bad from the individual viewpoint and experience. . . nevertheless it comes... for the big picture I believe we have very little control. . . for many areas of life and experience we have much control. . . it does not seem we have done very well even in the small areas that we can influence. . . if you wish to live then each time you are faced with a great change in your life you attempt to adjust. . . many do not wish to do this. . . they resist, maybe they are unaware they can adjust. . . whatever, that is the beginning of no longer living. . . we have spoken a long time tonight. . . I am pleased to be in your home. . . to speak to each other as human beings. . . the reaching out with the hand is very important. . . that is what my people need the most. . . once they know they are welcome, then they

will have the strength to face whatever else. . . we are
a strong people...

Narrative 13.

At forty-five and the single parent father of six children, this
Lao Lum man from the province of Champassak has had a
difficult time making ends meet. A recent widower, he has
relentlessly searched for full-time work to make a decent salary.
His sister serves as a surrogate mother for the children, and he
has a large extended family of single Laotian men and friends
who regard him as a "young elder."

We refugees talk of before and after. . . two times. . .
before the Americans and after they got to Lao, then
after the Americans left and before leaving m y
country. . . to go way back, I was born in the south
and lived on a big farm. . . we were never hungry. . .
we had food to sell and some to give to relatives and
friends who don't have the big farm. . . we have eight
children. . . I am the second son but the fifth child...
my father was married before so we had three others
with a different mother. . . we were all brothers and
sisters. . . I went to school for ten years in my
country. . . that is much school for my country. . . I
speak French, Thai, and I work hard on the English
now. . . My family was Buddhist. . . we didn't go to
church on Sunday like here in the United States. . . it
was different. . . what we believe is in our hearts....
we wish the blessings of the triple gem on to
everyone. . . even our enemies. . . the south is
different from the north. . . we have close family with
Thailand. . . before the Americans everyone looked
to the French or went to Bangkok for the new idea. . .
now, when the Americans came we looked to them...
there was much trouble and much talk in our

country... many wanted to be a country without the ties to anyone else. . . just good friendship with all country. . . others wanted the American side. . . others wanted the Chinese side. . . but many small people just couldn't understand it all. . . many were very confused. . . we saw much change. . . the airplane and the war did much damage. . . many people were confused that the same Americans who were very good to us in some way will at the same time destroy our country. . . I don't understand this... many good thing came to our people with the American. . . many bad came too. . . I can't say good or bad that they came. . . I am a guest in your country now, to criticize is not so good. . . after the Americans left, the new government was very hard... we couldn't get many things. . . they said everyone had to work hard to fix our broken country. . . it was too hard. . . everything was count[ed]. . . you got to have just enough to get by. . . the rest was taken or taxed. . . there was no future for me. . . for my children. . . the new government said the Americans were making war with us... not with the bombs. . . with food and building things and no new machines... they said the Americans wouldn't give money to fix the war damage. . . we didn't believe this. . . we think the Americans wouldn't do this. . . we know they are very rich and generous. . . we believe the new government to lie and keep all the money. . . there was very little when the Americans left. . . it was a sad time. . . we knew we could never go back to the old way. . . much had changed. . . we got the new way in our life and we needed those things now... I did not like the new government. . . we were sad with very little. . . we had to leave. . . you would be very sad to see our beautiful country so destroyed... we didn't want to wait for the new

government to fix things. . . it was too hard. . . we
leave for Thailand and hope the Americans take us to
there. . . our children will have the school. . . we will
have enough food. . . now I am here. . . away from
all that sad thing. . . I hope for the job. . . I hope for
the new life. . . maybe later I will go back to my old
country when it is fix[ed]. . . now I wait for the job...
we have no money. . . we have little to eat. . . I hope
the American will help me. . . I think from my heart
they will do this. . . we are a good people... we like
the American. . . we are friend. . .

Narrative 14

A former school teacher in Laos, this Lao Lum man has
relocated to California where a more equitable support system
of benefits awaits the refugee who is unemployed and disabled.
As leaders of the community, the loss of this man and his
family to the local Lao community was hard felt. He was one
of the few men acceptable to all factions in the community and
was a valued friend and informant during my fieldwork experience.

I studied twelve years in Lao. . . I was an elementary
school teacher, then a clerk in the army. . . I lived in
the capitol city, Vientiane. . . I have five children. . .
I speak French, Lao, Thai, and I am struggling to
learn English. . . it is a difficult language. . . the
sounds and the structure are different. . . French is a
help as the structure seem similar... I always wanted
to be a teacher. . . there is excitement for me in
watching young minds open like the flower. . . each
petal part of the whole thing. . . each lesson. . . Our
schools have been disrupted for many years... What
will happen to our people?... Many of the young
cannot read or write. . . What will the world think of

the Lao people? We are an old people. . . Few
Americans know of us except as the refugee. . . we
are more. . . Let's just say that when the Americans
came our world changed. . . it is difficult to
explain... the American world is bright. . . many
things came into Lao that we had never seen. . .
movies, television. . . much more electricity. . .
different food and clothing. . . also, Americans live
differently than the Lao. . . friendship, family, men
and women are very different in the American
world... some new things were good. . . others not...
we never knew which ones were best. . . we made
many mistakes. . . we forgot the basis of our religious
beliefs. . . the middle path. . . we left that path. . . it
is too late to go back. . . Lao is a distant mountain
with a deep river in between. . . we cannot go back...
I wonder how this came about. . . we wanted more
and more after the Americans came. . . it all
happened too fast. . . so many things are great about
your country. . . medicine, education, plenty of food,
health. . . now I think we wanted these same things
for the Lao. . . but we wanted to stay Lao. . . this has
not happened. . . by wanting these things we have
had to become Americans. . . at the same time. . .
not the same as Americans because we are the
refugees. . . we will never know if we made the best
choice. . . we can never go back... we left. . . it was
too hard. . . most of all we left for our children. . .
We hope things get better for our country.... for our
people. . . you must go there someday... even though
much is destroyed. . . you will still see its great
beauty. . . I was lucky. . . I spent only three months
in the camps in Thailand and then went on to the
Philippines for six months. Being a teacher. . . being
able to help my people also helped me. . . At first, I
went to another state for four months. . . a pig farmer

sponsored my family. . . When we arrived we lived
in an old cabin. . . it was cold. . . I went to work the
next morning and so did my wife. . . twelve, fifteen
hours a day. . . if I didn't work... I didn't get food for
my children. . . It was very difficult. . . we were
isolated. . . in a new country. . . the people thought
we should be grateful like slaves. . . we expected to
work, but not be treated like slaves. . . we stole
potato starts. . . my children went out and dug them
at night to survive. . . we had few clothes. . .
everyone was confused. . . we couldn't speak the
language. . . we didn't know what to do. . . months
went by. . . in some ways the experience was harder
on the mind than the camps. . . We didn't expect the
Americans to be this way. . . My arm got caught in a
mowing machine and was broken in several places...
The farmer and his wife put ice on it. . . I was in
great pain. . . still they made me work in the yard. . .
In a couple of days I was taken to a hospital. . . my
wife cried. . . she didn't know where I was going and
thought I'd never come back. . . I felt the same way,
too. . . They wouldn't let her come. . . she had to
work in my place if the children were to eat. . . The
doctor put my arm in a plastic bag filled with air. . .
then we went to the hospital. . . they set it. . . Two
days later he made me work again. . . I tried but it
hurt more. . . In the meantime. . . my son-in-law [in
Eugene] got a letter we wrote that a nurse mailed for
me (the farmer didn't know)... he sent money to the
nurse. . . she got us out. . . we took the bus. . . we
were afraid but happy. . . it was a long ride. . . we
didn't know what was ahead. . . Here we got a new
sponsor. . . life is better. . . people are good. . . we
are poor. . . we are willing to work. . . we don't mind
being poor as long as we are treated as human
beings... we have hope again. . . This is far away

from all we know. . . the language is difficult. . . our children learn quickly. . . we try hard, too, because we know it is important to them. . . a part of us will always be Lao. . . my heart lives there. . . a part of us has become so many things. . . Thailand, the Philippines, and now Eugene. . . we have become more than Lao. . . Our children are Americans already. . . so different. . . We hope to remind them of where their parents and grandparents grew. . . we want them to understand they can be the best of Lao and American. . .

Narrative 15

A thirty-one year old mother of three and head of a large extended family, this woman and her husband have been fortunate enough to maintain the equivalent of full-time work between them. In addition, enterprising teenagers in the family are available for seasonal work picking nuts, beans, apples, strawberries, etc. Focusing on surviving in America, all of their efforts are put towards maintaining the education of their children so that "they will get ahead."

We came to this place in the spring of May, two years ago... my heart felt so glad to see this beautiful green everywhere. . . my heart felt so glad and so sad. . . I thought of my home, our farm, the young green. . . much of what is gone. . . the airplanes and the soldier take it all away. . . But here again, my heart felt so happy. . . so I was smiling and crying. . . then we met our host family. . . we were afraid. . . how could they speak to us, and we to them? I hid in the bedroom for two hours because I didn't know what to do or say. . . I didn't want to look so stupid... I was afraid of everything. . . the bathroom, the food, the car, the dog, the shower, the dishwasher. . . Now when I tell this story we all laugh, but that is the real

truth. I was so afraid. . . I didn't want to embarrass
my husband... He speaks some English, so I
unpacked. . . everyone else ate. . . later I came out
for a while. . . they were all so happy to meet me. . .
I didn't say much. . . inside I was happy. . . Slowly I
became free. . . no longer afraid. . . I learned to take
the bus, to shop, to do many things alone... I studied
hard at L.C.C. [Lane Community College]. . .
Mindy was my teacher. . . she told me that women
here don't have to hid away. I didn't quite believe
her. . . it didn't seem right. . . Now I understand. . .
we all have new duties in this country. . . sometime I
miss Lao. . . my family there. . . other things not
here. . . most of the time I am o.k. . . too busy. . .
the children in school, my husband works, we have
other people living here in our house who have no
work. . . we share what we can, that is the Lao
way... I cook and do all the work. . . I am studying
English, I belong to a church. . . they are good
people, I go to the wat in Laos, but I never belonged
to a church. . . The children learn English in
school... they tell us something and we learn them...
Just a little once in a while I feel sad and deep inside
when I think of something... maybe my sister or my
mother. . . maybe something that reminds. . . then I
just don't talk. . . I stay inside until I think about
something else. . . we just try to live. . . to be a little
happy. . . to see our children grow. . . right now
that's enough for me. . .

Narrative 16
Twenty-two and illiterate, this young Lao Lum male arrived
in the United states with almost no transferable work skills. In
two years he has lived in six cities, moving from relative to
relative who support his young family while he earnestly tries

to find employment. With basic welfare grants expired, he lives in constant poverty and in fear of "future troubles."

> I am new to Eugene. . . there are no jobs in Portland, so I come to here for work. . . I have a wife and baby, I must work. . . That is what I want most of all. . . any kind of work I ask do. . . no matter what. Here I have friend and cousin. . . they are helping me. . . when I find a job I will help them back. . . I don't very well speak English. I understand more than I speak. I want to work bad. . . really. . . so bad. . . I am very sad not to work. . . a man needs work. . . this is what I want.

Narrative 17

Son of a Lao Lum man who worked for the Americans, this twenty year old Laotian male lives as part of an extended Laotian family in the United States. Enrolled in E.S.L. classes, he also works part-time as a custodian. More fortunate than a number of the other singles, there was a friendly Lao family, a former business partner of his father's, waiting to take him in as he negotiated resettlement. Formerly from the Vientiane area, he has eight years of school in Laos and had begun studying English there.

> Because of the communist we came here. . . they took everything away. Not at first, but then after a while there was not good life for me. . . no future. . . only work. . . my father was taken away to Sam Neva. . . there he worked very hard. . . too hard for a man of fifty. . . he had to help clean where the American bomb are in the field. . . very dangerous work. . . no pay. . . very little food. . . all punishment for all the extra money the American had give to him. . . while the American in Lao we are very lucky. . . my father make much money. . . Now

96

[it] is all gone. . . nothing. . . he stay in Lao. . . we leave for a better future. . . more education. . . then I go back for a Lao wife and bring her to here. . . We had many houses. . . now only one. . . all the other the government keep, they say we need only one. . . We have to grow some food now. . . before we could buy. . . my two brother, they here. . . my sister they stay. . . we are afraid for trouble to come to them in the camp. . . I want my family to be here. . . Work is very, very hard to find here. . . no job. . . not enough money to pay rent, buy food, make car payment, insurance, so many thing. . . I need the job. . . this is why I come to this country. . . to make a good new life. . . to save money. . . In Lao, I cannot save the money. . . not enough. . . Oh, the camp isn't too good, not so much food, clothes, good things. . . Wait many month to get out. . . the police very bad, very mean. . . take my gold Buddha image... not so very good luck for me. . . very hungry there. . . no money. . . I want to go to U.S.A... so now I am here. I hope for very good luck. . . I hope to learn many new thing. . . I worry about the job. . . can I do what they will ask? Sometime, I [am] afraid they will not like me. . . now I live with another family. . . they are good. The wife, she cook. . . I go to school to study the English... very difficult. . . I try, I know how very important is this English. . . If I speak enough I get the better job. . . Some people in the United States are very much friendly. . . other do not see me. They do not smile or say hello. I think sometime they don't like my black hair. . . I try to look [like] the American. . . that way they like me. . . no trouble from me. . . then a job and a better future. . . Sometime I want the house. . . not too big. . . I want the garden to grow the onion, the hot green pepper,

the little one we like, the tomato. . . This I like very much. . . Now I have the car. . . not so new but work very good. . . no trouble the Japanese car. . . I want for the good job. . . I think this will happen to me. . . that is why I come to the U.S.A. . . for the new life. . . someday in the camp I think I am very wrong to leave my country. . . in my heart I have great pain. . . I miss my family and house and friend. Now I think it is o.k. . . this city is better than the camp. . . better than Lao. . . I have a good future. . . I wait. . . when the new good future come, I am the happiest man. . . all the bad is gone now. . . this I pray. . .

Narrative 18

This sixty year old Lao man had relatives from Vientiane who settled in Eugene. Many times over the two years in the field I had long conversations with him about life, Lao customs, and Lao language. Each time he was careful to say "This is for your head and not for the writing..." Like many of the Lao I encountered, he felt very personal "explanations" were not to be written down. Through him I first clearly understood the relationship of the Lao on both sides of the Mekong River. A gracious host, he called me his "younger brother" and treated me as family, i.e., free to comment in private on anything from my bumbling command of Lao to questions of how American women were "in bed."

My story? I have not thought much about that. . . I am a busy man. A family. . . work. . . a wife. . . children. . . life is many things. . . too many to think about. . . let me see. . . We are farmers in Lao. . . we worked hard. . . we have many buffalo. . . a house. . . big, wood. . . my brothers, too, and their family live there. . . many children. This is good. . . they take care of the mother and father when old. . .

this way we are not alone. . . not like America where
the old are put away. . . I hope my children
remember the Lao way. . . we all work hard. . . it
o.k., this is the way things are. . . I am happy now...
I work, we eat. . . no war here. . . plenty of food. . .
children in school. . . they speak English good. . .
almost like Americans. . . they help me. . . my wife
don't speak. . . only Lao. . . she is good. . . we come
from Lao together... same. . . too much bombs. . .
no food. . . no school. . . fighting. . . new
government no good. . . That's o.k. . . . we leave,
come here. . . American sponsors good. . . they help
sometimes. . . I am not farmer here.... wash dishes...
this o.k. . . I want to work. . . English hard. . . not
same sound. . . I try. . . don't understand. . . I
work... don't think. . . just work. . . I [am] happy
when I work, don't worry. . . no more Lao here,
now... Lao gone. . . I die here. . . no Lao. . . that's
it. . . come and eat. . . my wife cook because you
come. . . enough talk. . . this our way... eat, forget
problem. . . life very short. . . die young if worry
much.

Narrative 19

A twenty-nine year old and father of three, this young Lao
Lum man from the Vientiane area has been employed full-time
since arrival. University-educated as well as having training in
the family business, he was able to transfer work skills quickly
and adapt to the expectations of American employers. Ex-post-
facto, he has expressed regret that he didn't have more time to
study English. Pragmatic and motivated, he has moved upward
from dishwashing to custodial work and on to a supervisory
position. With upward mobility he has increasingly referred to
himself as a Lao-American and seldom socializes with the
"refugee" community.

I came here for a new life. . . I learned English at the Lycee. . . I am not sorry to be here. I have a good job, not what I want yet, but a very good job. . . I have a family, children, my wife is happy. . . We know the life we knew in Laos is gone. . . Many of our people would go back. . . they don't understand the politics and history or economics... they miss their old lives and go through the motion of living here. . . they can't understand the culture. Some of us who were educated had the opportunity to learn Western ways, of course this helped us to adjust. . . these other refugees can't help being ignorant. . . What do they know? Time will change some of them. . . I associate with very few of them. . . my children will be Americans. . . this is the only way to be sure they survive. . . I have closed the book on my old country. . . everything we do is American. . . You know the old saying, "Do in Rome as the Romans do," the same applies to life here. . . It may seem hard to you, but what are my alternatives? I have a wife and a family. . . I had no chance left in Laos. Let's face it. . . regardless of their motivations, regardless of their commitment to the Lao people, the new government was going to have too much of a struggle without American help. . . We were a poor country. . . who wants to spend a lifetime slaving for an idea that may never come about? I only have one life. . . I didn't want to do without. . . with the hope that someday there might be an independent Laos... All the politicians are the same. . . economics is the game. . . we little countries can do nothing without consent of the bigger ones. You have to be on one side or another. . . aligned with a big country to protect you... neutrality is foolish... with a country half destroyed... and no money for repairs... Why talk of neutrality? Neutrality can't feed people... we

left by choice... I could have stayed... I wanted a
better life and I am getting it.... letters from Laos tell
of food shortage and many other problems... Laos
can't do anything with its back turned to the big
powers... They will starve Laos to nothing... what a
shame... You can see, I am not hungry, we have a
comfortable home. . . my children are healthy. . . I
have much here. I have no regrets. . . those that do
are those that don't understand how American
works... they still think as Lao's in America. . . that
doesn't work. . . it all has to go. I think many people
are unable to make that adjustment. It is a problem
most people didn't think about before coming here.
My brother had spent two years in Europe and he
explained the problems he had. We spoke in length
before we left our country. . . at first it was difficult
but I expected that. . . with a little preparation we are
better off. . . in just a few years I am now
comfortable here. . . I am saving to bring the rest of
my family here, not as refugees, but as legitimate
immigrants. . . People came here expecting the easy
life that Americans brought to Vientiane. . . money,
good times. . . good jobs. . . they have been
disappointed. I came here expecting difficulty. . . I
wasn't disappointed.. I am a university graduate and I
washed dishes for six months. . . you have to prove
yourself here. Nothing comes for free. . . later I
became a janitor and then moved on in the company
to a better job. I never complained. . . I never
mentioned the university or the hardship or
humiliation I was feeling to do this kind of work.
That's why I have been successful. . . you can't be
disappointed if you are realistic. . . the better
opportunity was here, I took the chance. . . Don't get
me wrong, I have no great faith in any political
system. . . there's big money behind all of it... all

those people in Laos working day after day to build a new world are in for a great disappointment. . . if a new and better world hasn't come about here in America, it won't happen anywhere. . . work, hard work, is the only way to survive. . . politicians come and go. . . great and little countries come and go. . . still we have to feed our families. . . that is what is lasting. . . survival is the main question for the small man. . . survival any way he can. . . that's why I'm here. . . to survive. . . that's a big word. . . it covers everything.

Narrative 20
In his sixties, this elder Lao Lum man recalls much of the history of modern Laos and remembers the Americans since their arrival in the post-World War II period. His stories of the Lao life and his obvious delight over telling them were a rich source of cultural information. With a good sense of detail and context as well as a great curiosity about life in this new country, he is making adaptations much quicker than many of the younger Lao men. On the other hand, he is at an age where he is free from the worry of having to support a family.

I am an old man. I have lived a long time. . . sometimes my wife asks why I have lived so long and never been sick. I say because I always work hard, try to be generous, and find something good in every man. . . You ask me to talk about my life and about being the refugee. . . can you sit still for that long? Can you listen. . . or will you be writing? I am not sure of what this anthropology is. I understand it to be the story of what happened to my people and how we became the refugee. Tell me, why is a farang [white man], an American, to write this story. . . why not the Lao man? [Please understand, I am not writing this story, I am like the pen, you are the hand.

What you say is the story!] It would be better for all of us if you tell the story. . . [I am only your helper with this task.] You must be very rich to have time to do all this writing. I am born in a small village many years ago. Some of what I tell you I am told by my parents. . . the rest is in my own words. My father was the farmer. . . in his day, most men were farmers. My father was Lao, my mother was Lao Issan. . . in those days we were all Lao. That changed, as many things in my lifetime. We have a good farm. . . everyone work very hard part of the year... the rest of the year we have a little easier. All of my life (until the Americans come), the French put the big hand on our country. . . many taxes. . . the oxen, the flint, even on the children. We have to lie about the number of children. I am lucky... m y mother could read and write and she teach all of us. We never go to school, only the rich could go. . . there [were] very few schools. I learn everything with my father... he teach me about farming, plants, and animals. . . and people. We go to the Wat [Buddhist shrine] and have celebrations. I want to know more. My oldest brother and his family live with my father. I go to work for a Chinese merchant... the Chinese own many businesses in Lao and Thailand. . . I save some money. . . go back to my village and start a small rice business. I marry and have seven children. . . Then the Nippons come and everybody talk about a free Lao. Many people... I think most. . . hate to have the French there. They make Vientiane the big city... make Vientiane more important than any other part of the country. Our part of the country is then put in a lower place. Many people. . . I think most. . . hate to have the French there. They make Vientiane the big city. . . make Vientiane more important than any other part of the country. Our part of the country is then put in a lower place. Many people talk of a free, independent Lao. . . no other country but our own to run our business. . . We fought out the Nippons and then were tired of the great French taxes. Let me think, about the end of July of 1945 we drive away the Nippons. All over the country a new government is happily coming about. . . we have a new constitution... the princes and other leaders want a free Lao. . . then again, some still want the French to stay and trouble begin. The French make the [Vientiane] king the leader over the whole country.... they buy him with the army. . . they want to kill all those who make us work to build bridges and roads, we have no time to work our own farms or business... everybody is fighting. . . then we hear about communism. . . it is all very confusing. . .t he French and the Americans call anyone not on their side communist. . . that was not so. . . many of us are not with the communist group. . . or the French and American group. What a fight. . . those are the busy days. . . you don't know who to trust. . . Those bastards the Thai join the Americans to bomb us. . . that's when the real trouble began. . . we knew we could send the French home, but the Americans? The Thai are a little people. . . they do mean things. . . they are not gracious. . . they turn on their own... you have to watch them all the time. Everyone knew the Americans to be tough . . . soon we found almost everyone except the French and American side working with the Neo Lao Itsala . . . not everyone agree on everything. Sometime in 1950 the Lao National Congress comes . . . then the prince Souphanouvang is elected leader. Many groups support him . . . this committee brings the schools to many areas of the country for the first time. They bring medicine and new farming methods . . . Still I don't like some things they do but felt they could be talked to and to work with once the fighting is over... and they are for the Lao first. . . not other countries. We spend many years fighting. . . my children and grandchildren have no time for school. Some parts of the country are bombed harder. . . we don't know then that it was only a drop of rain compared to the storm to come. In the middle of the 1950's, the Americans take over from the French. . . then come the bombs to many parts of the country. We are not against the Americans. . . we like them. . . we admired them. . . just want our own country. . . no one seem to understand this. . . more and more people move to the big city. . . the countryside is a mess. . . fighting here. . . fighting there. . . most of the destruction come from the airplanes. . . for many years they come every day. . . the airplane doesn't know a communist from a Lao, a Lao from a Frenchman. . . everything is destroyed when the bombs are drop. . . little ones, big ones. . . little pieces of paper that burn. . . the jelly gasoline that burn the skin, the powder and the liquid that kill the trees and plants. . . many kinds of death. . . all from the air. . . we never know so much sadness can fall from the sky. . . still I live. . . my first wife die. . . my second wife is caught on fire when a plane drop bomb. . . my third wife I meet in the refugee camp... over the war years many people become the refugee... first to the cities from the countryside, then from the cities across the border to Thailand.... Always I can remember my wife burns. . . no one help her. . . many nights she come to my head. . . even here in the U.S.A. I thought when I left Lao that would stay there. . . The refugee camp is very sad. . . everyone worry all the time... I am the old man. . . people help sometime. . . a little rice... some cigarette. . . and for two years I live in Thailand. I wait, so now I am here with my son and his family... this is very good. . . I am not alone. . . they are many family. . . they love me. . . I cannot work a big job, but I can still work. . . I plant the garden, I can cut the wood and do fix of things. I can watch the children. . . with the others, I remember the stories of our old country... our ways, our believes. . . I tell the stories. . . I know the songs. . . the people like that... they make me feel good because I know these things.. I am not an American. I live in America. . . I will die here. . . this is the last stop on my life journey. . . I am Lao, I do not live there. . . I will not die in my country. . . my mind is sometimes there. . . What can I do? I have to take the day as it appears. . . I cannot change things. . . I am only a human being. . . If I had my say I'd be home on my farm, I would live in my country. . . hear the old songs and the old language. . . see the old things I know and that know me. . . but this is not so. Now I look at new things, hear a new language. . . do thing a different way. . . that's life. . . one day at a time now. . . My grandchildren, they know more about your country than me. . . I listen to them. . . they have good eyes... they are smart. They tell me everything. . . then my son will say, "How do you know that, father?" I don't tell, but my grandchildren are the teachers. Who knows? Every day is a new surprise. I know more in my own country, here i know only a little. I don't have the whole life to learn over again... the others help. . . they are my eyes and ears... they tell how things are. . . this television, it is very good. . . I like it. . . I learn much about your country... I watch many things I don't understand. . . some things I don't known when to smile or laugh. . .

but when the others laugh, I too laugh. . . it makes
me happy, even if I don't understand. This is only a
small piece of my life I am telling you. . . many
things I once thought important are not now important
to me. . . Next time we can talk more. . . I think
now about many things. . . maybe another day you
will come and we can talk more. I have many
stories.

Narrative 21

Nineteen and learning English rapidly, this unaccompanied
minor, sponsored by a local church, has worked part-time, off
and on, since arrival in the United States. Overcoming many of
the distractions young Lao men his age have fallen into a new
arrivals, i.e., buying clothes, records, and other material things
to "be like Americans," this young man has focused on learning
the language and going to college. Described by his employer
as an "excellent and trusted employee," he has his sights set on
becoming an electrical engineer. Living with an American
family and being one of the few Laotians who have been able to
endure the severity of the changes in daily routine and
perspective on life, he is rapidly assimilating and is distinctly
different from most of the other Laotian youth.

Oh, what do I say? I don't know. . . I like music. . .
I don't think too much about Lao or the camps. . . it
is gone. . . I think sometime of my mother and
father... I [have been] gone a long while. . . they
don't know me. . . I was a little boy, only children
when I leave home. . . My mother cry, my father
send me away for a better life. . . to Australia or to
the U.S.A. . . no chance for me in Lao. . . nothing
left... too much hard work. . . not enough food. . . I
would have [to] go to the army some day. My father
want the better future for me. . . so I go to Thailand
with my cousins. . . I speak Thai so no problem. . .

easy for me to understand there. The Thai police took my money and watch. . . one man took off my clothes and locked me in [a] room by myself to wait... I lost my cousins and then another boy was put in the same room. . . we had no clothes. . . for two days we had to stay locked there. . . then the man say we can make much money if we stay with him... he say some men there will pay much money for us because we are young. . . you understand what I mean? At first we both say no. . . nothing like that... we got hit many times very hard. . . then no food for one day. . . the other boy finally say yes and they take him away. . . I never see him again... he tell me when were are alone he is afraid of pain, afraid to die, he want to live. . . even if he have to do what they ask. . . I still say no. . . they hit me again and again... I hurt. . . am very sore hurt. . . they do things to me I cannot say. . . then I get my clothes back and the police send me to the camp. There I was put with other Lao people. . . I never tell anyone these thing. . . you know, I hate the Thai, they are bad people. . . very mean. . . but I win. . . I am here... I work in the camp. . . first to get wood and make a little money. . . then to help clean building for the camp people. I learn some little English.... not too much. . . I hear that many Lao come to the U.S.A... they say people write the letter to tell of opportunity. . . This is where I will come, too. . . a church sponsor me. . . they take me here. . . I know nothing. . . I was afraid. . . I was happy. . . For two years I have come here. . . now I know more. . . I went to L.C.C. . . I work... I have a stereo and I love music. . . Oh, yes, I have music. . . Sometime I wish there to be more Lao girls. . . the American girls are not for me. . . very pretty, but not the same as what I like. . . some American are very good

friend to me. . . like a new family. . . here I know
Lao people and they are nice to me. . . I am still
young. . . my future yet is unknown. . . I think I can
stay here. . . learn more. . . speak more English. . .
get the good job. . . then, maybe find a Lao wife.
Sometime, not now. . . first to save my money, buy a
car. . . then maybe next year a girlfriend. My
sponsor say I have time, yet. . . I am having to have
time and be here. . . now I know my father to be the
right one. . . this is what he want for me. . . I wish he
could come here. . . Maybe someday, yes? Who
know the future?

Narrative 22
It took well over a year and a half to get this man to speak in
my presence. He was thoroughly convinced I was employed by
the C.I.A. A few months before the end of my fieldwork, he
shook my hand and said, "Now I know you are not C.I.A." I
asked him why, and he said that was his secret and some day he
might tell me if he "can ever trust" me.

He says he doesn't want to tell you anything about his
life... he wants to know why you are doing this. . .
he doesn't believe you. . . maybe you are C.I.A. or
the communist. . . He says this is his own business...
he doesn't want anyone to know his life. . . it is his
alone. . . He says he doesn't believe this
anthropology will be of any help to the Lao people...
He wants to know how much money you will get for
this and what the Lao people get from this. . . He
says no one will tell you the truth and you waste your
time and theirs. . . he thinks you are strange and
stupid. . . he won't speak any more as long as you are
here... his wife will offer you some coffee, but he
will not say any more.

Narrative 23

A former civil servant under the Royal Laotian Government, this man has worked part-time at various jobs since arrival. A lack of English and inability to do heavy manual labor at the age of forty-eight has handicapped his ability to obtain full-time employment. Optimistic when I first spoke to him, the last two years have been difficult as his ability to maintain discipline in his family and to contribute to their support has diminished. A marked change in attitude and motivation have set in after many frustrating failures.

I speak for myself and my wife. . . she will answer but I speak. We have the very good life in Vientiane for many years. . . very lucky. . . three house, farm, children in school, very good health. . . The American bring much money, a good job. . . with this new money our life is more comfortable. Otherwise we have to work the farm land and do many different things. . . without the American money our children will have no school. . . without the American money not enough gas or food. . . we work for the American. . . we don't want the communist. . . we want like the King to keep the American. . . we are small. . . with them we become big. . . I help with the U.S.A.I.D. . . so you know what? I am very proud. . . many people respect me because I am part of the American job. . . We have many American friend. . . they come to our house, eat, enjoy. . . life is so good. . . our city not bomb so bad like the country, but then the American leave.... very quick. . . in a moment. What do we do? We are the good friend to them. . . we do as they ask. . . we help to fight the Pathet Lao communist. . .yet they leave. This is a very big trouble for me. . . everyone know I am for the American and the King. . . This is o.k. for the rich man. . . he send money to Thailand

or to France. . . his family fly or leave by boat. . .
they are all safe. . . me, I have no money to send
out... only my houses and property. . . nothing left...
I have to leave everything. . . only the clothes on my
back and my family. I have about 350 baht [Thai
currency, 22 baht = $1.00 U.S.]. We are all so sad...
we do not want to leave. . . we must. . . one of my
children stay to live in my house. . . one of my
nephew take another house. . . some land we give to
good friend. . . me, I must go. . . they will not kill
me, but I will have no good job. . . I will have to
work hard in the labor because I am for the
American. . . my sons will go to the army. . . before
I play so they don't go. . . I don't want this.... I take
them to Thailand. . . we all go. . . my wife will not
stay in Lao if I am gone. . . we are married twenty
years. . . I have some girlfriend but only one special
wife. . . we come to Non Khai. . . there we are very
poor. . . we know a friend in Non Khai and he give
us a little money. . . not too much... very little, it
save our life.... our baby die there. . . we are sad.
All the other live. . . two years we are in the camp.
Oh, it was bad. . . sometime I [am] depress. . . what
can the man do? Wait, wait, wait. I even think
maybe I make the mistake. . . maybe to stay better...
I hear the story of people go back. . . some are o.k...
the new government doesn't kill everyone after all.
Maybe to stay better. . . my daughter write and say
come back. . . other say no food, no gas, no job,
everyone have to work very hard for a new country.
The war do much damage. . . we stay in Thailand and
wait. . . I [am] afraid to go back and work too hard...
I [am] too old. . . We go to the U.S.A. where life is
easy... where there is much job. . . where there is
plenty of food. . . no war. . . no hard work to build a
new country, already build and strong. . . we wait. . .

long time pass and we come here.... the church is
very good to us. . . we are very ignorant of what to
do. . . we know nothing, everything is strange. . .
sometime we laugh, sometime we cry. . . sometime
we don't know what to do. . . many new thing. . . the
church help us very much. . . find house, help with
food, give me part-time job. . . my children go to
school. . . we learn English. . . we meet many
people. . . we suddenly have many new families. . .
cousins, grandmother, friend to help. . . so we stay
here always. . . Later I lose my job. . . my wife go
to work. . . so very hard to clean the motel.... after a
year many friend no longer come to say "hello"... to
bring food. . . to explain what to do. . . Now two
year here we have a few friend. . . the church still
very good. . . very helpful. . . but we miss our friend
at home in Lao. . . we miss the market. . . we do not
know this language so well. . . we are different. . .
our family change. . . each day the children become
to like the American. . . I am now the strange man to
them. They do not speak Lao too much. . . they do
not talk too much to me. . . these words, this
language come between our family. Everything is
very expensive here. I own no house or land.
Sometime I no have the work. I cannot give the
children what they need. . . they do not look to me
with the special favor of father. . . I am small to
them. . . not important. . . the refugee. . . my
daughter will not bring the friend here. She say we
do not have the American custom. This very bad
inside for me. . . very much hurt. . . in our country
all people welcome to the house. . . more come, more
happy we are. . . share with all. I think the children
will be o.k. here. . . they learn the American way to
do very quickly. . . in a few year when they finish
school, when they are safe, maybe I go back to my

country. . . I miss my country so much.... better for
me to be the street cleaner, the servant, in a place I
know.... there I am somebody. . . here I a m
nobody... nobody see me. . . nobody know my name.
What good the house? What good to come here,
U.S.A., if nobody know my name? Is this not the
same as the dead ones?

Narrative 24
A very young Laotian woman, this sixteen-year old high
school student struggled through six interviews, with help from
her family, to develop the following statements. Her comments
about the family and the changes the traditional Laotian family
is experiencing at the interrace of cultures are both astute and
painfully honest.

It is hard to speak to you. . . first, because you are
American and from the University. . . and because
you are a man. . . and because you speak only a bit of
Lao. . . my English is not so good. I'm embarrass,
but I'll try. Sometime I think about being a refugee...
sometime not... I have many American friends in
high school. I am sixteen, everything is usually o.k.
when I am with the kids, but when I have to go to
someone house. . . or to the dance or party. . . I feel
very different, as much as I try, I am not the
American. Many things I don't understand. . . many
things they don't understand. In Lao it was different.
I was in the school and everyone did the same thing...
we all understood. . . lucky for me, my brothers and
father went into the camp with me. I was not alone.
I cry many hours... many days. . . after a while only
on the inside. . . I miss everything. . . most, my
friend who I will never see again. We had a big
house. . . we were never hungry. . . I had good
clothes. . . then the Americans left and took all the

money away and my Dad had no job.... in the camp
we had no nothing. . . we were very ashamed of not
to have clean clothes. . . everyone who saw must
think we are the beggar. . . you know, very poor.
My mother felt so bad. This was not so in Lao, that
is the very honest truth. We have many people in our
family here because many cousins can't get jobs. . .
my mother and father try to feed everyone. . . they
come to our house to eat. . . just a little bit, but
something for everyone. Sometimes we are hungry...
that's o.k. because we are better here than in the
camp. I have many dream. . . I want to have many
nice clothes like the American girls in school. I want
some new furniture for our house. . . I want my
mother not work two jobs and my father to have
one... everyone worry too much here. . . worry about
the car payment. . . worry about enough money for
rent. . . worry about enough food. In Lao we relax
more. . . we talk more and eat food with our
friends... we sing and dance.... here we have not so
much time for friends. I want to finish high school
and go to college. . . maybe someday I will marry
and have children... not until school is finished. I
don't want to be poor no more. You know, I mean
not to have enough money to enjoy life just a little
bit. I will work hard for that. . . I still dream that all
possible to be. They told us, who knows, anything
can happen in America. . . I will always miss Lao. . .
crazy thing happen to us here. . . sometime my father
is so unhappy. . . I don't understand... he want to
work. . . he is not lazy. . . no job. . . his English isn't
too hot. At home [in Laos] he was important, he
worked every day. . . my mother didn't work. . . she
cooked, helped with our school, shopped, and did
women things. Here she is a maid. . . she has to
clean the dirty hotel room every night. At first she

would cry before leaving. . . then my father would
feel sick. Now she says nothing. . . just go. . . but I
know. . . her eye tells you she is sad. . . she walk
slow to the door. . . we love her very much. . . she
never complain. . . everything to everybody...
nothing for her. My Dad is ashamed she has to do
this. . . he feel no good. . . he hit us once, but we
know he loves us. . . he waits all night for my mother
to come home. . . he never sleep when she works. . .
he just sits or talks with us. When we go to sleep he
cleans, cooks, or does some things for my mother. . .
we pretend not to see him because he is doing
woman's work. . . he wants to help. . . We all have
hopes. My brother got a job, he helps some. . . my
sister husband got a job, they help some. We all
share... what else can we do? Everyone understand
that things are not so good in America right now. . .
the American is hard to find jobs, too. . . so we wait.
Maybe by the time I am seventeen things will get
much better. I have a boyfriend now. . . his family is
strange, but nice. I feel good that someone things I
am nice. It is then that I forget about being a
refugee... when we walk or go shopping, or go to the
movie, I walk proud... I feel good. I am like
everyone else. My father tell me to enjoy being young. . . he says we get old very soon enough. . .
Do you understand English? [Yes, no problem.] o.k.,
I am speaking only two years. . . the language is so
hard. . . the most worst of all things. . . what to do
when you can't say what is in your mind and heart.
Sometime the American think we don't like them
because we don't say too much. . . not so. . . we just
don't know the right word. . . we still feel. . . want
people to hear. . . All in all. . . it is easy as time
pass. . . more English, more speaking, more classes
help us to figure out what to do and what to say. I

think it will be much easy for me than my Mom and Dad. . . they find it hard to begin all over. . . for me, I am still at the beginning. . . I still have many dreams.

Narrative 25

A husband and wife, thirty-seven and forty-one, respectively, this couple has taken their family to California for security. He found some part-time work in the city while he was in Eugene, but with increasing difficulties straining the economy of the greater community, this sole source of income and self respect dried up. A recent letter from the husband indicates both he and his wife have found part-time work and all the children are doing well. Despite the economic success found in California, they miss the small community where they knew everyone.

We are happy and not so happy. . . happy to be here... very lucky to be alive. . . five of our nine children are still alive. . . we have apartment, some food, and we work, very hard work, but we are lucky to work. We have friends, Americans. . . our church helps us. Most of the time we are so happy. Only a little bit of the time we are unhappy. Some days we miss Lao, we look for old friends but they are not here to be found. We remember our dead children and relatives. . . I miss my kitchen and my house. . . the old way. . . the big family. . . the festivals. . . the wat and the market. I most of all miss my oldest daughter still in Lao. . . she is all alone without us... what can she do all alone? [Now the husband speaks] Me, I don't speak very good English. . . there are not many men here to talk with... business, politics, news, you know, what men talk about. I have few Lao friends here. . . my heart is very lonely for my old friends. . . my farm, the old times. I know were

are very lucky to be here. . . please excuse that
sometimes I am very lonely and unhappy. This I
can't help... maybe when I can speak better your
language I will not feel so very little as I do now. I
miss feeling like a man. . . I have a very good wife,
good American friends, for that I am a very lucky
man. I try to forget about all the past. . . when I
remember, my heart hurts, my head, too. I'm
finished for now.

Narrative 26

Interviews twenty-six and twenty-seven are from the same
family. This interview is of the father, who is around fifty
years old. Both father and son speak passable English.

My children are happy here. . . they don't remember
as much. They try all the new things.. they are
getting very smarter than their mother and father. . .
The oldest son is unhappy. . . He cannot find an
American woman who behaves and stays with the
home and children like the Lao women. . . maybe he
will go back to Lao or to Thailand and find a wife and
then come back here. . . the other children are young
so they don't miss Lao so much. . . We have traveled
for many years. . . now here [Eugene] is home to
them. . . this is good. They speak English, study,
and will be successful. I hope they marry
Americans... the past is too much hurt to remember
here. . . they have new American chances.

Narrative 27

This interview is of the twenty-nine year old son of the man
in interview twenty-six.

I worked for the new government after the Americans
left... believe me, I know all about it. Things were

very bad. . . not enough food. I had to go to my
mother's house to eat. We were paid very little. I
was a policeman. Let me tell you, the government
wasn't that bad. . . I mean. . . it tried to do things,
but it didn't. Nothing worked. No gas, no food, no
nothing, really. How can you live under a
government like that? No nothing, you can't live on
that... I liked their ideas for life. . . but they couldn't
make them work. You can't eat ideas. . . nothing
worked. Nothing. They tired. . . it just didn't work
out. . . so we left. They didn't want people to
leave... if they left, then nobody would be there to
help put together things after the Americans left. I
wanted the new government to be successful. . . it
had many good ideas of the heart. . . food for
everyone, jobs, no cheating, schools for everyone!
They couldn't do this. . . many people left because
they didn't want to share what they had. The war
damage was bad, really bad. . . and of a sudden the
Americans took all the money away. . . that's it. . .
they said. . . we won't help the socialist. . . we
thought maybe we could go it alone. . . we couldn't...
America is a big country, they decided we couldn't
have the kind of government we want. . . so, if I have
to have it the American way, I might as well as come
to here where there is no destruction and a chance. In
Lao, our people don't have a chance anymore. They
say the Americans "lost" the war. . . but really we
lost because everything we knew was destroyed. . .
Nothing was destroyed in America. . . only in Lao.
So really, they have won because they haven't been
made to pay the damage. We don't know too much
about the United Nations. . . but if they were all for
the people in the world, they would make the U.S.A.
pay for the damage. Anyway, they don't, so what's
the use? I'm here now. . . I have to do things

different than there. Here I have no opinion. . . I
can't vote, I am a refugee. You know what that
means. . . we don't have any say. . . we have to smile
when we get stale bread and old clothes. . .
sometimes too big or too small... some few
Americans are very special. . . they don't see me as a
refugee. . . only as the man, the friend. . . the human
being. . . these people make my heart feel good. I
love them because they don't have to do nothing for
me. . . nothing. . . but they do. I would do that for
them if they need in my country. That is the Lao
way. Here, I'm not Lao, not American. . . sometimes
it confuses me. . . you know? At first I just watched
a lot to see what to do. . . how to act. . . not to be
seen as a refugee. I made many mistakes. Now I am
good at being an American. . . it is easier now than
when I cam to San Francisco first. . . Americans like
Lao to smile a lot. . . and not say much. So I do this,
except with my friends, with them I have opinions. . .
I talk, I ask questions. . . those are the Americans I
like the very most best. I'm still afraid of
restaurants... otherwise I do o.k. . . I'm going from
this city. . . no jobs here. . . we are eating very
little... For food, a little better than the camp but not
much more. . . so I'm going away. I will come back
when I have money. I like this city. . . not too big,
not too crowded, very clean, and not too many
refugees. Here I have to learn more English, that I
want. I like the community college [L.C.C.]. . . they
saved my life many times by helping with problems...
still, I have to go now. . . no jobs, you know... that's
too hard. . . we need food, gas, money for shoes. . .
maybe the future will be lucky. . . I think so. . .
when I'm lucky I'll come back here to my friends.

Narrative 28

A single parent and a relatively unskilled worker, this Lao Lum woman, age thirty-three, has managed to survive as a maid and as a cook. Throughout the three years she has made time to continue to study English and has become fluent enough to survive in the world of work. A modest, self-sacrificing mother, she has transferred most of her hopes and dreams to the one son who lives with her. Simultaneously she has continued to search for her other son, writing letters to official agencies and friends still in camps, in the hope of finding him.

I have to think. I have been here three years now. My husband died in Laos. . . in Sam Neua where he was sent away to clean bombs the American drop. It burned deep into my heart. I have two children. . . with my brother and his wife and others we crossed the border to the camp, we had very little. . . The camp, it was very crowded and dirty. . . not enough water to keep clean. . . I was so embarrass. . . Not like my own country where I had a big house, land, friends. What good is the house if you have no money to feed your children, no husband, no future? At first I prayed very hard for better things to happen, two times we moved because of war. . . many family and friend we now cannot find. . . the new government was too hard... everything changed. . . I like the old way and the King. My husband was a friend of the General Nosavan. He knew him from a little boy. The family of Nosavan would not help me... they "didn't know me" anymore when I needed the help. Little food, two children, no husband. . . What could I do? My sister came to the U.S. in 1978. She wrote and said things were very different here but not so hard. . . jobs, food, no war. The government far away across the country in Washington. . . not in your yard counting the

chickens. I gave my house to a cousin to keep.
Someday I will go back when I save money. I was
very lonely in the camp. . . and I am sometimes very
lonely here. In the camp I cried many times. . . I
was worried to come so far away to a new place.
They said there was no rice in the U.S.A. and all the
people eat sandwiches. I could not speak the English
language so well. I was afraid the American would
think I am stupid. Somehow I got here. My one son
is separated and we are lost to him. My other son is
here with me. I still look for my other son. I ask, I
write the letters, someday I believe we will see him
again. Someone in the camp at Panat Nikom said he
was sent to Australia. He would be fifteen now. He
was very handsome like his father. I came here. . .
first to Pennsylvania. It was very cold. I never knew
the snow, ice, and winter before. I did not know how
to walk on the snow. I was afraid. Outside
everything was gone. . . only snow. . . everywhere.
My first job was to clean houses. It hurt to clean the
other woman's house. . . but I was happy to make
money. . . then I didn't have to be ashamed and worry
about money from the government. I did not go to
school in Pennsylvania. I had no friends. My sister
send me money to come to here. We moved to here
by bus and were very happy to be with family. Oh
yes, I was so happy. Then she move to California. I
like it here. I work, I study. There is very much I do
not understand. . . I watch television but I do not
always understand. I hope some day to have another
husband.. no one yet. My son is in school. His
teacher tell him to make decision for himself. I want
to help him. . . this is the Lao way. . . he will not let
me. He says he knows more about the U.S.A. . . he
wants to be a singer. I want him to be some important man. . . to go to school, to take a good wife,

have the good family. He wants to stay single. . .
who ever heard of that strange way? This I don't
understand. The camps change him. Before he was
very good. . . he listened and was very respectful. In
the camp he met too many bad people. Here, the
good people do not talk with the refugee. In my
country I was the good people. Americans do not
understand this. There is no man here to talk to
him... or to say no. He won't listen to me. I have no
meaning as mother to him. He say "speak English"
or he won't talk to me. He say "be American." This
is very hard for me. . . very, very hard. Something I
can't change. Something I don't know how to do, I
am not the American. I am Lao. I am the refugee
person. What do I do? There are many things I don't
understand. I try. I try every day to learn more. . . I
can't make him happy. He wants to go to California
to live where the movie star. I don't want him to
go... he is my only family here. I cook everything he
love. . . still not happy. I go to the counselor, he
cannot help. He doesn't understand the Lao way. I
am too ashamed to tell too much. I hope everything
is o.k. soon. I miss my other son, my house, my
husband, my friend. . . here I have little. Food and
job are not enough. . . my alone gets very big. . .

Narrative 29
   Twenty-eight years old and originating from the area around
Ubon in the middle of the country, this man works two jobs as
he contributes to the support of his extended family. Like
many Lao men, he is frustrated over the shortage of young
Laotian women available for marriage in the refugee
community.

I'm not sure I understand. . . I don't know what to say. I put in my mind your questions about Lao, the refugee and here. Nothing together. . . many thought. . . first of my old home and family. . . as I think in the past when I used to be there. . . it seems so very nice and beautiful my country. . . here is beautiful but there is my home. . . where I was a little boy, where I knew many things so easy... not like here where I have to learn everything very new. . . We had a wood house. . . up high. . . you know how, with the many window. . . I live in my mother's house with my wife, she was very good to us. We went there to live until we had a house of our own in the future. . . We were farmers, my brother worked for the American, he made the most money and bought a radio. . . We had the bull, chickens, and the other animals. . . we grew the rice, the field was beautiful and very green. . . nice to look at. . . it make me very happy. . . We caught fish, too. My wife left my home to go to an American. . . I was very unhappy and moved to another town with my uncle. He sold ice and had his own shop. Later we decided to go away with the American because the new government was very hard. No gas, not enough rich, no new American thing. They say we all have to work very hard. They come to our town and talk to everyone. They say everything will be very hard because the American and the Thai destroy our country. some people were taken to the prison camp for a new education because they helped fight with the American or because they had too much more money than us. We decide to leave just because it was too hard. No future for me there. I want to come to the U.S.A. where all people are very rich. . . save much money. . . buy the nice car and house. I don't want to work hard in Lao for everyone else. No

sir. Not that way with the communist. . . it makes
everyone lazy. . . no profit for you. . . just for all. I
spent one and one-half year in the camp. I knew
nobody in the U.S.A., so I had to wait until a church
would take me here. The Mormon take me here.
After a while I go on my own because my custom is
different. They were good to me. . . but, you know,
no smoking, no beer. . . all that is what the Lao do. I
like to drink beer and to smoke. So I come to here
where I am far away. That way they do not see me
drink and smoke. I still write to them and feel them
as family. I am better here with my friend in Eugene.
I am not yet again married. . . but maybe later. I
don't understand American women. They are
different. They don't want to cook or clean or have
children. . . they are very expensive to have as the
wife. First you must support them, buy nice things
and do their work as well. This is not good. I want a
Lao wife. When I save enough I can go to Thailand
get my kind of wife.... some person to be good to me
and understand my way. American woman don't
even know how to cook rice. . . everything is sandwiches. Right now I have two jobs. . . as a
dishwasher and in the factory. I also help my friend
and his wife and three children because he has no job.
I live with them. They are my family here. We all
help each other. She cook the food I know. We all
understand each other. I don't think about the refugee
much. Right not I worry about the future. What will
happen when I get old and have no family? I know
some day I will have to go home to my country. . .
even if it is communist. . . because I cannot be an old
man here where no one knows my way. . . now I
work hard and save. . . later I will see what to do. . .
This city is good to me, some people here are very
good. . . I am doing o.k. now... Only when I think of

Lao am I very sad. . . do you understand that? Lao is
so very far away. Maybe I will see my country again
some day. I would like that very much...

Narrative 30

This traditional Lao Lum woman is in her late sixties. Her
comments about her life in the United States shed some light on
North American cultural values as they relate to the elderly.

> My new life here is very hard. . . I am not hungry....
> I have the apartment with my family. . . I am
> healthy... The hard is to know very little American...
> the language is very hard for an old woman. . . the
> city is very big and not like my town. . . the store,
> the cars, the people do things very different from my
> way. . . No one here talks to me... they do the
> business but they do not say hello, how is your
> family. . . or ask the question of my friend at home
> who know me and know my way. . . I do not go
> anywhere very much. . . no one to sit and talk to...no
> one to visit, no temple, no shop to buy things in my
> own way. . . The television speaks a different
> language. . . I do not know what is happening around
> me. . . I do not drive the car. . . my husband is
> dead... no one here to take care of me. . . my son and
> daughter are very good to me but not the same as
> having the husband or brother. . . Something I
> cannot buy here to cook. . . the stove is very dif-
> ferent, too. . . I am very old to learn so many new
> thing in this life. . . even the bird sound different
> here, they sing a different language... My old house
> was very big, my daughter and her husband lived
> with us... seven grandchildren. . . much land, cows,
> chicken, vegetable. . . I have much work to do
> there... clean, wash, cook, the garden, feed the

animal, many thing each day. . . My daughter and granddaughter help me, too. . . we cook rice, some friend and other relative come to our house to eat. . . many cousin. . . my grandson catch many fish for us... no rent to pay. . . the taxes but no rent. . . it is our house. . . I do not want to leave this house. . . I always live there. . . I know the spirit. . . they good to us always. . . so very good. . . My husband and one son die for the army. . . then when the new government come they say some of our land must be taken to give away. . . they say I have too much land... I need it all. . . big family. . . some land for my grandchildren. . . they take some. . . After a time my other son and daughter go to Thailand, then my other daughter and her husband, then some grandchildren and cousin. . . some friend leave. . . then my daughter and her husband want to go. . . What can I do? First I say stay with me. . . they say go to live with my cousin in Savannakhet. . . no, I will stay. . . then I cry. . . they leave in the night. . . I cry so hard. . . everyone go. . . no one know where... I am old. . . the police come to look for my daughter's husband... they say he take money. . . later my friend and her husband go to the Thailand camp. . . I decide to go. . . I give my house to my cousin. . . his son stay there to live... I take a little money. . . they come with me to the camp. . . there I find my daughter and some other family and friend... everyone is poor... we are happy to be together. . . I am old but strong. . .my cousin in Thailand lend us some money. . . this help so we don't starve. . . now I come here. . . I did not know the world to be so different. . . this world is so small for me. . . I am not sick. .. only my heart burns for my old home. . . my friend. . . I know I cannot change this way. . . here I am. . . still, my heart burns for the thing I

know. . . sometime when I dream I am happy. . . I
see my old house, my town. . . I am here two years
and one-half now. . . much is so very strange. . . I
wish to be happy again some day. . . this I hope for...
My grandchildren are happy here. . . they grow so
big, so healthy. . . they grow different in the head
than in Lao. . . some of this way I cannot
understand... sometime they hurt my heart by what
they say and do. . . my son tell me this is o.k. . . they
do not want to hurt me. . . they must be American. . .
I try to understand this. . . maybe in more years I will
understand this American way.. Oh, it is the very different way from the Lao way. . . from my way. . .

Question: Do you feel as though you are becoming American?

Only a little bit. . . almost all Lao still. . .

Narrative 31
A fifty year old, former merchant in Laos, this man has had
great difficulty finding a meaningful place in American society.
He has often expressed feelings of disempowerment, loss and
isolation.

You asked me to think of my home in Laos and why I
left... you asked about the camps. . . and then the
experience of the refugee in this new country. . . For
a few weeks these questions have been on my mind...
they are not easy questions. . . I have thought of
many bad times. . . Some I cannot express... others
would make so sense to anyone but myself. . . other
things I, of course, could say to no one. My country
was something I thought very little about until I made
the decision to leave. . . before that time I was busy
with life. . . never thinking I would like in any other

country, even when times were the very worst of all... maybe I thought I might live in some other part of my own country. . . We have talked at other times of the war. . . you know these things. I will try to tell, as you have asked, my own story. You know... as I have thought about these things since you asked last month.... I have change inside. This thinking has changed how I see myself. Now that I think about these things of my life. . . they become different from when I was just living them. To be doing something and to talk about something are quite different. My first thought of Lao is of my home. . . the house I grew in.. the wood, the kitchen, the water not so far away. Oh, I loved that house. . . it was safe for a little boy. I had my mother to take care of me and my auntie as well. We were not very rich or very poor. . . I enjoyed to play and fish and be with other boys, my brothers and sister. Sometime I went to the field. . . we worked with my father and uncles. . . later my father no longer worked in the field.. he advanced to a job working for the American company. . . this was good because he was getting older. I was young at the end of World War II. Everyone was talking about what would happen to our country. The French were there a very long time. At that time our own country seem to be a good idea. I was young. I had thoughts of young women in my head more than politics. . . I secretly wanted to see the French go home. Many people my age spoke of a new country. . . a free country. . . all Lao. Of course, there were many worries... What of the Vietnamese. . . would they cause trouble? Could we win against the French? We would drink coffee or beer and talk late into the night. At that time we didn't think too much about the American. We admired them. . . we heard stories of their country...

automobiles, big homes, and no sickness. We saw them in the movie. We knew they were very powerful. . . even the communists weren't against them at that time. Everyone worried about the French or the Vietnamese. I studied communist thought at school. . . we were allowed that in our country, you know. I was lucky to be getting a very good education because my father worked for an American company. What I studied about the communist and the communist people I knew were very different situations. Many times I understood and in my heart, hoped for the communists. They helped many people. . . started schools, taught agriculture, bought medicine where only the Buddhist priest came before. There were many people in my country who were very poor. . . could not read or write. . . and many children died of sickness. In some parts of my country war did great damage. The poor were with the communists and also many of the Yao [Mien]. When the French lost, the Americans came. It was different. . . there were some very High Lao who wanted them to help take the country from the communists. I believe these Lao didn't understand what would happen if they did this. . . they had good jobs, much land, they didn't want to give them up to the communists. Other Lao wanted the neutral government. . . this government didn't work. . . who can say why. Many men say the reason was this or that. . . I think it is because we listened to all the outsiders and each of them had a reason to talk into a Lao ear. This made some people greedy. We couldn't come to any agreement inside our Lao family. Over the years as a young man I was very confused. . . one month I wanted this, one month I wanted that. . . Our leaders all said confusing things... some we knew to be lies. Some people in our country became very rich. . . we could see that. My father made a good living. . . it changed my life. We became used to many good things that came without trouble. I cannot apologize for this. . . in some ways it made our life easier. Isn't that what we all want for our families? Only later, away from my country, after thought, do I see the price we paid for so much ease. I did not know I was changing them. I considered myself Lao. . . really, I was becoming like an American man. Inside. . . more and more. . . that's what I wanted to be. I never thought about that. Over many years our country was at war. . . during that time I married and became a father eleven times. Eight sons is a good record. My good feeling would become sorrow as some of my children became communist. Our family became divided. . . they argued with their own father. They accused me of "selling" the Lao to foreigners. That hurt my heart. My wife cried many nights. Two of our sons and one daughter went away. How do these things happen? Of course I didn't listen to them at the time. Now one is dead and the others are far away. . . I lost everything. When the Americans left, I stayed. Oh, our country was a mess. I believe any side that won the war would have had many problems. There were not many good-paying jobs when the Americans left. The new government was very hard. They didn't like the criticism but the politics. . . they were very bad like the Vietnamese. They made big mistakes. They wanted change very quickly. They were angry and bitter. . . angry because the Americans gave no aid for the damage of the war. Everyone agreed this war was not good of the Americans. They were bitter because they won. . . but they had big problems. What they wanted to do with the revolution they could not because of the war mess. They couldn't get at the Americans. . . so they were very hard on those who were on their side before. I think many people would never have left the country if these hard ways had not come. I knew I had to leave. I hated the communists for being so hard. . . I wanted to say, yet I know I had to leave. Somehow all of the Lao failed.... we failed to say together as a family, and so we had no care. There was much bitter hurt. All those years of fighting we should have stayed together. Maybe things might be different now. . . I am so far away from my country but in my heart I am still Lao. I hate the communists and the Vietnamese for taking my country. Yet, as I have thought about it. . . I do understand why it has happened. We were not generous with each other. . . any of the sides. Somehow, down in my heart, when I arrived in Thailand, I knew I had made the wrong decision. I didn't want to face that. I didn't want to admit I had made mistakes. I wanted to believe the communists had caused this. Only later do I see we were all responsible. So, here I am. Not a young man anymore... I am faced with very difficult problems. Still, in some ways, I am lucky. My wife and some of my children are here. . . I have a place to live and food to eat... even so, I do not belong. I am lost here to learn this American life. When I left I felt for sure my dreams would come true in America and everything would be o.k. Even if I do have food and a house. . . there are other parts of me that have no food and are starving. The Lao in me will not die. . . it calls to me at night to go home. I cannot do this... I am afraid, I am stubborn. . . I do not want to live that hard life. Then, I do not wish to live this life.... one where I am in a prison because I do not understand or belong. Right now I wait. . . my youngest son and his cousin will go back to Laos this year. . . they cannot stay here. . . they miss the Lao life. They will write and tell me if it is o.k., maybe I will go home. . . If I have a house and some food, then I will go home. I do not want to die here in this strange place. You see, I have done many things in my life. This is just the part you asked me to speak about. As the refugee, I do not want you people to think I am a bad guest. I appreciate what my friends and neighbors here have done for me and other Lao. But I do not belong here... I am Lao. . . How is it I had to come this far away from my home to see it as it is? I was like the blind man before. . . just living without thinking. If many of us go home, maybe we can change the way things are. Now I will take less... maybe I should have seen this way before. If all the Lao had demanded a little less of each other and gave a litttle bit more to each other, we might have remained a family. The price I paid for having so many things was to lose everything. . . then to have to leave... then to have to be a dead man in a body that lives in another way of life. I still hate the communist. . . but maybe I can learn to live with them. Television has told me there is little peace anywhere in the world. All their bombs and wars and fighting. I thought it I cam here I would never hear of that again. . . so you see, I was wrong again. Americans are people. . . they are not perfect. . . there are good and bad. I have seen the rich and the poor American people. . . everyone here is not rich or healthy. Everyone does not have the easy life. . . most of the refugee people have a very hard life here. I did not know this before. . . we Lao are as big as we thought the Americans to be. We are all people, we make mistakes. . . we do some good things. . . and the communists are here. . . and you seem to live with them. Oh, we have talked much tonight. There

are many more thoughts in my mind. . . my tongue is
tired. Maybe you will come to Laos if I go back.
You will be welcome there. The Lao are good to the
guest. If you go there your Lao will get to be very
good very quickly...

Narrative 32
This twenty year old Lao Lum man from the area around
Vientiane has in recent months requested return to his country
through the United Nations.

How can I say to these questions? I am not educated.
I think. . . but these are hard to make words for. I
am young. . . many thing I remember, but not a
story. Thing I remember. . . the light at the
celebration and the many candle. . . the food. . . so
many kind of thing not here. . . my mother and
sister... my father and my friend. . . my dog, my
father's horse. . . all of the wood and many open
window. . . the vegetable and to fish. My
grandfather went with me to fish. . . we went to the
market and he smoke. . . he buy for me something
sweet. The buffalo were in the field. . . the new rice
plant was very green and beautiful. Vientiane was a
big city for me. . . we live in the country. We did
not have the car. . . we had a cart. I left Lao because
my friend go. My family was very unhappy. . . they
say to stay. I did not want to work so hard. . . I go to
Thailand. . . we hear on the radio Asia the Lao. . .
they say it is a good life in the United States. . . much
money, good job, no problem. This is good to me.
Everyone in Lao work too hard for almost nothing.
The communist government did not take the house.
We had to give some chicken and food to other
people. . . I did not like this. I want to come to this

country. The refugee camp not so bad. . . not so good. . . nothing to do. . . just to wait. . . many people sick. I am very lucky. . . I am strong. . . no problem. I got skinny from no good food. . . but I am o.k. I wait two year to come to the U.S.A. When I come here it is different. . . very big. . . very confusing. . . I go to E.S.L. and try to speak the English. I cannot write Lao very good. I need to work for the money. How can I live with no money? I have a car. . . I have a part-time job. I would like the wife. . . not enough Lao women here. Maybe I will go to California next year to find a Lao wife. Many Lao women in California. . . Stockton. Someday, when I save enough money, I go back to Laos. That's o.k. for me. I was not in the army. . . I did no wrong. I can go back. . . now .. I want to be here for one year. . . two year more.. Later, when I have the children, I will go back to Lao. My sons will be living in Laos. My wife will be the Lao wife. I learn much in this country. This will help my family when I go home. I send money home to my father... I am welcome there. I am not afraid.

Narrative 33

As the seventeen year old son of a former civil servant in Laos, this high school student is rapidly assimilating into the American life. Convinced, at this point, that the only way to get by is to act like an American, he refuses to speak Lao. For him, "English only" is the way to learn about America. This has distressed his father, and a wide communication gap has grown between them.

I am a teenager. I was young when we left our home. I knew we were leaving. My father and uncles talked about it. My father had a very good job before. He

worked for customs... when the communist
government come to power he lost his job and had to
make less money. He was very angry. He owned
four or five houses. . . he had to give all except ours
to the government. I was in school when we left. I
studied English in Laos. We had a big house and
plenty of food. . . we had motorcycles. When we
left, my father sent some money to my uncle in
Thailand... we sold some things and gave some
things to our friends. My brother was in Thailand
working. Before the communist came he took much
of my mother's jewelry and some money to Thailand.
We took very little with us when we came across the
river. I was sad to leave my friends. . . but I was
excited to go so far away. We didn't tell our friends
what day we were leaving. We left at night. . .
everyone was afraid to get caught. At first we lived
with my brother... then the Thailand government said
too many Lao were coming over the they wouldn't let
people get work permits. Then my mother and father
and three children went to the refugee camp. Two
sisters and one brother stayed with the family of my
older brother. We spent five months in the refugee
camp. There was little to do. . . no school for the
children. . . there was nowhere to go, not enough
food. . . my mother cried. My father was angry some
days and hit us. Finally, we came to the U.S.A. A
church was our sponsor. . . they helped us get a
house. We go to that church. We are Christians
now, we are not Buddhist like in Thailand. My father
has a job. My mother works part of the time. I am in
school. . . my brother in Thailand sent us some of our
money from selling our mother's jewelry. We have
two cars, we have colored television. I want to go to
college. My brother and his wife are trying to come
here now with the rest of our family. They must

come as immigrants. . . not as refugees. Our church will try to help them. My father has told him he must become a Christian if the church will help him. I am an American now. I am not Lao. I changed my name to an American one. All my friends call me this American name. I never want to go back there. The people are ignorant, they are poor and sometimes they are dirty. They do not have the modern life we have here. This is so much better. Americans are number one. I am an American now. I hate communists. I will go back there and kill them some day. Then we can free the Lao people from communism. My minister told me the communists don't believe in God. Americans believe in God and they are free. Americans are number one.

One Family: A Profile

The extended Laotian refugee family in this profile consists of four households: a husband and wife who have separated for financial reasons, a daughter and her husband, a son and his wife, and a single son and his girlfriend. The wife of the first household, now in her late forties, lives in a separate apartment with five children who were born of her second husband, from whom she is separated for financial reasons. This man travels from household to household to stay with his "family." Included in this profile are the views of the eight adults mentioned above, as well as brief comments by some of the children, other extended family members, and friends. Three generations of Laotians are represented, covering a period of over seventy years. I have edited a great deal of material and consolidated interviews in order to restrict the focus to the experiences of this family. Indeed, due to the fluidity of the Lao community stemming from secondary migration patterns, I could have included additional materials involving people from other cities and Lao communities in the Pacific Northwest and California.

My intent in including the experiences of the members of one family was to provide multiple viewpoints and perspectives on the same questions I had asked the other adult members of the community to address in their life histories, while simultaneously attempting to record the changing structure of the family during this post-camp transition period. In addition, I asked each member to comment on typical days in their lives as refugees--in the camps and in the United States. This, to the degree that is possible, provided subjective comments regarding their personalities and experiences, balanced with accounts of daily schedules and behavior.

This family, the members of their extended family, and their friends in the Lao community demonstrate the complex sets of characteristics which the refugee population has to deal with. The setting is a middle-sized city of the Pacific Northwest in the Willamette Valley. Most of the activity transpires in two housing complexes in a relatively small urban slum area. From the outside, these buildings appear to be exactly what they are: box-like structures of the late 1960's built to accommodate low-income families. Absentee or non-maintaining landlords have let the properties deteriorate. The outside of the buildings is clean from refuse, but grassy areas, shrubs, and trees have grown wild and are not tended on a regular basis. Surrounding the complex are a series of industrial businesses and a major thoroughfare.

The Mother
This is a woman in her late forties. She is, by all appearances, typical of many of the older Lao women who have come to the United States. She generally maintains Lao dress, a white or colored blouse worn with the traditional si:n, or skirt. Conscious of her Lao background, she wears sandals or flat shoes, never sneakers or high heels. She never wears make-up, but wears jewelry her sister was able to buy for her in

Thailand. She was difficult to talk with, shy of speaking with an American man as well as a teacher. Her son acted as translator and after a dozen sessions we were able to put together this narrative. Like the other Laotians, she refused to speak with the tape recorder. She had made some notes before the final session. Off the record, she shared much that she requested not be put into print.

I was born in Laos. My father was a farmer and a merchant. There were eleven children in my family and I was number nine. My mother and father were very good to us. The boys and girls went to school for four or five years. Then the girls didn't need to go anymore. I can read and write in Lao and speak some French. We did not learn English in our school, so when I came here I knew only a very few words.

My life in Laos was not so bad. We had animals, we had plenty of food, we had land in the country. We lived not far from Vientiane. My mother was part Chinese but we all call ourself Lao. Our house was wood--high off the ground. My days as a young girl were not too hard. I helped to cook, I helped to sew, I helped with the vegetables. Sometimes when the rice is ready we all help in the field--everyone. My family was like the old way, not like now with everything changing. We listened to our parent. We help with the old one. Some of my children do not do this here.

My mother did not go to work on a job. Her work was the family, the house, the market, and to make cloth. We would visit with other houses of relatives and friends. Women would go to the market. We saw some French and American women but they were different. They never spoke too much to us and they lived in a different place. They ate with the fork and not always together. They always ate at the same time everyday.

I like the flowers of my country. Oh, so many and so many color. Not so expensive. Here, the flower are expensive. I grow some. We know there is a war and we know there are communists, but that does not bother us too much. My father sometime worry very much about the politics. We hear the men argue and fight for one general--this one or that one. I was young, I had other thoughts of a husband and of my life. We were used to foreigners. My father wanted for all his children a French education. However, it was too expensive.

When I marry, [this was her second marriage. She wouldn't comment on her first marriage that had produced her first three children.] I found a handsome man. He work for the Lao government. He speak good French and has an o.k. education. We have a big wedding. . . much food, celebration. I am very happy. My father pay much for this marriage. We have a nice house. Nothing is wrong. For a few years we are very happy. My life becomes more difficult with more war. Who knows what is happening? My sons are going to have to fight so we sent them to Thailand to work and study. This way they will not be killed. This will make me very sad. This begins to see our family change and live away.

When the American are there we make much money. Life is easy. . . so many good things. we get free medicine from the clinic because my husband work with the government. We buy more land for each of

our children when they get married. This I feel very
happy about. I have some jewelry and we save some
money. Not too much is hard for us. We are with
Kong-le and also the Americans. We used to be with
the French but they are gone so we have the
Americans to help us. During this time my husband
is very worried. He know that the Royal Army will
not win. We begin to send some money, not much,
to our family in Thailand. We think, maybe we will
have to go there for while someday. When the
American leave we are very worried. My husband
has a job but now makes less money. They take
some of our land and houses away because we have
too many. We want to wait and see so we do not go
to Thailand.

Life is very hard now. . . not enough food, almost no
gasoline for the motorcycle. We each can have only
a little bit of things each month, not enough like we
used to have. My husband is very depressed. He like
to make money like when the Americans are here.
He is very angry with the Vietnamese who come to
help the new government. He say this is not good for
Laos. He say these are the worst of the foreigners. . .
too hard. We listen to the radio [Radio Free
America] and hear the refugee in America say they
make much money. We think about this. We give
two houses to our cousin. One daughter will stay in
our house. We think maybe we will go to Thailand
and then to the U.S.A. to make some money until
things get better. I am very worried but my husband
say it o.k. Two sons are in Thailand. The rest will
come with us and some friend. We are very secret.
At night we go in the country and cross the river to
Thailand. My husband has friends who will meet us.
Something happen and the Thai police find us. They

do not send us back because they know my husband work for the government before. They take our money and jewelry. This is very sad. We do not take too much with us. . . now everything is gone except 600 baht. They take us tot he camp. Then many papers, questions. I am tired. We see a new life we did not expect. We build a house from the wood while we wait. It is a small and dark house. I am ashamed because we have very few of clothes. Not enough water is very hard to keep clean. This is not the way we like to be. We have so little.

My husband write to a friend in Thailand and he send some money. Things are a little better. From this time we wait. My husband and son go to classes of English every day. The women and children just wait. There are many fights and argument. People steal. Too many people in one small place. We cannot leave. We have to wait for permission from the U.S.A. Many sad thing happen in the camp. We live with too many people. . . very crowded, everyone unhappy, not enough food, not enough water, no jobs, no money. We wait to hope for a better life in America. Sad things are in our heads. We miss our house and our friends, our city.

Then we hear a church will sponsor my family. This is very good. So we are happy and we talk of many thing. My husband is so happy, too. We come first to California, then to here. We know nothing. . . we think everything will be o.k. with the Americans like when the Americans came to our country. We are very good to them. . . they bring much money. Our heads are very big with dreams of a better way of life. When we came here the church was very good. For one year it helped very much. My husband got a part-time job working with the trees. So my two sons did. Then we had a small house to rent. . . not enough rooms but we are very happy to have a home and to cook and have friend. I work a part-time job in the motel to clean.

Then the church does not help us anymore. We cannot be the Christian. We try. We like them very much. We are the Buddhist. We cannot change this. They were very nice but they no longer came to help us. My husband was hurt cutting the tree. He is forty-five and the work was very hard for him. He try and get very sick. They lay off my sons because they do not speak the English so well. This is not true but they do not fight the boss. I am the only one to work for a while. I work all night and I am very sick and tired. My husband is depressed and very angry. He does not want me away every night. Everyone is unhappy.

We have been here three years now. Very much has changed. My husband has no job yet. Sometime he works part-time. . . but not so very much. Other days he stays in bed or he drink the beer. He want to go back to Laos but that cannot be. He does not want to stay here and be nothing. He was a good man in Laos. Easy to live with... very good father. Now he is very sad. I am sad for him and my family. The Lao people are sad here. We cannot get jobs to make enough money for good tings. The husband must move to another house to get the welfare to feed the children. This is very bad. Not a father in the house for the children is not so good. We move many time. I am very lonely for my old life. I do not like to work to clean the motel. I cannot do for my family what I wish. My children play with bad children.

They are bad to their mother and father. They are learning not so good things in the schools. They smoke the marijuana try to act like the soldier. They want clothes, money, and new things we cannot buy for them. They change the name to English. Our son say he "hate" the Lao. We don't mind him to try to be American. We hope he will not hate us. They do not ask our advice for plans. They do not care so much for us.

We did not go to the English class for too long because we try to work and make the money. Now I am sorry. Too late I know I want to learn more English. So you see, we are here now. We are very poor. The Americans do not welcome us. They see us as the poor refugees. . . not as the friends they had in our country. This is hard for our hearts to accept. We thought no one to be so poor here. We thought there would be jobs. That's what the radio said. Which way is best? We do not know. To stay in Laos we would have to work very hard and have very little. Here we cannot work and we have very little. There we know the Lao language. This helps us. If things change in my country, I will go home again. Now I know how to live with very little so it no longer matters if I have too much. It is my husband that cannot go home. He hates the government and the Vietnamese. His heart is all sad. For now we stay with him. My daughter and her husband will go back in a few years. They are very good to me. They help me very much. I am happy they live near me. They give me grandsons.

My other children, except two, are more like the Americans. Maybe they will stay here. I worry so much. Our family is not the same. Everybody does

something very different. Nobody knows what to do.
This makes my heart so sad. Right now I wish for a
job for my husband... a good job so that we can live
in one house again. . . to have friends, to have my
family. We don't understand why the Americans
cannot help with the job. We will work very hard. I
am not young anymore. I hope before I die I have
some time to rest, to have my family and husband
back, and not to worry so much. I am always too
sick with worry.

Oh, yes, what I do every day. Nothing now. I have
the welfare and no job. I wait and worry. I wash the
clothes, I cook, I clean. I don't know where my
children and husband are most of the time and I worry
something bad is happening to them.

The Father
This man is around forty-five years old. He came here three
years ago with his family. He was a respected civil servant in
his own country, earning almost ten times the salary of the
average Lao while the Americans were there. He owned homes
and land. He was supportive of the French and then later of the
Americans. His sympathies were almost always to the extreme
right of the political spectrum, believing in the King and the
royal family. He was a nominal Buddhist. His stepson served
as translator.

You are my friend so I tell you some of these things.
I love my country very much. You know I hate the
Vietnamese. They steal my country. They take
everything. I hate them.

I was a very lucky man. I have the land and the
house. I have the very good job. See, these are my

papers. These tell you I was important. Look at my picture. Everything is very god for me. My father was the farmer. Not a little land but much land. I work hard, he send me to school to learn French. We do not study English then. Only French and Lao and some Chinese. Almost everyone know Thai, too. I went to Thailand many times. Before 1975 it was so easy to cross the border. No problems. I have many friend in Thailand.[Historically, the border between Laos and Thailand was open. Due to pressure from the United States and increased refugee migration, the border was closed in 1975.]

In my country I have a big house. Plenty of food all the time. My wife is a very good cook. Everyone welcome. Many American come there. We have many friends and relatives in Laos. They visit us. This is very good. We talk. We plan. We try to make the future good for our children. I send all my children to school, the girls, too. This way they learn French and English to get a good job. Then when I am old I will have some help from them. No worry for me. I work very hard to do this. I am not afraid to work for my family and friend. They like me. They respect me. I feel good.

It is a long story of the war. So many things I am with. This does not go so very well for us. When the American leave we think that could never happen. How can they leave us? Then there were no jobs for us to make enough money. The Vietnamese come to steal our country. They tell the communist those men who work with Americans have too much land and money. They take some of the land. I am very smart first and give each relative some land and a house. This way I cannot own too much. They take everyone's money in the bank and give only a little back. They say the general and the rich people take all the gold from our country when they leave. They say we must keep all of the money in the bank to help the country feed everyone and to run the government. I hate this. I work hard for my money. Now it is all gone. What can I do? I hate it so very much.

I keep my old job. . . they say I get one-fourth [of my previous salary] now because there is not enough money to pay. It is very hard to get the rice, the chicken, the gasoline. Everything is just a little bit. Everything is counted. This is a crazy life. How can you live like that? That government cannot do anything. What a crazy mess. We do not want to leave our country. We love our country. I am afraid to take my family to so far away. Then we hear the Radio America. Lao people say you can have much money, a good job, no problems in the U.S.A. They say come here. That's right.

They invite us to leave the communist community. What are we to think? The American bring much money to Laos. We believe them when they say life is so good here. We think about this. Then we decide to go. This is not so easy. We worry much... all the time. It is hard to leave your country, your friend, the things you know in your heart from being a little boy until now.

We give everything away. That's o.k. We know we will be better in the United States. We have friends in Thailand. They will meet us there when we cross the river. This did not happen. The soldier find us. I tell them I am a civil servant. I tell them. They laugh and say everyone say that. Still, they take our

money but do not hurt us. So now. . . no money, no
house, nothing. I do not tell my wife but I am so
depressed. O.K. We go to the camp.

The came is where I learn some little English. We
don't do too much. I don't understand much. All
these thing they say in class I can't picture in my
head. I go anyway. The Thai treat us like the
servant. I am not the servant in my own country. I
say nothing. I want to get to America. I close my
mouth. In my heart I hate them, too. We need some
help. . . nothing. I try to keep my family together.
Then we know we will come to America. I want to
send my sons for more education. I hope for a good
job because I work hard. On the airplane my mind is
very confused. . . you know, happy. . . sad. . . many
different thoughts. My wife I want something special
for. She is very good. . . no complaint. She help,
she say everything is o.k.

Three years now, Rob, three years. You know what
happens to the refugee here. You see. They do not
have to tell you how sad. How poor. I have no
job... no chances to make my family safe. First my
wife has to work. . . this makes me angry and sad. I
do not want this. I am the man. Then we have to
move to another house to get money. My family is
everywhere. One son here, one son there, my wife in
another house. I have no job. What is here for me?
American invite me here. You have to believe me
when I say this. I would not come if I didn't believe
their good invitation. They forgot me.

Here I am nothing. Not a man, not a father, not a
husband. Many days I feel crazy. I do not want to
be the dishwasher. Why do that? It does not pay me,

it does not help my family. No one knows I am a man. Some day, forgive me friend, I hate this country, too. I hate being alive. This is hard for me. What can I do? Nothing to do is hard for a man to do. Look around my house. What do you see? Not even a television. The man shouldn't live this way. I cannot read the paper. The language is very hard for me. When I walk outside no one says the "hello." I am dead and I am also alive inside the dead man. I don't know how to think like the American. My children do not respect me very well. I cannot help them. I beg my family for food, for money, for clothes.

In my country I was a man. Then change and I have nothing. Here I have nothing. Now I don't know what to think. I pray. I think. I watch. I don't know. . . I don't know. Maybe I will go back there someday. Maybe if the Vietnamese leave. I don't know yet. Maybe a better life will come here. My mind is not clear on these things. I have to wait.

The Elder Daughter

This woman is the third child of her mother's first marriage. The mother left her first child, the older sister of this woman, in Laos, where she lives with her husband and three children in the family house, keeping some of the family property. The third child, this daughter in the profile, came with her mother to America. She was accompanied by her husband and one child born in a refugee camp in Northeast Thailand. They now have a second son born in the United States. She is well educated by Lao standards, speaking passable French and English. Her language skills are valuable to other refugees in the community as they struggle with language problems. This ability landed her a job very quickly with a local social service agency. Although traditional Lao in behavior, she has overcome an

initial shyness with the public and with men to work effectively
in the community. She deals mainly with women, women's
problems, and with children. She has been instrumental in
helping families deal with the schools and with health
problems. Like her mother, she dresses in the traditional Lao
si:n and blouse. She wears no make-up. She is proud of being
Lao and very proud of her contributions to keeping her
extended family together.

You know my family. I grew up near Vientiane in a
nice house. My mother did not work there. I had a
very happy young life. I learned all the women's
things and I went to school. My father was very
liberal to let the girls get so much education. He felt
we could do it. I enjoyed school but I was very quiet.
Sometimes my older sister would answer for me. I
was very shy to everyone. My sister talked much.
People said I was pretty but I don't really think so.

In my house, there was much talk of politics. I don't
think you can see my father as he was at home in
Laos. His experience here has been very difficult and
very sad. He was very good to everyone. When he
made much money he made everyone welcome in our
house. He loved people to come. We had others,
what you call extended family, living in our house.
All the women helped with the cooking, the cleaning,
and all that. We shopped almost every day. When I
was very young, we did not have refrigerator or good
electricity. Later we did and then we didn't have to
shop for everything every day. Still, we liked to
shop. . . we saw other people, talked, and that was
very good because we didn't have the telephone. We
did a lot of visiting to other friends and relatives.

As I said, we heard much talk of politics in our home. Mostly of some Lao history, of our generals and armies, and some of the French and Americans. My father was not as quiet as he is now. He read the French and the Lao paper. He read the Bangkok paper. He went to Thailand. He knew many things of our history. He worked for the government. The women listen a lot and we heard many things. This was almost every night.

My mother was a housewife. That is something very different from here. She was in charge of the house and the finances. It has more prestige to be a good wife in Laos than here. She is a very good mother. She would do extra work if we had to study. She was glad all the children were learning in school. She didn't have the same opportunity. They say when she was a young woman she was very beautiful and when my father first saw her, he wanted her to be his wife. She laughs when we say this but I know it makes her happy. She still likes to look good when she leaves the house. She always told us to be neat and clean.

My brothers are all very different. The older two or three I can talk to and we are friends. The younger ones are more and more like Americans. Let me explain that being the refugee is very difficult. Your whole life changes but you don't know that when you leave your country. Everyone in the family is now changed. First, both my parents did not find here what they had hoped. Worst of all is my father who cannot find a job that makes him feel good. It has bothered him to see the family all broken up in different homes. He drinks sometimes and used to hit my mother. Now, because of some counseling, he will not do that. In stead, he becomes very quiet and says very little. He was on the American side and no one could say anything about the Americans in our house in Laos. He couldn't believe they just left. He could never accept the new government. When he heard Radio America he decided to go there for a new life. He felt the Americans would treat him well because he had helped them in Laos. This, you know, has not happened.

My mother has had to go to work. They have no common home. They have many problems, life is very hard, and they do not understand many things. So, my brothers, the younger and the older, have given them many problems. Only one, the oldest, gives them any help. He has worked hard to keep the family together in one way or another. He does things sometimes the Lao way and this is not so good here. My other brother thinks of his life, his girlfriend, he is like an American. He thinks it's the oldest one who is to take care of the parents. At first he would give no help. . . but now, he helps a little because there is a great need. The younger brothers are very confused. They don't know if they are a Lao or American. They cannot be either. A couple try very hard to be like their American friends. They took American names. They say they will never go back to Laos, that they like here, that they are Americans now. Because I have been in the schools I understand this. My parents do not understand very well and they are hurt.

I was happy in my country. When my parents said they would leave I decided to stay. Things were hard. We had very little compared to before but I didn't want to leave. My husband had a job and I felt we would be o.k. My father gave us one of his houses. We didn't pay rent. We had a garden and some rice fields in the country. We had a motorcycle and we could have anything of my father's when he left. Then my husband decided to go. We argued. He heard there was much money in America. Finally I said he could not go without me. So we left. I have not been happy about that. Here I work too hard. I always worry. My husband works hard but I still worry. There is never enough money. I am afraid for anyone to be sick. I worry very much for my young children. I want to go back to Laos before they get too old. My husband agrees there also. I do not want half my family here and half my family in Laos. I don't think my father can ever go back. I think my mother will stay with him.

There are so many problems here. Different from those at home. There we were worried for money, for enough food, but my husband had a job and we owned a house. Here I must live in a small apartment. . . we do not own a house. We have not made enough money to save. We wonder if we will be punished if we go back. Everyone says they hate the communists when they go to the camp or come here. We know this is the right thing to say. Actually they are talking about the government. Many Lao people here worked for that government. I can't say too much. In my father's case he really does hate the government.

Working with Americans has been very difficult for me. My husband doesn't like me to work so much. He doesn't want me talking to so many strangers. He is afraid I will become like American women. I know I won't. I am Lao. Many Americans say to me, "Tell that Lao boy his hair is too greasy, he must wash it." Sometimes they say we smell, or our homes are too dirty, or we shouldn't do this or that. They cannot understand how hard it is to do everything the American way. I do my job and I am quiet, but I hurt when I hear these things. In the schools they say all people in America are equal. I know this doesn't mean the refugee. Sometimes people talk slow or in part English before waiting to see if I understand English. Sometimes I laugh inside.

I have been very sure to be a good wife. . . to keep my husband. . . to have my children know a Lao father. I try to help my mother and father and brothers. My husband is good with this. He is very good to my family. Sometimes he is the only one to go every night for a few minutes to talk to my father, to bring cigarettes, to see if he is o.k. I am lucky with my husband. So, even if I have to leave Laos, I am lucky. I pray we will go back there someday. I try every day to visit my mother or to bring her here.

We don't own very much. We have a stereo and a television. Not too much clothes. Lao people do not have too much furniture in their homes. We like to sit on the rug. My family still eats the Lao food. Only in public are we like the Americans. Then we don't eat too much or say too much. Right now we are all hoping for a good job for my father so that the family can move into one house. Too many bad things happen with the children, the father and the mother all living in different homes. My mother and father are sometimes very lonely. I worry for everyone and sometimes I am sick from that.

The Elder Daughter's Husband

He has worked full- or part-time since he arrived, in various jobs including construction, janitorial work, and now in a factory. He is in his late twenties and speaks minimal English. Known as a hard worker, this man dislikes his wife having to work. They have a car, rent payments, and general expenses for a household of four plus extended family members. He is generous and well-like by everyone. He is healthy and takes pride in his good health and in being a hard worker. Although not educated, he has respect for education. He wants a better education, but work keeps him busy.

I came here because the radio said we could make good money and not have to put up with the communist government. I wanted to come for fun, too, because I was tired of all the problems in my country. One night when my friends said they were going, I said I would go. Just like that. My wife didn't want me to go. I said stay here for a couple of years and I'll come back with a lot of money. I had a job but didn't get much money. I worked for an American company and they stayed. She said, "If you go, I go."

So. . . we left. My house is still there with my younger brother in it. I can go back when I want to. The camps were bad. Then I thought I made mistake to leave. Too late. Then I came here and soon I knew it was wrong to leave. I work very hard here for nothing. You know I still have great trouble with English. I cannot read. There I knew everything. To tell the truth, it was very hard with the new government. We all know that it wasn't their fault. Our country was pretty messed up. When the American left, when many people left, there weren't enough people to do everything. Then we didn't have

enough for two years. There wasn't enough food.
Everyone was always hungry. Gee, I don't know. I
guess I was crazy, but I just wanted to leave. When
we heard the American radio say there was a better
life, I just said "Let's go."

Not I'm not so young. I have traveled. I have seen
many things I could not believe. Here I see so many
unhappy Lao people. I know almost everyone wants
to go home. Most of the time we don't talk about it.
My wife and I will go home in a few years. Maybe
sooner. I don't know yet. I am confused about many
things. I am sad to see my father-in-law so unhappy.
He was not like that before. He was very generous to
me. Even though I'm not so educated, he treats me
like one of his sons. I try to be good to him now.

The young kids are doing crazy things. I watch and
don't know what to do. No one helps them. Who
can? The Americans think everyone is o.k. because
we don't say much. When we complain, or when we
worry and go to welfare, they say we are trying to
cheat the Americans. They count every penny. They
are not generous. They make us feel like we are the
beggars. I will not go there. Other Americans think
our women are for them. They have no respect for
the way we think of our wives. That is why we do
not take them to many American parties. We take
our family only to the safe places.

I enjoy my car here. I like my stereo player very
much. Each one I will not take home [to Laos] so
now I will enjoy them. I have a very good wife. She
takes very good care of me. I look at other beautiful
women. . . you know that is natural to think when
you see a beautiful woman. Still, I don't cheat. She

is good for me. She came all the way here with me.
I always have her as my friend. She gave me two
sons. I am very proud of her. I want to take them
back to my country.

Lao families just keep moving. . . here, there. That
is because we do not belong to this country, we are
not Americans. Few men here act to me as an equal
friend. Some are friendly, but not as an equal man.
In my country we always treat the American person
very well. Special things to eat when they come to
our house. We are always glad to know them. Here,
too. When Americans come to our house we try to
do something nice. We know this is their country.
We want them to enjoy us. Do not think we are bad
guests here because I say these many things. I know
now that I belong to my country. Americans have
their country. I don't know why I thought I could be
an American, I am Lao. See what happens when you
are young and foolish? Who thinks about these things
when they are so young? Now I know. While I am
here I will try my best to learn everything. When I
go home I will know a lot. . .

The Oldest Son
    This man is in his late twenties. For the average Lao he is
generally well educated. He speaks fluent Lao, Thai, good
French and English. He is the second child of the mother's first
marriage. He left a "wife" in Laos. He lived five years in
Thailand. He lives with a girlfriend he sometimes calls his
"wife." Because of his relatively strong command of English,
he initially found himself helping as a translator for the family
and the community. For a couple of years he has worked with
a local social service agency dealing with refugee transition.

He dresses casually, almost "preppy" at times, and is described by his friends as generous and easy-going.

You should have asked me all these questions first before I knew you and worked with you. You are my friend. . . some things are easy to say to you and some things not. You know many things about me and my family, and we have done so many things together. I have translated for you and taught you our customs. You have slept in my house and eaten our food the Lao way. You have been to our country. All the times I translated the others' stories I didn't realize how difficult it was to think this out. For two weeks I have worried I cannot do it. I don't want to let you down. . .yet, I have conflicts.

I won't say too much about our home or my growing up. . . you have heard that from the others. For me, almost everything was o.k. until I went to the Lycee. Before that I hadn't bothered too much with politics. The things my friends discussed there were very different from the things discussed in my father's house. Exactly the opposite. It never occurred to me that the Americans might be part of the problem. I never knew too much about world politics. I believed what my father said and what his friends said as the truth. Then other students and some teachers talk about communism and capitalism. This was very hard to understand. I became very confused and very depressed. I did not want to believe what I was hearing. Even some of the monks say this.

The Americans were my great heroes. Since 1965 that's who I wanted to be like. I dressed like them. I learned English. I went to places where Americans went. I listened and watched. Everything they did was very interesting. They had nice clothes, cars, motorcycles. The women were beautiful. So, I got a motorcycle. At the Lycee all of that changed. Maybe I began to grow up. One friend said I lived in a world of dreams. The Americans are only people. I wanted to learn much more. I read and listened and tried to figure out what was happening. Our political situation was so confusing. Only later, after discussing with you about our history, did I realize everyone there was confused and pressured. Our leaders had little experience with world politics.

I did not know how hard the United States worked to manage and shape our politics in a way comfortable for them. I did know of Vietnamese involvement because of my father's hate for them. Anyway, the Lao people really lost. By not allowing us to select our own leaders, to develop a simple economic system suitable for our needs, to select the leaders we loved who wanted a neutral Laos, we lost it all. These were difficult years for me. In many ways I was sympathetic with much of what the Pathet Lao said... particularly about the need for a Lao system for the Lao people and for education for everyone. Everyone was fighting and no one trusted anyone. I believe we could have achieved our dreams of an independent Laos without all of that interference. Maybe it would have been hard to keep, but it would have been ours.

Oh, I almost went crazy trying to figure it out. I drank a lot of beer in those days, staying late into the night to talk. You know I was with Kong-le. He was in the middle and he was loved by the people. When he went to the Pathet Lao I didn't know what to do. Before that I believed some of the things the

158

communists said were o.k., but I was with the Americans. Then he said many of the rich sold us out to the Americans and the Thai. Now what? I had to stop and think a lot. You know that there was much trouble in my country by that time. Every week new stories, new problems. Politics kept changing. No one knew the truth from lies. Life was very crazy for us. Many of the Thai Issan [Lao] were beginning to say that the Americans should be thrown out of Thailand, too. So, what was a big fight in the Lao family over who would control the government became a bigger fight between the Americans and others. Let's face the fact, the Americans were strong, rich, and everyone knew it. When they were around, you had to be on their side. They controlled many things, jobs, and even the army. One time they stopped foreign aid to the army when the government of Souvanna Phouma wanted to be neutral and the country almost fell apart. By controlling our money, they controlled great parts of our country.... and our politicians. The Pathet Lao pointed this out all of the time and said, "See, you aren't free, you are under the Americans."

Most Americans don't know that a very high percentage of the people were for a free, neutral Laos. Many supported the Pathet Lao, but they had many real problems with the Vietnamese. The Vietnamese have been around along time and we knew them well. It's the Americans we didn't know well. If we had known some of the things we know now, maybe life would be very different. So most of my family stayed with the Americans. When they left, there were so many problems. First, who would believe they could be beaten? In some ways I was proud of the Pathet Lao for hanging in there and winning. Then I worried about what would happen. the Americans had said we would all be killed if the Pathet Lao won. This was not so. . . but many of the former leaders and military men were sent to reeducation camps. Life was hard there. Since they had screwed things up, from the Pathet Lao point of view, they should be willing to work hard to change it all. Until they showed a willingness, nothing was done for them. They were the very last priority. As you know, just now, eight years later, still some people are in the camps. We have heard the Lao government has said let them go to America if they want, we don't need them. Many of these men could never accept a socialist government, they were too high, too rich, too powerful to now have to consult the average people about what they want. They believe by education and birth they know more and should be the leaders.

So, when the Americans left, the country was really in trouble. . . not so much because of a socialist government but because of the war damage, of all the internal refugees, of neglect of crops and roads and everything else. Many rich persons took a great deal of money out of the country and left with the Americans. There were so many things to do and nothing to do them with. Our family stayed, believe it or not. My brother and I were in Thailand for a few years to study and save money in case of problems at home and if my father had to leave. We went back, hoping the new government would be o.k. Even though my father hated the Vietnamese who were helping the new government, he didn't want to leave our country. We are Lao. Between 1975 and 1978 things were really bad. The government was very slow to fix things up. They said the United

States and Thailand were working against them in the international banks and the U.S. refused to give any aid for war damage. We were a small, poor country. So, everyone had to do without. Food, gasoline, everything was scarce. At first we blamed it on the communists. Now I know that it just wasn't there. Not enough of anything. Almost everyone in the world forgot about Laos. People were disgusted. Then the Radio Free America began to broadcast, saying life is better in the U.S. We heard Lao's speaking about how they made good money in the U.S. Thousands of people thought a lot about this. Then too, you know we had those three years of almost no rain. This was very hard on everyone. Not enough rice is a very serious thing in Laos.

Well, you know what happened from there. People were disgusted. . . life was too hard in Laos. We wanted more. Nothing was going very well. So we came here. We really thought the Lao government would never make it. Now we get letters saying that things are still quite hard.... but getting better. We really didn't know this. All those years of war made people very tired. The new government said we must be strong to build our new country. We must sacrifice. We must not lose what we have worked so hard and suffered to win. People were tired. The better life was supposed to be in America.

When we came to the Untied States we were all very surprised. The church was good to us at first, but telling us not to smoke and drink was not so good. We just couldn't become Christian or Mormon. I haven't had it so hard here. I worked at different jobs. . . loading trucks, planting trees, until I got a good one. I work hard. But I came here with

English. Most of the Lao have not been so fortunate. Still, in my heart I have suffered very deeply also.

There are two things I can say. First, the Lao men feel very bad here. We are not equal. Everyone treats us as refugees. . . different than other people. It is hard to be normal and to be a friend when people treat you different. Then. . . many of us were not close friends in Laos. Here we are the only Lao and we have to be friends with each other. There are no good programs for Lao men. We all need a lot of help. Dishwashing jobs and loading beer trucks are not what we thought we would have to do for the rest of our lives. We were more than this at home. There are many problems when you can't find a good job, when you can't find Lao women to marry and have a family, when even the married men have to live in separate houses in order to survive. Most of the men here were on the American side. They feel cheated by what they are given, all they want is opportunity. Why should anyone care if all you can ever be is a dishwasher or a janitor? We drink a lot to forget this. We enjoy life while we can. Who knows what will happen on tomorrow? We have seen a lot of change.

For me, it has been the same and also different than the other Lao men. When I became a translator it made me more. All the time. . . anytime... people call my house. I go. . . to the hospital, to jobs, for anything that is needed. I try very hard to help everyone all the time. My people always come to me. Sometimes I am very tired. Then, the Americans expect me to know everything, explain everything, do anything anytime they ask. . . whether I like it or not. Everyone forgets about me, my life, my needs. I am a human being too. As a Lao, I still cannot explain everything, do anytime they ask. . . whether I like it or not. Everyone forgets about me, my life, my needs. I am a human being too. As a Lao, I still cannot explain all the Laos, what every Lao does, to the American. Also, I am sometimes having the same problems as everyone else. Yes, I have problems, even if I don't say so. I miss my country. I miss my way. It is hard having to be like an American all the time. I can never relax. You know, I got my dream. . . I'm here. Now I know I should have been satisfied with being Lao. I intend to finish my education here. To learn as much as possible. But then I think I will go back. . . if not to Laos then to Thailand. Language and culture are more than words and more than the outlines we get in cultural orientation. They are a way of living. American and Lao ways of living are very different. Some things I like very much about both. But I am Lao for whatever I may look like at work. I guess I just want to say that people seem to forget that I am not perfect. I make mistakes and I have much to learn. I must learn your ways. You do not have to learn mine. How is that equality?

Being here is not all bad. I do not wish to say that. Some Americans try very hard to be good to us. But we are always reminded we are different. We know people can't lead our lives and do everything for us. But why did the United States invite us here with the promises and then make us feel very low when we ask for these promises. Maybe all the Lao weren't unhappy with Laos and wouldn't have come here if they hadn't thought this to be a better life. Is it not better to be at home, among friends, where you know the language. . . even if you are poor? That is better than to be in a strange land where you are poor, can't speak the language, have few friends, and are not really welcome. I have very bad depressions sometimes and I worry about my people, my family, my life, what is happening. I want to be happy, have a family, have enough food. We all worry about getting sick or dying. . . it is too expensive in your country. We are thankful for what our friends here have done, but we don't belong to your country, we have to go to our own home. Down deep in my heart I worry that may not be able to happen.

The last thing I feel I need to say about my life is that when I have been your interpreter and translator, I have seen and heard so many things about my people, our country, the war, politics, and about being here that my head is filled. I have gotten to see through everyone's eyes. I have become a part of each of the Lao here and also very separate from them. When you first came I didn't believe you. I didn't understand what you meant when you said b y listening to each person's view. . . telling each story from their own mind. . . we could see a bigger story. Now I know. I am so sad sometimes, Rob. I am so sad to see and hear all these things. It is very hard for me. I feel like a very old man in my head and heart when I think of these things. I am not the same. Some part of me looks at the Lao and at the Americans and is always asking questions about what is happening. When you are gone, who will I talk to about these things? I say, when we go back to our country you must come. Then you will really see the whole picture. There is a part I cannot give you here. You must go there to be a part of it. You must go to the camps. [In 1982, I had my first opportunity to travel to the refugee camps in Thailand.] Then you will see it all. If I had a good education here and was important, I would write a book or make a film. I would have everyone tell that we don't need to kill or to war, that we should each have our own country, that there should be enough food and clothing for everyone. I think I have seen enough food and clothing here wasted to give to all the Lao people. No one way of living is right. My teacher, a monk in Laos, told me the story that all the flowers of the garden manage to live together. They are not all the same. Different colors, different sizes, some alone and some in groups. People can be like that, too. I often wonder why we don't know that. It seems so simple.

My mind is very tired right now. It is hard to believe that all this time has gone by. That we have talked to so many people. Done so many things. We have become friends. You know, some people here say you will be like the other Americans. In time, when this story is finished, you will forget us. You will be important and we will still be refugees. I don't think that is so. Like me, you are changed. I can tell by the way you listen, the way you speak, by the movement of your eyes, by the way you ask fewer questions and still know what is happening with the Lao. I know, although you have not said, you feel some of our disappointment and sadness. At one point, you know, were worried for you. Sometimes you began to think and act like the refugee. You were arguing with other Americans for us. We were afraid for you. You know how the mind can go crazy when you get that way. You are special to us because you know these things. Your heart has deepened. It is bigger. so, I say you will not forget. You cannot because a little piece of Laos is now inside you. I am this way too with America. When I go back, a little piece of me is America. If only we could. . . all the people of the world. . . have a little piece of each other in our hearts. Then no more refugees. Everybody could be happy at home.

One of the Younger Sons

This young man is faced with the typical kinds of choices the young Lao must make in the schools. In his early teens, he struggles back and forth from being a Lao refugee and being a young person in America and wanting to be a part of things--to be liked and accepted by his peers. He is in constant argument with his family, plays with what his mother calls "bad boys" and is disrespectful. He is small for his age, and darker than many of the Lao. He has picked up a repertoire of "swear" words and uses them frequently. There have been many problems with his teachers and he has already had one minor encounter with the local police.

I do what I want. I am me. Sometimes I use my Lao name. Sometimes I use my American name. I am tough. I take care of myself. I get what I want. I can do the school work but I'm not so interested. Some things interest me. Then I try hard. Other time I do what I like. Maybe in a year or two I will go back to Laos. Anyway, you know that the Americans think we are refugees. We don't know anything. The teachers and other people sometimes talk to us like we are six years old. Boy, I get tired of that. Just because we don't speak English so well doesn't mean we are stupid. Look at my Dad. He is very smart but everyone here makes him seem to be ignorant. He was very good to us in Laos. Here he can't do much. Nobody gives him a chance. My other brother thinks he's American already. He's nuts. I go to the same school. He just doesn't see people still call him a refugee, even if he has nice clothes on. Only the bad girls want to have a refugee as a friend... not the good ones everyone likes.

I have some friends here. Some Mexican, some blacks, and some white ones. They all think I'm tough. I have to be or they treat me like a refugee. Everyone things the refugee way is the same as the Lao way. This isn't true. All they know is what they see. Our people are very different in Laos. I don't know a lot about the government, but I know the people are different. We have a good time there. We had a big house and friends and we knew everything. My Dad was important. We had many people and friends come to our house. Everybody would eat and talk. This doesn't happen here. Many of the people are depressed. They hid from the Americans. They are ashamed they don't have houses and things anymore. They don't act the way they did in Laos. They don't have enough money. They worry about rent and bills. There are many fights. Maybe everyone likes my brother better because he acts American and says he is American. I know how sad he feels, too. He like this girl and she would laugh at his name. So he changed his name. No change in her. That's what I mean. She still thinks he is a refugee. Well, I'm just me. If they don't like me, it's o.k. If they get tough I'll kick their ass. That's right. I don't like that. But I'm young. I don't want to be come depressed and sad like my big brother's friends.

I think I will go back to Laos someday. Just to see how I do there. I want to go back to my country for a year or two and see my old friends and where I can speak Lao without worrying who is listening. Then, if I do stay there, I want to go to the community college and have a landscape business. This could help my Dad, he is very good at that. This could help him to feel proud again and to have all our family together again. Right now, I want to have some fun. I don't think that's so wrong. Even though some people say I am bad... I stay out late or smoke some pot once in a while... I am not bad. I know what bad is. The American's haven't seen how bad some people were in the camps. I saw many bad things. I won't do those things.

I know I am skinny and have different eyes and black hair. So what. I don't want to be like all those television people. I'm not a punker, either. Inside I am a good person. People who really know me can tell that inside I am good. I try to help at home. I don't yell at my mother or father. I don't steal. I have some dreams for the future but I am not telling anyone right now. I have to wait and see. Besides, I'm young, man, I need some time. I have many things to learn. Not just what the American teachers think is important. When I agreed to talk to you I was going to give you this story I wrote for English class in school. I thought you were going to ask me how much I like being in America. That's the first thing everyone asks. No one asks did I like my own country. Everyone asks about the communists. Well, this story I wrote isn't true. I got a B+ because the teacher liked what I said. Never once did he ask about me. How I feel, just me. Well I'm telling you about me. I'm the most important to me. I think a lot and even though I don't say so to my teachers, I read the papers and magazines almost everyday. My Dad can't explain many things to me. My older brother works hard to bring in money. When we have time to talk we discover that both of us are learning different things and we tell each other. He is now going to the community college and working. We explain a lot to our Dad but he gets impatient. He is used to knowing a lot more and he feels small to ask us.

Well, what else? I think it's sort of crazy that you write all this stuff. I only told you a little bit about me. I don't want you to think that what I said is all of me. I can't tell you everything about myself. . . if I do that you have power over me. I don't know some things about myself yet, so I can't say much about that. Right now I'm waiting. I don't know what will happen to me. That's it for now. I can't help you with anything more. I have more thinking to do. That takes time. Sometimes long, sometimes quick. I have a crazy head. It doesn't always give me the answers when I want them. I'm getting by, day by day. Some of them are good, some not. How is your Lao coming? I just thought of a joke. Maybe I'll write a story like you are doing. Only I'll ask the questions to Americans. I wonder how they will feel, if they can answer. Maybe then they will understand that when people ask you a question, you don't have to answer. You don't have to give them anything. If you do, then it is a present. Writing it down isn't reason enough. Listening to it and thinking about it is just as important. We learn all these things about being equal in school. they put us in special classes for the dumb ones. They don't listen. They tell. So why talk? If others don't listen to your side there's no point in telling anything. You keep the rest inside to protect it. That's why some people think I'm tough.

Middle Son

This middle son, for the sake of stability, has chosen to deny his Lao background. Ashamed of his parents and family, keeps a separate identify away from home. Faced with difficult choices, he has put the past behind him. These decisions have created frictions between himself and his brothers. In addition, his parents feel they have lost him to the Americans. On the other hand, they believe this is the only way he will get ahead in the United States. He remains an outsider, isolated from his primary culture and not yet fully accepted by Americans.

I don't want to talk very much about Laos or the camps. I remember some things like our house, our family, friends I used to play with. I remember what things looked like. . . all green and brown... but different from the green and brown of here. I had many friends. I like the motorcycle of my big brother.

The camp I don't think about too much. I had a good time playing with my friends but sometimes I know bad things happen. I don't think much about that place now.

Here I am American. I have changed my country. Americans are the best. All my friends, except my cousin and my brothers, are Americans. I do American things. My haircut is American. I work part-time when I can to get the money to buy these things. I always try to talk in English. I have to try very hard every minute because many friends at school call me Lao. I know they think I am a refugee and not as high as the other Americans. I wish my skin was whiter and my hair not black. Black hair is no good. I can change this but not now because of my father. He doesn't understand anything at all. Really. . . they are too old and they think like they still live over there. We don't. We are here. I sit on a chair and eat at the table. I know how to go into the restaurant and order. I am not afraid. If you act afraid, people know you are a refugee.

I won't sleep in a bed with anyone anymore. Now I sleep on the floor. Americans don't sleep in the same bed. I shower every day, see, I brush my teeth and they are white. Americans like this. Some girls do, too. They like me. This makes me feel very good. I watch everything and try to do everything just right. Everyone calls me by my American name. When they have to say my Lao name it is too hard. So now I don't say it.

Americans don't understand the Lao things of my family. I keep them away. I take the bus or walk. That way no one sees my father. Some of my family want to go back to Laos. If they go, I will stay here. They can't make me go back there. I am American and this is where I will stay. I will have a house and a car here. I want to go to college and be a doctor. Then people will like me.

When you came here I didn't want to have to talk to you. I hate questions. Everyone asks the refugees questions. I am not a refugee. If you let me say what I want to say like Americans do then I don't mind talking to you. So that's why I talk about America and not the other places. They are not important to me. My older brother says some day they will be. . . I don't know that. I don't care. I have enough trouble right now trying hard to be American, to have my school friends like me, and to get the things I need. My father doesn't understand this. He won't even try to learn more English. He will always remain a refugee. . . ignorant, if he doesn't try. He can't stop me. I am strong in my mind about being American.

Maybe I will go to the army when I'm older in a few
years. I don't know yet.

There is indeed more to the story of the individuals in
Section I and to this family than the interviews and statements
convey. Because they are still in the process of adjusting to
and coping with the struggle to maintain the basic physiological
survival needs, there has been little time for them to think about
what was lost when they left home, and what has yet to be
secured here to compensate for that loss. It is apparent that
almost all of the members of the Lao community suffer to some
degree from a loss of primary culture context, i.e., an
environment where the things they know, the behaviors they
have learned, the responses that have worked, the institutions
they have been "schooled" to deal with, collectively have
meaning. Loss of language for both preliterate and literate
Laotians has had profound implications. There is a tremendous
feeling of loss over not being able to "read," particularly among
the professional class. Many of the men and women were
literate in Lao and French. Not being able to read denies them
access to contextual information and the status that information
carries with it. Denied this, heads of families and parents find
their roles and their power diminished, and children are often
given no direction within the home pertinent to American
culture. This is highly stressed population and many of its
members have not developed the internal mechanisms to cope
with that stress.

The Lao Family
The paradigm for the family carried with the exodus from
Laos is varied. Lebar and Suddard (1960) characterize the
"ideal" arrangement in the Lao setting as consisting of a nuclear
family not unlike the model we find in the United States. They
note that the extended form of the family is not uncommon.
The family unit is generally represented by the male head who
in turn represents the family in village politics and business.

The wife often runs the household and generally has considerable say over the management of family finances. Married sons and daughters may live with either set of parents in extended family until they can afford a home of their own. Work is usually divided along lines of gender: the men do the heavy work in the fields, besides hunting and fishing; the women concentrate on the domestic tasks. All members of the agricultural family generally help with planting, trans-planting, and harvesting.

I found the similar models existing in the households of the Lao refugee community. However, almost all of these households, with only a few exceptions, were extended families. This arrangement compensated for the break-up of nuclear families as the result of resettlement and facilitated the inclusion of singles into family units where they could live and adjust within a support structure familiar to them. Roles, however, have and continue to undergo profound changes.

Due to the impact of the recession of the early 1980s, it was nearly impossible for many of the male heads of household to find employment. Many found part-time or seasonal work, but this would not support the family. On the other hand, over fifty percent of the women in the community found work as domestics in order to supplement family income. As women often became the sole breadwinners for long periods of time their exposure to the greater community increased. They began to interact with more Americans and to learn more English, and began to break the traditional pattern of working everything out with their husbands as well. The men, in particular the age group over thirty-five, have been the last to begin to accommodate to the new system. They are the group that has learned the least amount of English, and ostensibly have had the most difficulty with cross-cultural adjustments.

One Lao refugee characterized the traditional Lao family during this interview:

The family is important to the Lao. It is almost everything to us. We teach our children to be polite and to respect the older people. Even the younger children have respect for the older children. We love our children. The father is the outside head of the family. The mother is also important and is the inside head of the family. They are responsible for how the children learn about life. When there is trouble, this is where the child comes for help. Many of our children live with us after they get married. This gives them a start on life. We like to have many people in the home. Sometimes even we have family members who we call "cousins" or "aunts" and "uncles." They may not be related but because we like them we call them that. The young ones learn at home how to cook or how to plant. The home and the family are very important. It disturbs us that it is not quite the same in the United States. We see changes that hurt us. Many American children do not obey or listen to their parents. Their parents do not teach them. They give them to the school to be taught everything. This is not our way.

Family structures continue to change as the children begin to acculturate, as some Lao men and women marry Americans, and as single men and often entire households shift residences from one state to another in search of employment and other family members separated by the war. Many of the original Lao refugees who arrived between 1979 and 1982 have moved to California where the welfare system is more compatible with adjustment problems, and where there is a much larger Lao population to draw on for support in times of need.

CHAPTER III

INTERPRETATION: A PERSONAL JOURNEY INTO THE LAOTIAN REFUGEE EXPERIENCE

We were worried for you. Sometimes you began to think and act like the refugee. You were arguing with other Americans for us, we were afraid for you. You know the mind can go crazy when you get that way...

Laotian refugee, 1983

When I go back, a little piece of me is America. If only we could. . . all the people of the world. . . have a little piece of each other in our hearts. . .

Laotian refugee, 1982

Now I understand that it isn't only the Lao who are children to the American way. Also, the Americans are children to the Lao way. . . but now, we are here in your country, so we appear as the children. . .

Laotian refugee, 1982

Why am I here? Today it all appears ugly and confusing. The customs, the language, the problems, the whole damned process of doing fieldwork is becoming a strain. I can't figure out why I left the security of the university to do this. . .

Field Journal, 1981

176

This is a record of a journey, not of someone else's, but my own. It remains a brief transcript outlining the events that transpired as a result of continuous anthropological fieldwork during the years 1980-1985 when I attempted to partially acculturate and to "live" the experiences of Laotian refugees who had come to one small corner of the United States of America. Furthermore, it was the concurrent chronicle of antagonizing internal struggle which radically altered my perspective on American culture, on our species, and on my own life. This internal conflict generated by the fieldwork experiences was a catalyst for the following questions which lay heavily on my mind as I reflected upon what occurred during that period:

By what right are we educators and anthropologists empowered with the privilege of 'studying' the intimate lives of other human beings who, as new arrivals in a society which devastated their homeland, are dependent on our goodwill?

Once we researchers probe, question, interpret, and then record a final "product" clothed in the respectability of a nonexistent academic "objectivity," by what right and to what purpose do we lay open the naked reality of other human beings for the privileged to examine? What will we do with this knowledge? How will these human beings benefit by our use of it? Is anything sacred to the anthropologist-academician?

Beyond the question of morality in research, how does one begin to understand and to justify being a member of a powerful educational system and a respected anthropological tradition that, quite simply, almost universally refuses to recognize or examine their respective contributions to the devastation our society perpetrated on the cultures of Southeast Asia?

Last, beyond the horrors I have found my own society to have been party to in the devastation of Laos, what has the educational process done to me, and to other Americans? As we remain silent, our technological society continues to participate in the devastation of other pre-technological cultures, using the same old excuses for the same demented reasons. This silence carries a responsibility of its own.

The analysis that appears in this chapter was conducted in the anthropological spirit of reflexivity. That tradition in anthropology, the discipline which gave birth the ethnography, is critical to understanding this work. Within this context, the personal cultural and historical events and experiences which influence the ethnographer become a crucial part of the fieldwork and analysis. The emphasis on participant observation interaction with informants and translators, and the unique result they produce, creates the framework for understanding the total fieldwork experience. I bear full responsibility for the tone, focus, and emphasis of the material as presented. Much of what I experienced and learned can never be translated into print.

Four years in the field required a marriage of anthropology and education as I was involved in a series of human interactions using ethnographic methodology and the experiences of my own cultural heritage to identify the participant structures which reflected the Laotians' post-camp experiences. This generated a variety of questions and perspectives which enhanced my involvement and, I believe, brought me closer to the experiences of the Laotians. Analysis became a reflection of the total endeavor which included the experiences and perspectives of the ethnographer and all other participants.

Adult Laotian refugees were faced with a variety of decisions and problems as they encountered American society. They were forced to make choices for themselves and their families between what they knew worked for them in Laos and systems in the United States with which they were almost totally unfamiliar. The experience of choosing between the old and the new proved most difficult and often impossible for many adults. In particular, lack of facility with English, cultural contextualization, little schooling, and lack of experiential information, often led to disastrous consequences. This was, I determined, a key factor which few community organizations identified. Refugees generally accepted they had much to learn about the United States. The reverse however was not true. Unfortunately, the schools, social service agencies, and community structures weakened both the greater educational experience and the formal schooling by usually failing to include, compare, and build upon the previous life experiences of the Laotian adults as they attempted to learn about and to integrate with the mainstream culture. It is difficult to make choices without being able to identify what the choices are and what the consequences of those decisions will be. Cultural information, given out of context and hence without any real meaning within the perceived reality of the refugees, often confused the decision-making process.

I found that only a small percentage of the professionals in the community had been trained to work with adults, and even a smaller number who had even the remotest understanding of Laotian culture. Many, in the words of one Adult and Family Services worker, maintained the attitude that

> they have to adjust to our culture. I'm not here to teach them anything. I'm a steward of the public monies. . .

From my perspective, many educators, human service personnel, and bureaucrats approached the refugee population with a sterile efficiency which demonstrated a general ignorance of the extreme difficulty Lao refugees have in approaching bureaucrats or understanding how to gain access to our human service programs. The Laotians were often discouraged by the lack of help forthcoming from the individuals and agencies upon whom they were dependent for critical information. It was difficult for me to explain the lack of a "generous nature" in many Americans that, at least at first, the Lao people expected to encounter.

One Community

Eugene, Oregon, is a medium-sized metropolitan area with a population of roughly two hundred thousand. The ancestors of its European-American majority settled the region in the middle of the last century after displacing the original native population. This city, not unlike the rest of Oregon, is characterized by a low percentage of non-white minorities.[1] As the county seat, Eugene boasts of a recent multi-million dollar urban renewal project which has restructured the center of the city with treelined shopping and entertainment facilities.

In the area there are three major school districts, a state university, a community college, and numerous independent trade and professional schools. A complex set of human service agencies--local, county, state, and federal--attend to the needs of the populace. A clean city, located along the banks of the Willamette River, Eugene has numerous parks, recreation areas, and wilderness sites both within and close to the major urban area. It has been named one of America's most livable small cities. It's predominantly European-American majority controls the social and interactive norms that other's must adjust to for survival.

Laotian Refugees

The Laotian refugee population of Eugene was primarily composed of two hundred and six individuals. Both nuclear and large extended families contributed to nine cluster groups of families composed of relatives and close friends. These individuals were from two ethno-linguistic groups: ethnic Lao

(Lao Lum), and Mien (Yao). The ethnic Lao began arriving in late 1978 and the Mien arrived in 1979.[2] The Laotian people originated from the provinces of Vientiane, Khammouane, Savannakhet, Saravane, and Champassak. The Mien population originated in the provinces of Phong Saly and China's southern province of Yunnan.

The greater percentage of the Lao Lum originated in Vientiane and Champassak. Those families and individuals from Vientiane were usually well educated in comparison with the rest of the Lao population. The province of Vientiane is the seat of the old French colonial capital, which is also named Vientiane.[3] With a population around two hundred thousand, similar in size to Eugene, the individuals from the capitol were somewhat urbanized. Many of the men had been employed in the civil service with the French, Americans, or the Royal Lao Government. A number were multi-lingual, speaking Lao, and alternatively some Thai, French, Vietnamese, and English. The greater percentage of the adults had attended primary school grades through six, and many had also attended some of the secondary school grades six through nine. In addition, a few had specialized training in the military, civil service, or at the Lycee.

The people from Champassak, in the south of Laos, originated from a rural background. Provincial and less educated than their eastern counterparts, the men had more education than the women. still, few men had gone beyond primary school. Almost all of the women had no formal educational experiences. The schooling provided in this rural area came from Buddhist monks who taught on the village level within a tradition dating back thousands of years. A Theravada Buddhist country, Laos' traditional education has been centered in the village wat and the family. This education is oriented to practical needs, primarily those related to functioning within rural Lao society.

The Mien population of Eugene originated from an entirely different tradition than that of the Lao Lum. Having lived close to the Chinese border, they represented about five percent of the Laotian population before the 1975-1981 diaspora. They are closer in identification to their cultural and linguistic relatives in Yunnan, China than to the Lao Lum. Arriving in 1979 with a great deal of local support and publicity, they have enjoyed a more successful economic transition than the rest of the Laotian community. In addition, they consider themselves a part of larger families of Mien throughout the Pacific Northwest and maintain frequent interaction with these groups. A few of the male heads-of-household spoke Lao and Chinese. Most of the women received no formal education. Their educational problems were unique and they posed a challenge for local school personnel in having come from an oral tradition. Americans tended to notice them more because of their exotic and interesting dress. They, more than the other Lao, fit American stereotypes of the exotic refugee population. During the time this study was conducted, they comprised six households which together formed one large extended family.

Demographics

Community Census, 1983 (statistics from June 1982-June 1983

Number of Individuals in Community................206
  Males...124
  Females 82
Number of Adults, Sixteen and Older...............107
  Males...63
  Females..44
Number of Children Fifteen and Under..............99
  Males...61
  Females..38
Number of Families 67
Number of Extended Families..........................9

Education

Community college or high school classrooms in Lane County have often provided Laotian refugees with their first explanations and explorations of North American culture. The educational experiences available to adult refugees in Eugene have been largely restricted to the same community institutions. These local experiences offers a wide range of traditional program, from basic English as a Second Language and pre-vocational training for the non-literate to more sophisticated programs tailored to individual needs.

Seventy-eight percent of the male Laotian refugees and eight-six percent of the female Laotian refugees received less than a high school education in their homeland prior to resettlement. The majority of these individuals had not studied English before.

TABLE 1
EDUCATION IN LAOS IN PERCENTAGES

Gender	Less Than High School	More Than High School	High School
Male	78	19	3
Female	86	9	1

TABLE 2
LOCAL INSTITUTIONS WHERE REFUGEES HAVE
STUDIED

Institution	Percentage
University	0
Community College	86
High School	14

Eighty-six percent of the Laotian population have studied at one time or another in community college programs. A number of younger students, fourteen percent, have studied in the high schools. As of yet no Lao has graduated from high school and no local Lao refugees have been enrolled at the state university located in Eugene.

TABLE 3
EDUCATIONAL CHARACTERISTICS--LANGUAGE BY
PERCENTAGES

Gender	Speak Functional English	Read Write English	Literate in Native Language	Attended One Year or More of ESL
Male	47	12	57	66
Female	45	8	38	70

Since resettlement in Eugene, sixty-six percent of the males and seventy percent of the females have studied English as a Second Language for at least one year. Only twelve percent of the men and eight percent of the women read and write English as of 1983. Fifty-seven percent of the men and thirty-eight percent of the women were literate in their native language.

Employment

Obtaining employment has been one of the most difficult problems for the Laotian community members. Laotian refugees originate from a culture where the work ethic and value system are significantly different from North American values. Many individuals have had problems making the necessary adjustments expected by American employers. Integration into the American workforce was additionally hampered by the language barrier. These difficulties aggravated a tension expressed throughout the local job market during a period of disturbing economic recession in 1982-1983.

TABLE 4
REFUGEE EMPLOYMENT PROFILE*

Status	Percentage
Employed, full- or part time	39
Employed, full-time	25
Employed, part-time	14
Unemployed	59
Retired	2

*These figures reflect the general patterns during the 1982-1983 economic recession.

TABLE 5
REFUGEE OCCUPATIONS BY PERCENT*

Occupational Status	Percent
Professional	0.5
White Collar	2.0
Blue Collar	36.5
Unemployed	59.0
Retired	2.0
Total	100.0

*Based on averages for all adult males and females over sixteen years of age in the Laotian community between the years 1981 and 1983.

The majority of the employed Laotian community, thirty-six and a half percent, have worked as blue collar workers ranging from dishwashing and motel cleaning to janitorial and cooking jobs. Unfortunately, due to the limited nature of local employment opportunities, work generally centered around domestic help, wood products and related industries. Many of the skills and occupations learned in Laos were not transferrable to the new community setting. A representative list of skills and occupations refugees brought with them reads as follows.

Occupations and Skills in Native Country

Bank Auditor	Photographer
Bank Teller-Clerk	Policeman
Beautician	Priest (Buddhist)
Brick Layer	Sculptor/Artist
Carpenter	Seamstress
Civil Servant	Secretary
Commercial Fisherman	School Teacher (Lycee)
Construction Worker	School Teacher (Primary)
Electrician	Soldier
Hospital Worker	Tailor
Housewife	Tenant Farmer
Landed Farmer	Translator
Manual Laborer	University Student
Merchant	Watch Maker
Personnel Manager	Welder

186

Occupation and Skills Acquired in the United States

Assembly Line--Factory	ElectrostaticPrinter/Assembler
Babysitting	Educational Aide
Cabinet Maker	Fast Food Employee
Cannery Worker	Flagman
Case Manager/Counselor	Florist/Greenhouse Worker
Cook	Forestry Service Crew
Dishwasher	Garbage/Sanitation Worker
Gardeners	Self-Employed Craftsman
General Restaurant Help	Shoe Clerk
General Utility	Social Service Aide
Library Assistant	Toy Factory Employee
Maids--Hotels, Motels	Translator
Maintenance--Industrial	Tree Planter
Nutritional Aide	Tree Thinner
Packer/Truck Loader	Vegetable, Fruit, Nut Picker
Pantry Worker	Veterinarian's Assistant
Park/Recreation Assistant	Warehouse Worker
Road Grader	Wood Products Worker
Secretary/Clerk	

Over time, many individuals acquired two or more of the skills above as seasonal, part-time, or full-time job opportunities arose. New job acquisition was facilitated by on-the-job training through the local community college as well.

TABLE 6
PRECENTAGE OF REFUGEES HOMEBOUND OR
UNEMPLOYED SINCE ARRIVAL

Gender	Homebound	Unemployed*
Male	2	36
Female	89	31

*This does not count occasional day labor field picking jobs.

A substantial percentage of the community has yet to find long term employment. Language barriers, physical infirmity, psychological problems, and a tight job market all contributed to the problem of unemployment.

Due to a comprehensive pre-vocational and pre-employment program coupled with job development services initiated by the local community college in 1983, some Laotian refugees have found employment. Significantly, by the close of 1983 over forty-five percent of the Laotian community had left or was in the process of leaving Eugene for areas with better employment prospects. State Adult and Family Services officials encouraged secondary migration to states with better programs and services.[4] Most moved on to California where they had friends or family, where the state provides for refugee transition, and where over forty percent of this country's Southeast Asian refugee population is located. At the close of 1983, fifty-nine percent of the Laotians were still seeking stable employment.

188

Environmental Situation

TABLE 7
ENVIRONMENTAL STATISTICS OF ADULT
COMMUNITY MEMBERS BY PERCENTAGE

	Own	Rent	Car	Motorcycle	Med. Ins.
Laos	87	2	12	46	0
Eugene	0	100	48	3	2

All of the Laotian community rent apartments or houses. To this date no family has purchased a home. This is in great contrast to the percent of individuals who owned their own homes in Laos. Most of the Laotians, forty-eight percent, own cars. Again, this is in marked contrast to the situation in their homeland. However, many of the members of the community, forty-six percent, owned motorbikes or motorcycles in Laos. Few had medical insurance in Eugene and none in Laos.

TABLE 8
ORIGINAL SPONSORS AND CURRENT STATUS OF
CONTACT BY PERCENTAGE

Sponsor	Percent of Community
Churches	62
American Family	11
Laotian Family	17
Laotian Friend	21

Status of Contact	Percent of Community
Active Sponsor	12
Inactive Sponsor	88

A high percentage of the Laotian refugees in this community have lost contact or maintain very little contact with their original sponsors. Less than twelve percent of the population still maintains strong ties with their American sponsors. Many of the refugees were sponsored by church groups who now maintain a minimal contact. Secondary migration has played a significant role in the separation of these relationships. Sponsor burn-out has had some impact as well.

Respondents and informants interviewed during ethnographic fieldwork participated with full consent. All of the members of the local Laotian community were interviewed during the years of 1981 to 1984. The profiles and demographics I have presented are representative of the community during that period.

I was left with many thoughts when one Laotian refugee asked me,

> . . .for what reason do you put down all these numbers? How can these numbers tell the Americans how we are as humans, as people? I do not understand the American importance of numbers. If you are to know anything about the Lao you must start with the heart and stop the counting. . .

Government Agencies

Local government agencies, in particular the Adult and Family Services programs, which most of the refugees depended upon for services during their first eighteen months here, proved time and time again to be indifferent in their treatment of the refugees. Bilingual translators were employed who, living up to their reputation in the community as trained agents of the program, literally spied on families, reported additional income, and created both a fear of and dislike for other agencies and for the government. This greatly colored the initial educational experiences as refugees worked at figuring out how our society operates. One refugee said to me,

> I will not go there. They have no respect for me.
> Believe me, they make me feel so small. They check
> every penny, expecting us to be lying. This is what
> the communists did when they took over our country.
> They counted every chicken. That's why I came here,
> to get away from that. So, what's the difference?

This kind of institutionalized insensitivity, the rigid and often inappropriate application of the letter of the law, created an atmosphere where vital information sought by the Lao from would-be refugee service providers could not be obtained. Refugees learned to be cautious. Even though they were often ignorant of the law, they developed a general fear and mistrust of bureaucrats and avoided them whenever possible. Time and again, the difficulty of adjusting to this new cultural situation was exacerbated to the point of despair as government employes either failed outright to do their jobs as mandated by the 1980 Refugee Act, or stretched the interpretation of the law to the disadvantage of the refugees. The inherently racist structure of these American institutions frustrated and prohibited the kinds of human interaction with which the Laotian people were familiar. Professional "objectivity" was used to cover up the failure to meet the human needs of the refugee population.

As an example, a particular Laotian family was singled out for excess scrutiny, abuse, and neglect as the bias of Adult and

Family Services personnel filtered down into the politics of the Lao community. One family member explained,

> They don't like our family. We have an old family argument with their translator. They say she is Lao. We know she is Vietnamese who speaks Lao. There is a great difference between the two which Americans do not understand. So, they give us a hard time. What can we do? My father won't go there. We need some things but he won't go there. They said bad things about our family to everyone. They think whatever the translator says is true because they know nothing about our people and our way of doing things. They weren't with us (politically) at home and they are not with us here. . .

I personally witnessed many acts of ignorance, callousness, and inflexibility that highlighted bureaucrat efficiency to the point of caricature. Because of this, individuals lost benefits, people went hungry, families were deprived of medical attention. It was not uncommon to keep a refugee waiting for hours while "other priorities" were taken care of. Paperwork took precedence over human beings. This was incomprehensible to the various needy individuals. Time and time again, the Lao mentioned the lack of "heart" in the way American officials conducted business which was critical to their lives.

Other incidents which I witnessed graphically illustrate these points. The first entailed a meeting of local social service personnel, Adult and Family Services personnel, and a state-wide team of cross-cultural experts who had come to the community to assist with resettlement problems. One of the Adult and Family Services personnel put his feet up on the desk as he spoke to a Lao man from the state team. Culturally, there could not be a greater insult to a Lao. Professionally, in American culture, it is extremely rude. This man was indifferent to the fact that, by any standard of measurement, the

Lao man he was speaking to was his educational and professional superior. The Lao gentleman spoke five languages, studied in France, and had been an international diplomat. To the provincial American social service worker, he was only another refugee. With this kind of ignorance, how can one expect respect from the refugee community? The Lao man later said to me,

> Don't worry about it. I know you were angry with him. Remember, my job here is to help my people. So, I have to put up with this ignorance. It is difficult, but that is the position we are in here. We need the services of this agency. My pride is not worth the price of losing these services for people who are in great need of them. . .

Another incident which demonstrated this callousness also took place in a city-wide meeting for service providers. Bilingual translators representing Adult and Family Services were from upperclass Vietnamese families, neither having languished in refugee camps and both having flown over during 1975 when the upper middle-class and the rich left with American help. Trained by Adult and Family Services to work with later arrivals, they were making fun of the Lao as "lower" than the other refugees. Their jokes about cleanliness and ignorance were shared by the American Adult and Family Services personnel present. These are the same translators upon whom American supervisors depended for information about the Lao community. This information contextualized the decisions they made concerning Lao lives and resettlement opportunities. The economic power these individuals held was enormous. If they did not like certain people or families, they would not translate for them or they would translate from their own needs or perspectives.

Across the Lao community, the majority of the members related with fear and suspicion to the agency that was theoretically there to help them with adjustment. The Adult and Family Services people had great power over the lives of the refugees. They could have a person declared qualified for "survival" funding, or they could declare a cut-off or a sanction (loss of funds for a period to teach responsibility). They could deny education programs, medical care, or emergency assistance. They could deny access to programs by failing to have essential information translated. These possibilities became commonplace occurrences for the Laotians. The overwhelming impression I was left with was that these public assistance programs were more of a reflection of the struggle between the federal and state governments to see which one could do less, than a response to the needs of the refugees. These bureaucrats, untrained and unprepared to understand the immediate needs or the culture of the Laotians, neatly arranged and rearranged the lives of the refugees to make them conform to the regulations and restrictions of the agency. The Laotians had no choice but to attempt to conform, to change, to accommodate. Ultimately, many could not, and they paid a steep price. Every refugee paid some price in this process of accommodation. Few Americans realized the extent. It was a one-way street for the refugees until they learned to develop a public face and an aggressive posture when dealing with bureaucrats. Few Laotians seemed prepared to do this during the post-camp period. Culturally, many were unable to change their valuing in order to accomplish these transitions. Laotians who worked for these agencies often found themselves in culturally conflicting situations.

The Schools

Most of the adults over sixteen either attended the local high schools or the community college. In general, I found a positive attitude among the Lao towards the local schooling experience. Comments relating to the performance of the teachers or the effectiveness of the facilities ranged from approval to deep appreciation. However, this raises the question of what real basis of comparison the Lao had for making these judgments. One has to examine the antecedent educational context they were familiar with to place these appraisals in context.

The educational tradition the refugees carried with them is characterized by Chagnon and Rumph (1983) as "centered around the village wat." It is a record of male-centered education with a heavy emphasis on traditional Buddhist values. Informal consent on the part of the Lao elite, who filled most of the administrative positions during the French colonial period, contributed to an appalling neglect of the educational needs of the majority of the Lao people.

With the coming of independence in 1953, there occurred a parallel development in education. The Royal Lao Government clung tenaciously to the old French system which required instruction in French. Under this system Lao was treated as a foreign language. However, at this same time we find the Pathet Lao reaching out to the rural populace and creating a new system which focused on adult literacy as well as on the formation of primary schools in which Lao was the instructional language and where Lao history, politics, and customs were taught.

Chagnon and Rumph further delineate the situation in 1975 as the new government assumed leadership:

> Less than 20% had completed six years of schooling; less than 2% had finished the full twelve years. . . there was a critical shortage of qualified, experienced Laotian teachers. In addition, thirty years of war had seriously impacted the education of the few that accessed the system. . .5

On the local level in the United States, the programs in the community college were the places where the majority of the adults attending school were concentrated. These programs focused on language training and acquisition as well as on some cultural orientation sequences which were designed to expedite the mandate of the Reagan administration which emphasized rapid assimilation into the work force. As a staff member at the community college, I found the educators willing, but the system generally unable to provide the specific in-depth training the Lao population required to build bridges cross-culturally. The inherently racist bureaucracies of these institutions were not developed to allow for the flexibility and sensitivity required to respond to the delicate needs of cultural accommodation. Upon arrival in 1978 and 1979 many of the Lao were sent by their sponsors to work immediately and thus never had the opportunity to attend school. This was a bitter bone of contention among the Laotians as expressed in this statement:

> I did everything I was asked. The others and most of the Vietnamese didn't do that. . . they went to school. I worked in a mill. Now the government says I can't learn English because I'm here over eighteen months. This isn't fair. Once I was laid off the new employer won't give me a job because I have bad English. I can't have a job because I can't speak so good. What do I do now?

I had the opportunity, as a teacher trainer and as a member of a regional team of multicultural educators, to compare the educational programs of this particular city to other cities with a Laotian refugee population. To a great degree, the high school and elementary schools were entities unto themselves. Special classes were designed for the teaching of English as a Second Language. In comparison with other schools, they were average. Programs were focused on the needs of the

Vietnamese population which reflected a problem nation-wide in dealing with the Laotians. Cultural and psychological needs of non-Vietnamese ethnic groups, such as the Lao and the Kampucheans, were often ignored. Laotian students had to compete with Chinese-Vietnamese, who were often model students. The different needs of each population were not adequately addressed in materials development, teaching strategies, or other areas pertinent to education. As in other schools across the nation, the question was raised as to how much preparation the local educators could have had as they were faced with a burgeoning Lao population between 1978 and 1984. Given the state of teacher training in the United States, multi-cultural awareness has never been a priority. Compared with other schools in the nation of the same size as those in this community, Laotian bilingual translators were used relatively early on the local level. However, they were also the first victims of budget cuts and sometimes were victims of educators who had not confronted the racism in their lives or that inherent in the structure of most American institutions.

A fundamental problem arose as we explored just what class of people were employed as translators. Often enough a different class of individuals, usually those who benefitted the most by the American presence in Laos and who possessed a strong affinity for French or Western culture, were enlisted to interpret for the others. Culturally, these individuals were viewed as bureaucrats and elitists, and were often unable to elicit truthful information from members of the refugee community. Although viewed as bona fide Laotians, these translators took on a quasi-American status and were placed in a special category of relationships within the Lao community. They were recognized for "knowing" about American culture but, unlike the status conferred by the American community in response to its own needs and purposes, these translators were not the real "leaders" within the Lao community.

Despite a barrage of special events arranged by some of the "special" programs for refugees in the public school system, the community was well aware of an "us" and "them" attitude. One of the Lao men put it this way:

> We don't talk to the teacher in our country about school. That's their job. I have another job. It would not be right to go there and question. . . We become embarrassed an ashamed when they ask of things we don't know. . .

Often American educators perceived this as not caring on the part of the Lao. This was demonstrative of the great gaps in both communication and cultural understanding which separated American teachers who had not had Laotian cultural orientation from Laotians who had not developed an understanding of American cultural structures. What disturbed me was the fact that the Laotians were expected to make the adjustments for both parties involved in the experience. Often parents were inclined to tell the teacher that there were no problems for fear of losing face. Parents in the refugee households often received notes from the school explaining programs and/or homework. What local educators failed to realize was that the context was often missing. Laotians could not always identify "problems" within a North American cultural context. The Lao parents had not received training or had not been here long enough to understand the particular value Americans place on school behavior and competition. They, too, needed orientation for the process of becoming American parents and for the special roles of American parents in relationship to the schools. Lao parents had been repeatedly called on to make choices and/or to give support for a cultural process or institution they did not understand and for which they held no context.

Assumptions that the American style of teaching and learning was the best way to support the Laotians while they attempted to acculturate have yet to be examined and proved effective. Although a number of Lao youth have acquired a greater degree of proficiency in English, none have graduated from high school. Future longitudinal studies may reveal more about the impact of current methodology and programs in public schools. One thing we have learned is that refugees should not be grouped in the same classroom with special education students. There is a great difference between the needs and realities of refugees and the needs and realities of the developmentally disabled. Special and regular educators need to "re-think" what they have done to the refugees as they have assumed them to be "disabled"and used on them the methodology that behaviorists have intended for the developmentally disabled in U.S. society. In particular, the majority of "special educators" working with the Lao had no previous cross-cultural training. A majority did not view culture as an issue.

The school buildings and the teachers were impressive to the new refugee. Since most Laotians did not come here with an understanding of American culture and what to expect from the school system, they generally accepted that what the schools were doing was right and that the burden lay with them, as refugees, to respond appropriately. In the words of one Lao adult,

> I don't know all these things. My children are learning different things than I know of. Some things they do I don't like. Our children are losing respect for their parents. They do not ask for our help about life questions. This is not the Lao way. We sometimes don't know how much of the American way to let them learn. What if we go home to Laos? They can't forget everything Lao. My husband says we are in America now. These teachers are educated. They know what is right for America. So, we have to do it that way. The children must learn how to be Americans. . .

To a lesser degree than in government agencies, but to an appalling degree for educators entrusted with the complex task of "schooling" refugees, I found a significant lack of professional preparation concerning the teaching of the adult and of Laotian culture among local educators and administrators. I found a corresponding lack of preparation on the part of most local educators and administrators in the basic understanding of their own culture, the role of education in the acculturation process, and to what purpose they were doing what they thought they were doing in the classroom. Teacher preparation was appallingly deficient in this area. Often courses were taught with the specific class content as the priority, rather than a focus on class content in context and as a part of the holistic adjustment process for the refugee. In fact, many teachers contributed directly to refugee confusion. Programs, such as the Distar process, deny context which is critical for cross-cultural understanding and adjustment. Why learn a new language if the teachers fail to present a meaningful context within which one can function as a full adult?

This does not, however, diminish the individual efforts of numerous professionals who, despite an inadequate reception on the part of the system and a callous execution of legalities by some community programs, managed to create some meaningful experiences for the refugee population and for themselves during the acculturation process. The real educators were the single identifiable force in the American community that the refugee community could consistently look to for help. The term "my teacher" had a very special meaning and place in the vocabulary of the refugee. Anyone who had taken time to become involved, who had seen the few but extraordinary teachers who sought out help to understand the "Lao way" and attempted to respect the refugee adults as full human beings experienced the joy of cultural negotiation and mutual attempts to understand each other. Each grew as a cooperative experience unfolded. Those precious few provided a haven, a shoulder to lean on, a helping hand. They were the ones who, as one Lao leader suggested, "...put their hands out first."

These people were an inspiration for me as I watched them teach and share beyond the limitations of the schooling process. They learned about Lao food, Lao customs, and, to the best of their ability, about the Lao as they perceived themselves. Simultaneously they expected and helped the Lao to do the same in relation to their lives and to American culture. They asked the Lao to reflect on their needs, to express their frustrations, to explain and to examine what they experienced. They took chances and they became involved. They did not restrict themselves to one method. They used many and were flexible and pragmatic as this complex set of human interactions required. They looked at language, history, and culture from a total ecological perspective. One could easily identify those educators, for they were those to whom the refugees returned after classes were long concluded, over certain holidays, or any given morning. Often they would bring a plate of spring rolls or some small gift. They brought their "new" children to show to their "old" teacher, and in time of distress, need, or confusion it was often this teacher, this friend they called on for direction. That voice on the other end of the line, that smile while greeting established a life-line that was of major importance to the refugee. Having taken the time to learn to say "hello"in the native language and to remember the real name of the students as well as to pronounce it correctly was the kind of experience that held many a refugee together during a period in which many of the strongest became unglued. One refugee clearly stated,

No one ever know how good I felt when I heard my teacher say "good morning" in my language. Then I knew he cared. Then I knew he understood how hard it is to learn a new language. Then I used to tell him a new Lao word and I felt like a real person. Then we could laugh if he made mistakes. There was no blame, just to learn. He helped me, too, to understand that being a man is different here. You know the ways of these things are different in my country also. These things were very hard for me to understand. Really, only an American can explain the American way of doing things. If this doesn't happen, we don't know what to do, how to act, what to look for. So, then we do things the way we know. We talked about this. He told me how important it was for my wife to go to school. Now my wife and me can talk with these things to my children's teachers. We didn't do things this way at home. At home, the teacher is the expert. Here in America, everyone says what they think. This teacher taught me more than words, more than we could find in the dictionary. He helped me to understand. He is a friend. . .

Changing their relationship with traditional patterns of education and interaction was a challenge for the Lao as well as for Americans. This experience had repercussions across the entire community. Due to a long history of inadequate education during the French colonial period, the Lao were unable to develop a strong competitive educational value. Only a small class of elites were educated. They had a monopoly on knowledge and power. Now that has changed. Unfortunately, that change began to take place at a quicker pace for the children than for the adults. The young were very quick to recognize education as a tool for upward mobility. Because they were required to be in school, they were exposed on a daily basis to the educational system and the values contextualized there. The adults, often enough, sacrificed their own potential so that the children would "get ahead." This meant that the parents sought work as a first priority. Indeed, our government required them to do so. Some children remained at home to take care of younger siblings. Although culturally appropriate for the Lao, this practice was often condemned by North American educators who failed to realize and understand the deep culture involved.

Health Services

Unique to the community was the county health team. Two nurses, understaffed and overworked, took on the formidable task of identifying the health problems of the refugees, informing the local health service community about uncommon and often unheard-of illnesses, and of educating the refugee community to American culturally expectations and conceptions of health. They had the additional task of educating American doctors and health personnel to the special problems of the Lao refugees as well as of their cultural attitudes towards health and health care:

> The doctors finally gave us the green light and asked us to help with identifying problems. Many refugees were afraid of doctors, preferring home remedies. . .

> Some doctors were afraid of refugees. They held cultural prejudices. They were afraid of contracting diseases. . .

> At first we had a difficult time getting doctors to treat patients. Many still refuse to take on refugee clients...

A list of the range of treatments this team dealt with covers the spectrum from malaria and hepatitis B to multiple intestinal parasites. On home visits these women basically dealt with or referred to the social service community the health needs of the Laotians:

I didn't speak any Lao. We became real good with sign language. We drew clocks to inform them of the times they had to take medicine. An interpreter wasn't always available. Even when an interpreter was available, few have been trained in cross-cultural explanation of medical terminology. Try explaining T.B. or iron deficiency in the blood when there are no comparable terms in the language. Sophisticated equipment and medicines often generated a fear. We had no control over them once we left the home. Sometimes they would take all the medicine at once, instead of daily. Sometimes they would mix medicines and old herbal medicine treatments. . . However, they always treated us well, with respect and great kindness. . .

Traditionally, the Laotian people bathe daily. They associated this ritual with being physically and spiritually clean. However, their understanding of "germs" was entirely different than in the West. Lebar and Suddard (1960) indicate that prevailing food-handling techniques and eating habits have been sources of infections. Lack of refrigeration in Laos as well as the consumption of raw pork and raw fish contributed to parasite infections. They found that studies of school age children determined that "over 70% were infected with one or more parasites."[6] The custom of serving meals in a common bowl and dipping hands into the communal bowl created additional problems. Even though hands were washed before and after, the water used was often contaminated. The Laotian refugees carried or acquired many of these parasites in the refugee camps and on their journey to the United States. As one of the county nurses observed,

As the years have gone by, we have more materials in translation and we do have more interpreters. Health, however, is related to so many facets of life. Sickness is not the only aspect. Preventive medicine and cleanliness by American cultural standards are also important. Strange enough, the people coming in from the refugee camps in the past year are bringing more health problems than before. . .

Often parasites located in an individual could not be identified, as they were totally new to the American body of medical knowledge. This created both fear and frustration on the part of local physicians. As a consequence, some refused to work with refugee patients.

Beyond the health problems mentioned earlier, two important categories were almost entirely overlooked. First, it was important to recognize that all of the refugees suffered periodically as a result of the psychological adjustments that had to be made while adapting to American culture, language and values. The development of cultural context is not an easy task. This was further complicated in cases where the whole range of psychological disorders found in any population were transferred cross-culturally as Lao and American attempted to understand each other. No effort has been attempted at this point which addresses these needs. It is common knowledge that refugees suffered from loss of language, culture, familiar environment, and prestige. Furthermore, those individuals who spent a prolonged period of time in refugee camps had an additional set of problems to overcome. The totality of these complications have yet to be contextualized or addressed. According to one health nurse,

Questions have been raised if we are even capable of identifying all of the psychological complications that the average refugee experiences as he or she faces adjusting to American life. There is also the question of what each one has to give up. How much can a given individual give up. We know each person is different. We don't have any scale of measurement in order to identify expectations! In many ways each of the refugees must experience schizophrenia to some degree as they try to figure out what's happening to them. We have no way of identifying or responding to these irregularities. Everything we do is hit or miss. I've spent a lot of hours agonizing over the problems we encounter and cannot respond to. Then, I suppose, there are all of those we can't identify and never see. . . This experience has made me look at my own culture. . . and, it has raised more questions than answers. . .

The second area of concern is nutrition and diet. The transition from traditional foods, fresh food shopping, minimal storage, and balanced diet to shopping in American stories, buying prepared foods, and dealing with the plethora of "junk food" available was enormous and difficult. The whole range of problems that developed around diet and nutrition have to be understood within a cultural context. The diet of the marginal wage earner is different than that of the affluent. This was not transmitted in an understandable manner to the local refugees during the initial period of contact with American culture. One nutritionist conducting a survey of the dietary practices of the Laotians in Eugene was aghast as she found pregnant women consuming more candy bars and coca-cola than vegetables and meat. Junk food that was chemically based is more affordable than meat, eggs, fruit, fish or vegetables which were part of the Lao traditional diet.

Overall, this area of the refugee experience was probably the most neglected. Important factors to consider were financial problems--good food was too expensive for large Lao extended families who lived in marginal poverty; lack of education and nutrition information translated into the native language was also a problem, as was the lack of skilled health workers trained to deal with the complexities of cross- cultural health problems and adjustments. The low priority of health and health-related problems in relation to the emphasis on rapid assimilation into the work force created problems associated with resettlement that the government failed to address.

By 1987 there were still no Lao doctors available to the community, even though there were Lao doctors in Portland. There were no real health education programs in the community. The county health program had been drastically reduced and was expecting additional cuts:

> We haven't even begun to deal with the real problems like dental care. Who can afford it? Many people need medicines they cannot afford. . .

The degree of frustration expressed by those health workers was only surpassed by the degree of their commitment. They were among the invisible members of the community who, in spite of a bureaucratic and callous system, aided and nurtured the refugee transition process.

Neighbors, Co-workers

In contrast to the formal human services agencies which officially deal with the refugee community, a unique and unpredictable phenomenon appeared time and again as Laotians and Americans negotiated in the local setting. Despite a lack of knowledge of each other's cultures and of the politics involved with refugee resettlement, and beset with language differences and an inability to communicate in depth, many Lao people met Americans who were sensitive, considerate, helpful, and often protective. It was these individuals who went with the refugees to the welfare office and left feeling the same frustrations in relation to the bureaucracy as did the refugees. It was these individuals who drove Lao families to the market or took them to church. Hundreds of times I witnessed human beings from very different cultures struggle to understand each other as they were thrust into close proximity to each other as neighbors. Comments by Americans relating to this experience captured the complexity and intensity of these exchanges that occurred on a daily basis:

This is all very strange for us. We didn't know any Laotians before they moved next door. At first we were worried. You know, we heard a lot of stories about their eating dogs and cats, about the diseases they have, and about the way they live over there. We thought maybe they didn't know how to use toilets. So we just kept to ourselves.

They were only here a couple of days and the wife came over with some egg rolls. We didn't understand too much she said, we all did a lot of head-nodding and smiling. It was really awkward. Then she left and we weren't really sure about eating them. You know, maybe they cooked a dog or something. My daughter goes to school with some of them. She said she had them at school and they were good. So we ate them. No one died as you can see.

My wife and myself began to talk things over. We decided to bring them back some filberts from my brother's farm and some mint. Hell, we couldn't have done anything better. It really made them happy. The woman asked for some mint roots and we got her more. She planted them in a pot by her door. She also planted other stuff. Other neighbors began to see they were just pretty normal people--they speak a different language, they look a little different, but they are good people. We began to talk more.

Believe it or not, we even helped them with English and things. I never thought I'd be teaching anyone anything. I was a bad student in school.

They've been here as neighbors almost two years now. We've been over there, they've eaten here. Last Christmas we had them here. We had a good time. When they had their Lao New Year celebration, we went to it. In fact, I remember seeing you there. All in all, if I had to say anything, I'd say it this way: I think these people have really been screwed here. We went to the A.F.S. with them and they really treated these people awful. I gave them a piece of my mind. This guy works hard, he's a janitor. In his country he was some sort to official. He's not too proud to work. When I saw that I knew he was O.K. He'd do anything for you. She works part-time. She cooks, sews clothes, has a garden, and they are clean. You can eat off the floors over there. That's not what we expected. Our kids get along O.K.

All in all we don't have any problem with them. I know some of these people come over here and have real problems adjusting. It hasn't been easy for these people but they hang in there. As we can talk more English together I find they are really O.K. As I said, it was pretty hard at first. Did you know they fought on our side over there? Hell, we ought to be doing everything we can for them. They lost everything. My wife and me thought that if that happened to us we don't know if we could go to some foreign place and start over. These people got a lot of courage. I'm glad I know them. . . oh yeah, my dog is still alive. We laugh at how stupid we were to worry about that. . . .

Another American summed it up this way:

> Hey, I'm not going to say that everything is alright
> living next to these people. There are lot of
> problems. They tend to have a lot of visitors, they
> have a lot of gatherings on weekends--they all seem
> to come to this one apartment. We went over and
> talked to them and it was no real problem. The guy
> understood. They're fairly quiet most of the time
> now.

I had an attitude. I still do in some ways. My son
was over there (in Southeast Asia). These people
don't really bother no one. They helped me change a
tire one day. Another time I was invited to one of
their celebrations. I went over and had a couple of
beers. It was strange. Everyone was talking in their
language. Those who spoke some English spoke to
me. They treated me special there. I didn't stay long
but I was glad I went over. Inside their house was
like anyone else's. It was clean. That made me feel a
little better. I don't worry about them living next
door. I know if I need anything they'd give me a
hand. They are a generous people. Real easy going.
Hell, they can hold their beer. Their ways are
different. They cook a lot of different food. I used to
think all those smells were strange but now I don't
even notice it.

Last spring I was sick and the guy next door had his
wife send me over some food--rice and meat. I
thought, few Americans would do that for a neighbor
they hardly know. I'm not saying we're close friends.
I'm just saying they are pretty ordinary people when
you get to know them. One thing--they are real good

to their kids. I guess they all lost a lot of family during the war and they love what kids they have. I watch them as a family and it reminds me of the way things were when I was a kid in Ohio. The family is really important to them. They weren't so bad once you get to know them a bit. . .

This spirit also manifested itself in several projects I was privileged to be a part of while working with the Laotian community. For example, many Americans worked with the Family Garden Project which helped to establish family garden plots for the Lao to grow fresh vegetables like they had done in Laos. Americans with no previous exposure to the Lao worked side by side to till, to plant, and to grow food. This type of experience transcended the barriers a given culture may construct and reduced the process to common, shared denominators. Humans were learning from other humans, sharing and enjoying. In the final analysis, after all was said and done, I believe it was those kinds of experiences that helped most to sustain the Lao during this difficult period of adjustment. Unfortunately, there were not enough of these encounters.

City Agencies

At the conclusion of this study, the city of Eugene had yet to develop any effective system to deal with refugee problems during resettlement. Although refugees had to appear in the courts, interact with police, firemen, landlords, and tax collectors, no official translators had been hired by the city to insure that the rights of the Laotians were protected and that adequate information was gathered when decisions were made. Instead, the city chose to rely on community college translators, when available, to help solve problems. These translators were already working overtime for their community. The translators spent many hours working for the city without pay. As a result, most of the time no translator was present to represent the needs or perspective of the refugee. This caused enormous problems and generated anxiety and hostility towards refugees on the part of civil servants and city personnel who could not communicate with refugees when problems occurred. An excerpt from my field notes of October 1982 illustrates this problem:

> Being in court with a refugee is a "Kafkaesque" experience. The judge asks questions, the refugee nods, smiles, and looks at me. The judge looks at him, looks at me, and asks if I can communicate the question. We talk. The judge asks another question. The same process transpires all over again. Fifty-five minutes of this kind of interaction transpires. Then the judge asks if the Lao has anything to say. Confused, fearful, not understanding, he lets out with a barrage in Lao. A stunned and confused judge lets him finish. Then he looks at me and says, "What did he say?" Another conference. Frustration all around. All this over a simple traffic violation that happened because a policeman couldn't understand what the Lao was trying to explain and thought the man was being abusive. . .

This was a simple case. The judge finally gave him the minimum fine, more out of frustration than an understanding of the problem. The inability of city agencies and personnel to respond to the basic needs of the Laotians created enormous adjustment problems.

Those responsible for the resettlement experience seemed to have overlooked the American community on the local level. Instead, they put a great deal of time, energy, and dollars into relatively ineffective educational programs which emphasized rapid assimilation into the work force. I remain convinced that a broader educational experience based on an understanding of cultural ecology, effective public relations, emphasis on problem solving and decision making in context, as well as opportunity for involvement by Americans in the traditional organic community experience might have helped to make the post-camp period for the Lao less painful. The human factor was greatly underestimated. Community education and mechanisms for realistic acculturation did not exist. The courts, the police department, and the fire department remain as blatant examples of this neglect. In the courts, justice thinks and speaks English only.

The few human beings who extended a hand to the Lao were not enough to counteract the many with prejudices, with erroneous understandings of the Lao, with an unwillingness to give the Lao a chance to adjust, with an axe to grind or ignorance to overcome. The latter were, by far, more numerous than the few who took a chance. Community, knowing one was a part of the life of one's neighbors, was an essential aspect of the traditional Laotian cultural experience. Not being accepted by many Americans, being left on the periphery of American life, while coping with the loss of traditional community caused great mental anguish and feelings of isolation for most Lao. One young man stated the problem in this way:

> To me, every American lives in a lot of little worlds, sort of like boxes. The American goes from box to box to do whatever he has to do... church, school, home. They don't mix together very much. You can see the new baby in the glass cage... and the dead also go into a box. In Laos it was not that way. Everything was together. Neighbors had a special place. It was one big box instead of many little ones here. It is easy to be very alone here. I don't like this too much. It makes my heart sad. For this thing, I miss my country. . .

The "Experts"

> At the core of each person's life is a package of beliefs that he or she learns and that has been culturally determined long in advance of the person's birth. . . the world is made coherent by our description of it. . .[7]

Educators and anthropologists have written extensively about the impact of social institutions on traditional communities and on the process of acculturation. In particular, some anthropologists have analyzed schools in terms of their cultural congruence with the culture they serve (Kimball, 1974; Cohen, 1975; Carnoy, 1974; Ogbu, 1974; Kozol, 1980). Jules Henry's micro-ethnographic studies of the United States urban classroom culture conclude that they are the extensions of the dominant Anglo-Saxon middle class culture projected into the school setting (Henry, 1975). Essentially, this means that the system of reward in the classroom and how reward is to be learned as well as the criteria for student success are all influenced by cultural factors that more often than not are foreign to the immigrant community. Ogbu (1974) observes and analyzes the problems of ghetto schools and the loss of primary culture identification for many of the students. Spindler (1976) raises questions related to the concept of cultural congruence and the relationship of the immigrants to the United States national culture which is trying to integrate them and change their value systems, specifically:

1. Are the schools agents of the national culture?

2. Can the cultural integrity of immigrant groups and minority individuals be preserved as integration and value retraining occur?

Spindler's model provides a theoretical framework for the study of acculturation/assimilation roles in community settings. He states that institutions are instrumental activities, i.e., they retain their credibility as long as they produce results that are reasonably congruent with social beliefs, needs, and expectations. In times of change, schools become focal points for the introduction of new information and most often the results produced may not be congruent with traditional cultural needs or expectations. School, community, and national culture alter traditional cultural aspirations. Recent literature related to the experience of education within a cultural system is replete with models for the study of immigrants and acculturation. Bernstein (1970) examines the sociolinguistic approach to assimilation; Gamio (1971) investigates the experience of assimilation of Mexican-Americans into American culture; Cohen (1965) looks at the role of culture in relation to the educational setting; Glazier, Nathan, and Moynihan (1963) expose the myth of the melting pot theory; Higham (1975) records the assimilation of Jews in urban America; Taylor (1971) presents a detailed account of European immigration to the United States; and Pullen (1981), in a brief study of the Portland, Oregon Southeast Asian community assesses work related aspects of the first eighteen months of assimilation.

Numerous studies from classic literature related to immigration and assimilation provide models for urban ethnography. Jacob Riis (1890, 1892, 1902) researched immigrant experiences in urban slums; Oscar Handlin (1951) presents a sensitive analysis of the problems the new immigrant encounters through detailed examination of the history of immigration; Solomon (1956), Higham (1955), and Jones (1960) provide accounts of immigrant synthesis.

Educators and anthropologists have yet to participate in in-depth and shared exploration of the Laotian refugee experience as they confront acculturation and assimilation. In particular, the literature search indicates that no studies exist that thoroughly examine or record the events of the post-camp refugee experience and assess the long range implications for the Lao refugee or, in fact, for the dominant North American society.

Some educators have stressed the need for a technique of instruction that encompasses a process of "humanization" of previously dehumanized individuals. A dehumanized, highly stressed condition has been reflected in the behavior of great numbers of the refugee population in the period following release from the refugee camp environment.[8] Because most of the Laotian refugees are non-literate in English, educators like Paulo Freire insist upon a concept of education for these individuals that is compatible with human dignity and responsibility. Furthermore, they encourage the use of methodology that incorporates the concurrent study of language with concepts and experiences meaningful to the adult learners within the total ecological context of their daily lives:

> In so far as language is impossible without thought, and language and thought impossible without the world to which they refer, the human word is more than mere vocabulary, it is word and action. . .[9]

Freire refers to the world of the illiterate as a culture of silence in which the masses are mute, prohibited from taking part in the transformation of their society or from acquiring self esteem. He indicates that the nonliterate must experience and understand more of the culture and the society into which he or she is expected to integrate and to which he or she must adjust the sum total of his or her life experience.

In the context of national development, a number of anthropologists and educators identify an implicitly assimilative function for education institutions rooted in economic determinism--a stance expressed by Carnoy (1974). From this perspective schools as instruments of development inherently collaborate in the breakdown of loyalty, support and identification to kin groups, extended family, ethnic groups, and other models of traditional solidarity not congruent with the capitalist model for industrialization and progress (Cohen, 1975; Shimahara, 1975).

Sinclair (1923) in his classic study of American education develops this thesis in more depth:

> We have allowed the education of our youth to fall
> into the absolute control of a group of men who
> represent not only a minority of the total population
> but have at the same time enormous economic and
> business stakes in what education it shall be. . .[10]

He further asserts that the American educational system is an "instrument of special privilege" with its main function to perpetuate a capitalist system rather than the education of humankind. The monopolization of college and university boards by other than academicians establishes an "interlocking set of directorates" which stabilizes this mission and creates a uniformity.

Kozol (1980) raises questions concerning what is transpiring within the educational process. He alleges that research is a "self-perpetuating process of delay" and that parameters are placed around research by those who determine what questions may be asked, what research is acceptable, and what resources and references are legitimate:

> The school serves the state. The interests of this state
> are not compatible with private ethnics or

unmanageable dissent. The stars and stripes are not
above the door for decoration; they tell us, in the
clearest possible terms, the name and motives of the
owner of the structure that our learning shall inhabit
... 11

Kozol further cites the dependency of higher education on large
state and federal subsidies as evidence of the fact that the
universities are obvious extensions of the lower levels of state-
controlled education. He asserts there are "ten times four
thousand students in black, poor white, Spanish
neighborhoods" of the large American cities who will never
have the opportunities of the "privileged" but for the "accident
of color, cash, and birth.12

Professors, in the words of Kozol, are "with rare exceptions,
free to argue or discuss whatever they like, as long as this is
confined to words and discussion." Education that focuses on
social change is another matter. He maintains the present
system neutralizes the active thinker and doer, co-opts
meaningful examination of the issues, and perpetuates a system
that attempts to keep the energy and activities of everyone and
everything within its sphere of influence in a position beneficial
to its smooth operation. He concludes by saying that through
neutralized "discussion and investigation," American education
dilutes reaction and removes us from "... the things we do, the
sights we see, the agonies we empower..."; he charges that it is
an atrocity that even to this day, when the record of our role in
Southeast Asia has been thoroughly documented, we still
"cannot say that how we effortlessly kill" is evil and real.13

Cultural negotiation with the Laotian refugee population
during their post-camp interactions with North American
culture generated the following conclusions:

A. The resettlement process frustrated both refugees and Americans in the following areas as cultural interaction unfolded:

1. The complicated bureaucratic structures and personnel of American governmental agencies, social service projects, and the schools were unprepared for the influx of Laotians. This created tensions which inhibited the smooth transmission of essential knowledge during this initial adjustment period.

2. Most agency personnel were not prepared to identify the cultural or psychological differences between Laotians and other Southeast Asians. Laotians, more often than not, were treated as if they were Vietnamese. This contributed to erroneous assumptions on the part of Americans working with Laotians in the schools and in the community. Erroneous assumptions led to the transmission of inadequate or incorrect information.

3. Synchronicity of action, perception, or thought between members of the two cultures rarely occurred.

4. Laotians arrived in the United States with high expectations for success, reinforced by American promises made in Laos or by American personnel in the refugee camps. Reconciling the myth of living in the United States with the realities of living as a refugee was difficult and depressing.

5. Families and relatives were not kept intact during the refugee resettlement process. Becoming more aware of relatives or friends resettled in another part of the United States often led to secondary migration. This movement disrupted initial ties with Americans

and frustrated sponsors and other members of the American community.

6. Sponsors of refugees had almost no preparation for that role. Responsibilities were not clearly defined by the government. Idealism over being a sponsor became secondary to the complexity of involvement required when dealing with refugees. Many sponsors burned out or lost interest within the first months or year. This often left refugees without essential contacts and advocates within the American community.

7. Different and/or conflicting value systems between refugees and sponsors created both frictions and disillusionment. The expectations Christian denominations had for Buddhist Laotians were frequently unrealistic and impossible for the Laotians to adjust to. Prohibitions on smoking, drinking beer, and coffee or coca-cola were almost universally rejected by the refugee population.

8. Americans immediately began to identify groups of Laotians living in one locale as a "community." In fact, most of the refugees were thrown together by the circumstances of resettlement and were not a community by the usual definition. Americans expected the Lao to respond through internal community structures that were not present. The Laotians were, in fact, undergoing experiences where they were just beginning to think about and to identify the complexities involved with organizing internal self-help mechanisms.

9. American bureaucrats did not leave time for leaders to emerge who understood both Laotian and

American culture. Instead, they often relied on the leaders from the old country who, in many cases, were too old or were unwilling to lead the Lao communities through the necessary steps for successful acculturation. Or, Americans created "new" leaders to suit the political and economic purposes of this culture.

10. Too many Laotian refugees arrived too quickly during the period from 1978 until 1982. This strained already tight budgets during a time when the economy of the United States in general, and Oregon in particular was undergoing a severe recession.

11. The city of Eugene failed to establish translation services which were essential to insuring the basic rights of the refugees as they attempted to access the courts, city services, and other agencies.

12. Inadequate health screening in the refugee camps exacerbated the problems the medical community experienced as new diseases, problems, and concepts of health had to be dealt with by both Laotians and Americans. The city almost totally neglected this critical area.

13. Expectations by the schools and social service agencies were often unrealistic. Laotians were expected to identify problems, make choices and decisions about matters for which they lacked adequate contextual information. Often they were expected to respond to situations or materials that were not translated or that had no previous cultural context for them.

14. Social service regulations and American definitions of the family tended to break down traditional Laotian structures as well as eliminate traditional self-help mechanisms within the community.

15. Time, and relation to time created major problems for Laotians and Americans alike as the Laotians were expected to adjust to the American definition and perception of time.

16. Superficial changes in Laotian dress or social acquiescent behavior were mistaken by Americans as evidence of basic acculturation. This led to assumptions that the Laotians were ready for complex roles at work or in the community. In fact, it needs to be demonstrated that the Laotians have even begun to acquire an understanding of the deep cultural meanings, structures, use of language and behaviors essential for survival in American society.

17. Enormous language barriers need to be overcome. The Laotians, quite simply, have not had enough time to obtain adequate language training and fluency. American educators generally failed to connect language, culture and history as refugees strove to understand the ecology of North American culture. American educators who fail to consider both context and connections cannot teach these essential perspectives to Laotians.

18. Laotians were disappointed with the level of American response to their needs. They had expected American people to be more generous. They often found the governmental agencies and bureaucrats to

be mean and lacking in the heart they had hoped and expected Americans to display.

19. Laotians were faced with an entirely new spectrum of values. Choices were difficult to make. Often there was no choice. This was particularly difficult for older Laotians as they simultaneously observed the young becoming Americans at a rapid pace and the dissolution of the extended family rapidly approaching. They perceived the American family structure as weaker and less sensitive to the elderly.

20. Laotian adults needed training with decision making in the American cultural context. Americans often confused the Laotian lack of understanding of how decisions are made within North American culture with an inability to make decisions.

21. Laotians were in need of understanding the roles of parents and expectations of parents in relation to the rest of American society.

22. The experience of being a refugee forced adults, worried over the success of their children, to sacrifice their own learning potential in order that their children might succeed.

23. Work was invariably a priority over education. The Laotians were well aware of the economic situation in the United States and feared not being able to support their families here.

24. The agencies responsible for resettlement and the local institutions responsible for training and schooling failed to consider the Laotians' previous

experience as adults. Consequently, the adults were frequently treated as inferior or as children. This was confusing as well as painfully demeaning for the refugee adult.

25. Consumer education was sorely lacking as Laotians grappled with the problems of what to buy, how to buy, when to buy, as well as with the American system of currency, banking, and saving for the future.

26. Community educators, high school personnel, and community service personnel expressed frustration over the lack of articulation with cultural experts on the university level. They viewed the university as a repository for valuable expertise that was not often available to them on the local level. Many university educators were unaware of the local refugee population.

B. Challenges lie ahead for the Laotians and the Americans in the following areas:

1. Laotians seek to keep the family unit intact while Americans' values assault it. The Lao have a great respect for the elderly, something they found lacking in American culture. They had difficulty accepting the independence and lack of responsibility for the parents on the part of American youth. Laotians found abhorrent the American custom of putting old folks in institutions.

2. Laotians are working at developing community structures, self-help mechanisms within the community, and a trust for other factions within the Laotian population.

3. Laotians are adjusting to new roles in American society while deciding what portion of traditional Laotian values and culture to retain.

4. Laotians are examining parenting in a new society. They are seeking ways to keep relationships between child and parent viable, between family and society alive.

5. Americans must develop programs focused on in-depth education of the Laotians in the critical areas of physical and psychological health.

6. Americans and Laotians have much to learn about each others' culture and system of values: many Americans have yet to accept Laotian refugees as equal human beings.

7. Americans and Laotians must work together to develop community bi-lingual and bi-cultural teams that will attempt to solve some of the problems and adjustments created by the acculturation process.

8. Americans and Laotians are reexamining their original assumptions and expectations of each other as they share with each other the responsibility for creating a successful acculturation experience. This includes further exploration of the physiological and psychological aspects of adjusting to each other.

9. Laotians have to become more involved with the American community. Americans have to reach out with a helping hand when that happens. That help must come in a form other than a basic material response.

10. Americans must accept the fact that the pivotal role the United States played in the devastation of Laos was real and remains real in the minds of many of the refugees. Unwillingness to talk about this did not diminish the conflict this created for refugees.

11. American educators, sociologists and anthropologists need to develop strategies and materials for teaching that account for culturally specific assumptions about how the English language is spoken and contextualized.

Recollections from the Field, 1980-1984

In retrospect, both the spirit and actuality of daily experiences are often transformed by post-facto analysis. Despite a detailed field journal, the attempts to encapsulate the events that transpired during and as a result of my fieldwork with the Lao community from 1980 to 1984 are at best smooth stones cast across the surface of a deep river, creating ripples that expand, interact, and then become absorbed by the subtle and ever-changing flow of time. Comments made by various Laotians relating to our exchanges express this more succinctly:

> When you watch us, how do you know what is the truth and what is not the truth of the Lao way? Maybe we want you to know a certain thing, so we do a certain thing. You may not even know what the real thing is we wish to hid. Sometimes I think that as you watch us, you do as we do. If we laugh, you smile. We do this, too. . . you know, when we watch T.V. When we are with Americans, if everyone else laughs, we laugh. Even if we don't understand. Now I understand that it isn't only the Lao who are children to the American way. Also, the

Americans are children to the Lao way. If you ever
go to my country you will understand what I mean.
But now. . . we are in your country, so we appear as
the children. . .

If only we could speak as men. Two men shouldn't
have to have a third man between them as they speak
of things from the heart. This is very difficult for me
not to speak English. The words are very different.
Only the words and experiences of my country can
tell you what I have to say when I speak from the
heart. . .

I cannot pretend to understand the Lao Lum or to speak to
their experiences. Hemmed in by limitations of the linguistic,
educational and perceptual focus of my own culture, the
fieldwork became an expression of my meandering,
negotiating, and occasional glimpses of "otherness" as I briefly
entered into the lives of the Laotian refugees. Simultaneously,
they were striving to bring meaning and order to their initial
experiences with American society:

Right now we are very poor. . . we try hard. . . we
belong to the Christian church. . . we do not smoke
or drink. . . I am worried for finding work. . . a man
should be able to support his family. . . they tell us
times are hard here right now. . . that many
Americans are out of work. . . We did not expect
this. . . we thought everyone in the United States had
a job. . . We did not expect to find the same
problems that we left in our country. . . Who would
have dreamed that words like communism,
capitalism, democracy, mean very little when you are
hungry or sick...?

Like ripples generated by the skipping stones, our circles of experience converged, allowing for intermittent synchronicity. Nevertheless, whatever I had thought I had come in search of soon became secondary to the immediate realities of being an anthropologist and an educator, a member of a privileged class having the option to "study" another set of human beings totally dependent upon the class which, in their eyes, I represented. One Lao man, expressing some confusion while attempting to comprehend fieldwork and seeming to perceive it as not having to work for a living, stated: "You must be awfully rich to have time to learn how to read and write so that you can 'watch' for a living..." Initially, as the participant observer, I had no real place in the community. My first task, despite a well-circulated letter written in both Lao and English that explained my position, was to convey to the Lao people what I was attempting to accomplish, or at least what at that time I thought I was doing.

In the beginning, it was immediately apparent that my presence was an additional burden to a people beset with myriad adjustment problems. During the post-camp period, the refugee population faced a series of on-going orientations and dilemmas which at best complicated daily life, at worst presented seemingly insurmountable obstacles. Individuals and families experienced rapid developmental and cultural changes; they attempted to straddle the gap between an essentially agricultural experience in Laos and the technological experience in the United States while simultaneously attempting to recover from a war and the subsequent confinement in refugee camps in Thailand, Maylaysia, or the Philippines. Roles changed; Americans had complex and often confusing expectations and perceptions of refugees and refugee experience; the Laotian refugees were physically distinct from other new Americans and bear the stigmas attached to the Southeast Asian war; and lastly, on a more personal level, they struggled to develop some identity that bound those experiences and facilitated immediate direction as well as long-range survival.

If one was to understand the Laotian refugee resettlement experience in context, it became critical that an examination of the historical antecedents from which this experience developed be included in any discussion. To separate the events of America's Southeast Asian war during the period 1954-1975 from the resulting exodus, diaspora of refugees, the periods of resettlement and cultural negotiation would deprive those experiences of their historical meaning as well as lead one to conclude that being a Laotian refugee in the United States was an isolated phenomena rather than the consequence of a more complex global economic process.

In preparation for the fieldwork, two years of preliminary research, a pilot study in the Laotian community, and extensive preparatory coursework provided direction for the eventual long-term experience. During those years, and in the four preceding them, I had been active with the refugee community in the Pacific Northwest as a trainer of educators and social service personnel working with refugees, as editor for a model of Refugee Survival Competencies developed by a team of Pacific Northwest Community College educators and representatives from social service agencies, as a curriculum specialist, as a media consultant for the preparation of English as a Second Language videotapes to be used in Southeast Asian refugee camps and, finally, as a cross-cultural consultant regarding the refugee population's experience of negotiation with American culture. Those experiences helped to identify a specific target population, to focus on appropriate background information, to consult with representatives of the Lao community as a proposal for research was developed, to identify an appropriate site, and finally to select a research methodology appropriate to the refugee experience and the questions related to it.

During the early stages of cultural negotiation I found myself struggling to focus on and to record the developments that were transpiring in the lives of the Laotians. Despite a batter of anthropology and education courses, a reasonably flexible field plan, and the feeling that I was prepared for this experience, it began to occur to me that very little could have prepared me for the extent of involvement that intensive participant observation requires of the involved learner. My field notes of late 1981 reflect the beginning of a shift in consciousness as I began to struggle with my role, with the question of traditional definitions of objectivity, and with what I was attempting to accomplish:

> I'm here. I'm watching--often twelve to fifteen hours a day. I'm recording what I see and I've generated a couple of hundred pages of notes, observations, and questions. I'm feeling extremely frustrated and isolated as I spend most of my time with the Lao. After the initial excitement of moving to a new town, I'm faced with the reality of getting to know the Lao. I'm damned scared of failing, of missing the essential points, of getting too involved and losing my objectivity. All of the romantic notions of fieldwork quickly vanishing, I find the Laotians difficult to deal with. Gestures, relationships, habits are all very confusing. They answer my questions politely, but then lapse into quiet Lao to discuss them without including me. I am often left with the feeling that I am entertaining them. My translator-informant does a lot of interpretation. He doesn't always translate exactly what people are saying to me. He says he's protecting me. I hear things he doesn't translate. Our relationship is awkward. I know I'm not getting to the heart of things. I find myself doing all the mechanical things. . . almost obsessed with the process of gathering demographics and personal data in order to balance the frustration I feel over not communicating as a human being. Numbers, locations, institutions, structures are all fine--but I came here to be a part of the human experience and I

know I'm an outsider. I've taken refuge in my notes, charts, genealogies. Formal anthropological "training" may not be adequate to understand this experience. . .

The first few months in the field yielded an ever-growing body of basic demographic data. In other areas, I struggled with myself and my training as I attempted to assess what I was doing and what was happening to me. Attempting to be quasi-Lao left me stretched between two worlds. In time, I began to realize that the transition from normal everyday comings and goings at the university to immersion into intensive fieldwork distorts the researcher's life and perceptions. Over those long, lonely Christmas holidays I came to the conclusion that I could no longer "look in" from a safe distance, hidden behind an objectivity I believed my tools and training provided. In the final analysis, I was the instrument that had to be made functional. I realized that I had to take chances and lay aside my fears of "too much" involvement. My field notes of Christmas Day 1981 record the circumstances that I believe led to this breakthrough:

It's Christmas Day. I spent the greater part of the morning with a Lao family. I was invited over for some food and when I arrived I found my host plus several extended family members sitting about talking. Sticky rice (naa), chicken and beef, assorted vegetables, hot sauce (nampla), and some sweet cakes were served on a mat in the middle of the living room floor. The women prepared the food--the men ate and talked separately. I asked of the holidays at this time of the year in Laos. It was explained to me that many people have celebrated a holiday at Christmas time since the French came to their country over a hundred years ago. It was more of secular holiday for the Lao than a religious one. We spoke of American

Christmas--the different ways in which it is celebrated. There were some questions concerning the appropriateness of gifts--to whom one gives gifts. In Laos, it was explained, the boss at work, policeman, and other officials were sometimes given gifts. One individual explained that the Lao here in the USA would get together, cook some food, drink and talk--glad to have a little time off from work, if employed. He explained some of the other people would feel very bad (baw di) because there were many unemployed and could not afford to celebrate much. Some of the people 'bought' or made gifts for sponsors and for American friends. In this particular household there were none of the trappings of Christmas, e.g., wrapped gifts, Christmas tree, lighted candles, etc.

Thought, recorded later that afternoon, reflected back upon the phenomenon related to holidays:

I thought this afternoon about being able to afford a holiday. Strange enough, the depth and extent of the poverty these people are experiencing is not always visible. Americans have a tendency to think in extremes where poverty is concerned. If you aren't obviously destitute, or if you have not lost all of your pride or find it difficult to express your needs, then it is generally assumed all is O.K. A classic case is one of the translators I have worked with. He dressed fairly well, although I know most of his clothes comes from Salvation Army stores. He lives in a rented house and drives a fairly new model car. He is employed. To see him on the street or at his place of work, one would not realize he lives marginally. One finds his $500-600 salary is the major source of support for over thirteen individuals, not including

those extended family members that come and go
because they have no food. In addition, there is some
food stamp help and one partial welfare payment.
Rent is $375, the car payment is $150. The car is
necessary for the job, for transportation, and for
family and community emergencies. In the final
analysis, the family eats very little. Rice is the
staple. Meat is seldom seen on the table. The family
survives without medical care, afraid to get sick or to
have to go to the hospital. They are in constant fear
of being evicted because of non-payment of rent.
Because they have been over here eighteen months,
the family's benefits have been reduced to minimal
levels, certainly not enough to feed, clothe, and
provide the necessities for seven active children of
school age. Sacrifices are made on the part of the
adults so that the children are properly dressed for
school and for interacting with the American
community. One individual told me, "I put the paper
[cardboard] in the hole of my shoe. . . you see, no
one can see this when I walk. . . only see the top..."

The translator referred to previously is considered one
of the more successful Lao by the local American
social service community. Americans don't see the
behind-the-scenes story. He has too much pride to
share his problems with his employers. He does the
same work as his American counterpart, but he makes
less than one third of the salary of the other. In effect
he is the resident Lao expert on the staff of the
institution where he works. He receives no benefits;
the American does. He has been called upon at all
times of the day and night to translate with no fee
involved. Local police, courts, etc., feel free to call
upon him, so they can "understand his community."
He has become tired, close to burned-out. His co-

workers forget that he, too, is dealing with the same adjustment problems of other refugees. He wants to go to school, but he can't afford it. He worries how his family will eat. Few of these concerns are apparent to the local human service community.

The house I visited this Christmas Day was sparsely furnished. One couch, a chair, a television set. The kitchen had a table and two chairs. Almost everyone sits on the floor rather than the furniture. One the wall was a poster advertising a local beer, some National Geographic magazine pictures of Laos, and a Buddha tucked onto a corner shelf. The floor was carpeted with a wool rug. The television was in constant use, the sound turned off while people were engaged in serious talk. Over thirteen people sleep in two bedrooms and on the living room floor. The house was clean, even by the strictest of American standards. Needless to say, it was always crowded. There was very little privacy, and people were forced by the necessities of survival to adjust to very limited personal space. At the moment, the parents in the house aren't sure if they will be able to "stay under the roof." New welfare cuts have devastated the extended family unit and they are penalized for having other adults living in the household. In essence, they are penalized for sharing in their traditional manner. Many cannot make it on their own. The psychological and cultural security of living together in an extended family is being destroyed by American cultural expectations. And I've become involved.

My notes further indicate that during that period I had thought a great deal about the Christmas rituals of North American culture, of watching from within the Laotian structure from a totally different perspective. I felt it to be an empty ritual, lacking much sense or meaning when viewed from the outside. I was alone, caught between the rituals of Christmas and the rituals of fieldwork. Neither made complete sense to me at that time. I wondered why I was there, what I was doing, and what of value would come out of this schizophrenic process.

The year 1982 presented a host of new opportunities that would ultimately enhance and expand my fieldwork experiences. By the early months of the year, as a result of the development of a close relationship with my primary informant-interpreter, I made friends within the Lao community. However, the primary obstacle that seemed insurmountable was explaining to the Lao the meaning of participant observation, anthropology, education and what we call research. There was just no place for someone like me in the schematic of their daily lives. I felt like an exotic pet, wondering just who was studying whom. Later on I would find out that some of the members of the community thought I was part of the Central Intelligence Agency, sent to spy on them. One friend finally told me he had thought that "... you were a secret spy for the A.F.S. [Adult and Family services] who watched what we were doing with our welfare money"; others thought I was a policeman, another thought I was a member of the army, and so on. This soon changed, as in February 1982 I was hired as a consultant to the Lane Community College Refugee Program where I was to help develop a cross-cultural community team which was to deal with refugee problems and concerns during the post-camp adjustment period. This new role provided the opportunity to become more involved, with the emphasis on participation. We were doing things together. The "research" experience became one of mutual exploration and interaction.

As a member of the Eugene social service community, with a readily identifiable role, I became more acceptable to the Laotians. I had a specific role, and relationships could be formalized within a context that was understandable to the

235

refugee population. I was not longer just an anthropologist-educator (something which generated much suspicion), writing a "story" about the Laotians. As one Lao man said,

No one tell the truth to story writers. Everyone thinks over the story and tells it like he thinks it sound best. He tell it so he always look so good. . . Everyone is a story writer. . .

I became Mr. Rob, the counselor, the person who would help to explain the "American" way and to assist the community with adjustment problems. This role served as a visa for exploring the remnants of Laotian culture the refugees tried to maintain within American culture. It also provided avenues of access to homes, community interactions, and areas of privileged activity that are exclusive to the role of counselor. This daily exposure and growing insight helped me to begin to sort out the various and complex elements which composed the refugee experience and contributed to the greater synergy they were expected to deal with. Slowly, over the months and years, I became accepted as an integral part of that experience. Early on I decided to hold off on the survey questions and formal open-ended interviews. Instead, I intended to develop a rapport and a comfort level around my presence in the community. In addition, I wanted to ascertain, to as great an extent as possible, that the community understood what I was trying to accomplish, and to generate dialogue while simultaneously providing individuals with the time to think about their experiences with resettlement.

Over time, it became a familiar sight to have me about, asking questions or participating in "men's talk," which often covered the whole spectrum of life experiences from politics and religion to what qualities a "good" woman must possess. The fact that I was studying Laotian language and culture was taken as a community project and responsibility. People became involved with me, eager to teach, to share, as well as to offer feedback and suggestions on my language acquisition. They wanted to be sure I was learning the "Lao" way of doing things. Through this interaction they were able to "give" to me. By this time, I was working with three translators and a variety of informants in order to accommodate various factions in the community. People preferred their trusted friends as translators. This sometimes created confusing transcriptual problems. Clarification depended upon my personal relationship with the translator and his or her command of English. However, in every case, I double- or cross-checked with other informants and translators to clarify and/or verify translated materials and my understanding of them. Both translators and cultural informants became more attuned to the tasks and to each other as we worked closely together. This was reflected through relevant and realistic questions and transcriptions as the project developed and as friendships expanded.

The intensive involvement within the Lao community created profoundly deep personal relationships which were crucial to the documentation and experiences recorded in this study. As a counselor, job developer, and community organizer, I spent untold hours involved in a wide range of community activities, which included weddings, parties, family gatherings, attendance in court, emergency visits to the hospitals and clinics, intercession with difficult and often hostile government social service agencies, and a variety of other activities. On a personal level, I spent thousands of hours talking to people individually or in small groups about their problems, about the difficulties related to American culture, about frustrations and disappointments, and about the homesickness generally felt around the time of special Laotian holidays or at times of crisis. Death and sickness were a catalyst for thoughts related to a fear of dying in America, "a place far from home." A brief notation from my field journal during 1983 captured the essence of one such moment:

I was surprised to find so many Lao at the hospital. Several were in the waiting room, some visiting, and I had met several outside the hospital watching the children for those who were inside visiting. Everyone knew she was dying--I realized I was the only American there as I entered the room. For a relatively tall Lao woman, she looked like a small child wrapped in a white sheet. This yellow-brown Laotian woman was a direct contrast to the sterility of the room. Six people were standing around, not talking, just to be there with her when she died. Every once in a while someone would go to hold her hand. She didn't remember me. She looked up as someone whispered in her ear and gave me a brief smile. I thought of my own mother, of death, and what it must be like to die away from what is familiar and known. The Laotian men and women created a buffer zone of reality, a common denominator for her to relate to as she died. This small group of human beings lent a warmth and personal touch to a sterile and frightening environment. She spoke once in Lao to one woman and it was later translated for me as "...she said she is going home to Laos soon. she knows her spirit will go there to be with her friends and family. She said she is tired and can't work to stay alive in America any more. . . she is happy to go home..." Realizing it was important that I had come but also aware that I didn't belong--that I was an outsider--I left after a discreet visit. This moment was distinctly Lao, for the Lao as they shared communally the death of a loved friend in an alien environment. . .

The loss was quiet, the pain was internalized, life went on within the refugee community. One could not afford the luxury of extended personal grief. Several days after she died I was invited to a small meal in her honor, "not a celebration and not a wake." Over forty adults came together to talk, to share, to be mutually reinforced. Discussion was mostly centered on life in the United States and its problems, and on the question of "going home." There was discussion of the "new" government in Laos, their hatred for "communism" and loss of their property. With her death, a household and a family struggled to stay together. The husband and children did not have the familiar traditional structures of their home culture to support them during the period of loss. One felt an uncommon wisdom in that room that night, a wisdom wrought of trial by fire. I could not help but think of how much we have to learn from these people about life, about our species, and about ourselves. I also wondered if our entirely different perspectives on life, our different cultural experiences, and the lack of mutually understood and identified points in time and space were conducive to open dialogue or would allow a sharing of that wisdom.

In time I came to understand that beneath the reality of surface impressions of the Lao there existed a landscape and a geography expressive of their primary culture, language and experiences which engaged in a continual dance with the new culture and language of America. These encounters generated all sorts of clues and signals which indicated that synchronicity between the two cultures was a rare occurrence. My heart, my ears, my intuitions and informal experiential learning were often as important to the experience of recording, analyzing and understanding as were my eyes. Configurations of friendships and relationships, the willingness to speak openly or within a group, change in dress or appearance, acceptance or rejection of new ideas and experiences would change according to time and event. Any situation had to be viewed from a variety of vantage points including, sometimes, the events of the far distant past as well as aspirations for the future. I had to constantly look for the "other" things that illuminated the tacit structure and messages that are an integral part of the experience of any cultural and linguistic encounter. Directly affecting my role and any information I was privileged to receive was at worst a mistrust and at best a lingering disappointment with the Euro-American. As close as we became, these feelings, combined with chronic unemployment and increasing inability for many Lao to keep their families together created an environment where the truth of any matter was difficult to come by. The fragile nature of the postcamp state created a lingering tension. Across the board, almost every adult Laotian I knew found some difficulty understanding the behavior of Americans, and feared "telling" too much. They also struggled with sorting out their own experiences as they attempted to discover who they were becoming.

As friends and as individuals, we shared the questions and struggled for understandings of adjustment to a new culture. Over beer, over coffee, across the desk, working in the garden, walking along the river, moving furniture, barbecuing chicken, in numerous settings and in various psychological and emotional states, we labored to bring meaning to what was transpiring on a daily basis. Ultimately, across the parameters that cultures construct, it was individuals who dealt with understanding, accepting, and effectively communicating with each other. Sometimes we were successful, other times we drew a blank or a stand-off. There were tears, anger, smiles, and quizzical faces. As we attempted to use language to think about, organize, and speak we found there were times when effective communication proved impossible.

What I feel was the very first acceptance of me by the community best illustrates the differences in culture and the difficulties generated by the cultural negotiation experience. My notes detail that first night of being on the inside:

> It's winter. The rain is crashing with those big, cold drops that February rains in Oregon are known for. I'm having a quick coffee before going to a gathering at the home of one of the Lao leaders. I'm not sure

what to expect. I've been a friend of his son for months--he's been my closest and most reliable informant. This is the first time I've been invited to their home. He made it clear that I'd be the only American there, hinting there were things for me to learn and see that he couldn't speak of directly. I'm feeling anxious, hoping that I handle things well. I'll write my impressions down later.

[Later that evening] Well, I'm home. . . it's about 2:30 a.m. I went there tonight with "demographic" knowledge of the family members and most of the people present. I knew their ages, past occupations, basic political sympathies, and a host of current adjustment problems. I knew that the mother in this household was from a "higher" family than the father. He had been a civil servant in Laos and both were considered rich in relation to the average Lao. All of their children were schooled in English, French, and Lao, which automatically made them part of the five percent of Laotians who received that kind of education during the French or American colonial periods.

I didn't bring a notebook tonight. My translator advised I just come and be a part of things, to watch, enjoy, and then we would talk it over later. Pulling up to the curb in front of the house my stomach was tight. My friend came to the door as I rang the bell. I had passed through a white picket fence, across a well-groomed lawn with rose bushes as I was on my way to the front porch. Just like any other suburban house, ran through my mind. As I entered, two younger brothers of my Lao friend, whom I had met before, greeted me first in Lao and then in English. Everyone was helping me to speak Lao. Suh-by dee (hello)... Hi, Rob. . . The hallway to the house was lined with shoes and coats. I took off mine as well. As I entered the living room there were about thirty men sitting on the floor around a series of woven mats. On the mats were food, beer, cigarettes, etc. As many were smoking, the room was heavy with clouded smoke. People were talking and only a few heads raised as I entered.

My friend took me over to his Dad where I was greeted and asked to sit down. Several others stopped and said hello; I knew almost everyone in the room. I had met with them for one reason or another over the months, under varying circumstances. Seeing them together, as a group, was a totally new experience. I was immediately aware of being the outsider. . . how little I knew.

With typical Lao politeness, a bottle of good whisky was produced and each man took a little whisky from a communal glass, drank, and then turned the glass upside down to show due respect. This was repeated across the room one-by-one until all the men had toasted me. My friend's father took the bottle from person to person.

Later, I was to learn that I should have been the person to do that. In time, as I grew in understanding of Lao custom, this ritual and others would become secondhand. Fortunately, due to some planning on the part of my translator-friend, I had brought a bottle of good whisky [Johnny Walker Red] with me to the gathering. [Needless to say, I was happy to be one of the later arrivals. Eventually I would have the experience of arriving earlier and having to drink a little bit (noy neung) of whisky with each new arrival.

It certainly is a good way to keep the researcher from asking too many questions or from being too observant. It is also an excellent device through which tension is reduced.]

The room was painted white. There were no pictures on the walls. In one corner a two foot Buddha was placed on a stool. Fresh flowers and fruit were on a tray before the statue. A candle was lit in a small red glass. Later I was told the television couch and chair had been moved out to make people more comfortable.

The natural rhythm of the evening continued and groups or individuals conversed about life, politics, and daily experiences. The women and girls stayed in the kitchen, cooking, talking, and occasionally bringing food to the living room. This was to be a special occasion for me as it would be the first time I heard the Kene--a bamboo reed instrument special to the Laotians. Occasionally one of the younger men would play a song and people would stop to listen. At those moments, I watched faces--away in thought, smiling, tuned to the sounds of the Kene echoing across the room. This experience transcended the living room of a suburban family home in America. I felt moved across time and space to another place far distant--the smells of food, the sound of the Kene, the men sitting close and talking around the reed mats, for a brief moment maintaining touch with and reinforcing their primary cultural realities.

As the evening wore on, I became increasingly cognizant of a shift in focus. Discussion became more serious and in a rather spontaneous manner, the host finally said he had invited me here so that we could talk about being Lao:

Mr. Rob has asked us to help him understand Lao people . . . Lao language. . . Lao ways.

[Discussion centered on what was the best possible manner short to going to Laos to live. A series of comments were made by individuals present]:

. . .You can't really know Laos here. We are Lao, yet we are sometimes different here. . .

. . .Everything is changed in Laos. Laos is gone to us. . How do we tell anyone what it was before the wars. . . it was so beautiful. . . we had everything we needed. . .

. . .Maybe the best way is for each of us to tell a little bit of our own lives, of where we lived, and what happened. This will help Mr. Rob. . .

The translator-informant, by making the latter statement, brought a bit of focus to the discussion. His Dad started with a story that lasted well over two hours--individuals interrupted, clarified, confirmed, and I found the first of my oral biographies emerging. Talk was lively, animated, and contagious. This group experience, which we would repeat dozens of times over years, became a catalyst for exploring issues, defusing frustrations, clarifying confusions, and reconciling different perspectives. It helped to develop a sense of trust, confidentiality, and a willingness, within the confines of the communal experience, to touch on subjects and areas of experience that were personal and which left the individual vulnerable. Throughout the evening we took a good look at Laos from their perspective.

Before going home, one Lao man asked, again, why I was writing all this. I attempted to explain that their experiences and perspectives were important, that if they were recorded now then they wouldn't be lost to their grandchildren who would be American and not Laotian. This way the grandparents and the grandchildren might be able to understand each other. I explained that the more perspectives we had on Laos, on the camps, on the war, on coming and adjusting to America, the better we could deal with helping Laotians and Americans adjust to each other. One man interrupted me and said, "We are all like the puzzle. Mr. Rob must see many of the pieces. Then he puts them together to get the big picture. Then we can all look at it, too..." I realized that no one in the room had the full story. This helped to center my efforts and to reinforce my feelings that the oral history approach would be invaluable. Much of what I heard either contradicted the readings, the anthropological studies, the accounts of the war, or touched on areas that these reports had not and could not have included. What left me feeling excited was the fact that the community [at this point, men] felt this project to be useful. Another man said, "...only a Lao could tell the true story, but we don't know how..."

Later on, more than a year later, one of the participants would tell me:

I'm eighteen. I learned more about my country and what happened in these talks than I knew at home. I was fourteen when we left. Earlier we didn't have these talks because everyone was afraid of the war and too busy. Now I know more. I want to go home someday and do some things in Laos. I feel cheated that I can't do them. I didn't know so much or maybe I wouldn't have come here. I have no grandmother or grandfather, no animals, no farm, no house, and only my father. My mother is dead. I don't know how to be American or Lao. I have to go back to Laos before I can know. Then I will decide what way to be. . .

Another man commented:

This talk, it disturbs me. I didn't know I could miss my country so much. Maybe it isn't big or important, but it is my country. Here I am like a visitor in a strange house. I cannot relax. . . I must always watch to be respectful, to do the right thing. . . there is no place to be myself. To be with people like me. This makes me very tired to never relax. . . [and finally] . . .Many things I have heard my friends say that also happened to me, especially how I feel inside now. . . while these things of the refugee were happening I did not think about them because they kept me very busy doing them. . . now I think about them. . . I am different to myself as I think about them. . .

I believe I had my first real experience within the family, the extended family, and the Lao community that revealed the Lao were struggling to keep aspects of their primary culture alive under extraordinarily adverse circumstances. During the remainder of my fieldwork, this particular evening would serve as the model, the moment when I first identified the underlying structure of this community. The complexity of these relationships, the importance of interpersonal dynamics and their importance to the process of acculturation, the critical role the extended family played in maintaining some sort of social stability during the post-camp period of transition became key "pieces" in the puzzle of the refugee experience.

As fieldwork progressed beyond the first year, I became excited over being part of a dynamic which was, for me, a new approach to the recording of history. My relationship to the task of writing about these events was developing along parallel experiential lines. The Lao decided what was important in their lives and I was privileged to record it as they lived, felt, and shared their interpretations of it. These are interpretations and experiences of ordinary men and women who have rarely been taken seriously or considered important. This is the process that Kozol (1981) refers to as "history from the bottom up," the workers, the family members, the people who have struggled for a living. The value and the credibility of these histories lies in the fact that the individuals of the Lao community decided what was important from their perspective. Ironically, in the development of realizing that they indeed had something to say and that their comments were important, they often prefaced stories with comments such as:

Oh, I've never done anything important. . .

I can't say this very well. . .

I was only a farmer in my country. . .

I have not had as big an education as you. . .

My story is not so important. . .

One of the critical problems was to convince refugee people that what they had to say was valuable. Once this was perceived as a means to make a contribution to their community, they invested a great deal of time, energy, and thought to the task of organizing their experiences into a sequence of events that made sense to them and which I could record. They taught me the meaning of the power of community voice within their cultural context. For many of the adults I worked with, this was the first time in their lives that they had been called onto review their own experiences and to account for them in some manner. They very act of self-examination was always a difficult endeavor and they almost always conducted this analysis within the context of the community. The honesty and openness with which these human beings shared the details of their experiences was humbling. Each of these human beings was generous with time, patience, and understanding as we grappled with the process on interpretation, translation, and differing perceptions of the world.

Often, as I read back what I had written, or when I asked for clarification or additional comments, people would reflect upon parts of their presentation or focus in on some comment or event through such statements as:

Thinking of these questions makes me see myself clearer now. . .

I see myself differently now. . .

Please change those words to say this. . .

I was very lucky in my life in Laos, I didn't know that then. . .

I didn't understand the war, the camps, or coming to America. . .

I was a bad child. My mother and father gave me everything. I'm very happy my children are not as bad as I was. . .

There was a healthy ability to laugh at oneself and sometimes at the ironies that life produces. At the same time, it appeared that everyone I spoke with was aware of the seriousness and the complexity of the sequence of events that began with the decision to leave home in Laos and ended, for the moment, in this community in Eugene. Finally, as one woman confided to me:

> Many of these Lao I do not like too much. If we were at home in Laos, I would not talk to them or have them come to my house. But now we are the only Lao here. So we have to help each other, we have to stay together. We still need each other. . .

I came to the realization that what Americans had labeled the Lao community was, in reality, not a community at all. It was a group of widely diverse individuals and extended families who shared in common the decision to leave their primary culture, even though the reasons leading to that decision were different. Ultimately, time and events would find them thrust together into a new situation where they had to attempt to be supportive of each other for basic reasons of survival. In the beginning, they were not a community. They were displaced Laotians with little personal relationship to each other.

Excerpt from my Field Journal, Spring 1983

> . . .Children are standing in the doorways and on the front porch--playing, watching families and food arrive--everyone dressed in best clothes--then watch as I edge my old station wagon between two newer model cars. I'm feeling tight and apprehensive--a strange mood for a person who has thought he was "at home" in the Lao community for the past couple of years. The struggle is internal. I realize this will be

one of the final large gatherings I will be attending for a while. The necessity to complete this fieldwork and to remove myself is beginning to create conflicts.

. . .I know all of the faces that will be waiting inside--they are friends with whom I have worked, prayed, played during this period of transition from Lao to American culture. Not so long ago I found myself so involved that I was contemplating marrying a Lao woman. Feelers out to the family in the traditional manner were positive. Today--of all days--when I have been extended the singular honor of being invited hours earlier than other guests to be present at and take part in intimate family and community celebrations, I feel most like an outsider. I'm aware of this special honor while simultaneously trying to suppress the awareness that despite this honor, I am the one who must view himself as the intruder, or at best an outsider. . .

. . .I'm carrying fruit and flowers--partially in respect for time-old Lao custom and, certainly, to demonstrate a respect for my "teachers"--purple and white, lilac and snowball, fresh from my garden. The fruits have ben carefully selected to include the varieties the Lao enjoy. I'm socially correct--yet consciously uncomfortable. In many ways I'm afraid to let go of my fieldwork. At the same moment I realize it's basically over. I know that eventually I will have to remove myself and return to the world from where I originate. . .

. . .At the door--some of the teenagers are gathered in a small group--mostly young men--talking and socializing, waiting for special or favorite relatives and friends to arrive. Some are dressed in designer jeans--flash--mostly the young males. A friend comes forward extending his hand to say hello to "Mr. Rob"--the name the Lao community gave me in the early stages of fieldwork. Others take my hand-- come over--touch my shoulder--smile. There is an air of festivity about the crowd of people. Young as they are--given their already intense immersion into American culture, I am struck at how uniquely Lao, how incredibly gentle they are as they welcome and attempt to make me feel at home. I scan the eyes and smiles and find a bit of tenseness abating. I unconsciously slip into their world.

. . .From inside the living room--my friend and major informant--moves toward me through the crowd. We are old friends--this fieldwork experience thrusting both of us together as we mutually explored the Lao refugee and the American during this negotiation of cultures. It has changed both of us in irrevocable ways. The task of identifying, perceiving, translating, and interpreting has been co-celebrated. Any synthesis product will be a result of this unique relationship. He smiles--indicates he is "really glad"I brought flowers--testimonial to his correct choice of friends and successful attempt to "educate" me to the Lao manner of doing things. Significantly, I hadn't been asked to bring anything. The Buddhist monk had arrived from Portland earlier in the day. Since he was "more important" than the one who was originally supposed to come, more people were coming and the host didn't have enough flowers. These would help him to save face.

. . .Since there are no daughters, the host's oldest son takes the fruit and flowers--filling in for the mother who is suffering from post-camp schizophrenia. She is "quiet" today--focusing on the priest. I, too, focus on the monk who is seated on an ochre piece of cloth. All of the furniture has been cleared from the room and it takes on the aspects of a large temple hall. The wall-to-wall carpeting on the floor has been covered by bamboo mats. This scene strikes me as a classic example demonstrating the Lao refugee condition in the Untied States--a juxtaposition of the "old way" carefully inserted into a modern suburban house--the former generally accommodating the realities of the later--rough edges apparent when looked for.

. . .I sit on the floor near to men my age. Not all the way up front with the elder men and not at the far back with the teenagers. Generally people are seated in a semi-circle with the monk at the center of the two ends. They have come to celebrate a late "Lao New Year" and to participate in a respite from the constant effort to adjust to the American way. The monk is chanting. There are two large statues of the Buddha-- one of bronze and one about three feet high of wood. Numerous smaller images line the floor to be blessed and returned to niches in the home. Papers with special writings and some Lao money are burned in a bronze dish. This, as is explained to me, is symbolic of the dispersal of the old--cleaning out the old year to get ready for the new. More prayers--some in chorus by the group--and the ashes are placed in a hug bowl--there a stainless steel kitchen bowl replaces the decorated bowls used in the "holy" water. More prayers and chanting. For a brief period--I forget I am in a small house in Oregon--I am carried back to the kinds of ceremonies I witnessed in Southeast Asia months earlier.

. . .Then the monk takes a long-stemmed purple iris and dips it in "holy" water--he proceeds to travel around the room, dipping the flower in the water and sprinkling a few drops on each person while praying for a "good year, good health." As it began--so it comes to a quiet ending. Soon the priest stops to make a general prayer and then leaves the room. He is going to visit a small group who have separated themselves from the larger Lao community and refuse to come to this house. The sandaled feet, ochre sheet, bare legs, and shaven head suddenly seem totally out of context in this living room. It is the other celebration where no outsiders will be welcome. Soon he is gone--replaced by a more party-like atmosphere. People exchange fruit, hard-boiled eggs, wish each other luck. Special strings called bati are tied around each other's wrists and the wrists of teachers and respected members of the community. This binds the individual spirit to the higher community spirit.

. . .Shortly American guests began to arrive. Beer and whiskey arrive at this point as well. Food preparation begins in the kitchen--women talk, laugh, sing, and chop meat and vegetables. American music is put on the stereo and it is loud. The younger people are enjoying the change in pace. Some of the older people look bewildered--like the monk they are out of context in this setting. After a bit of socializing, drinking beer and some whisky, people sit down across the room in preparation for a few "speeches" before dinner. Guests are formally welcomed. The old year is briefly summarized. Then gone. The new year begins with endless round of food and lots of laughter, talk, and celebration.

The ensuing months witnessed the beginning of my gradual withdrawal from full time activities with the Lao community. Formal duties in the social service world were carefully transferred either to Laotians or to caring Americans. In order to reflect upon the experience, to gather my thoughts in final preparation for completing the study, and in order to come back into my own world, I had to step out of the fieldwork experience. I stood, for a brief moment, at the razor's edge where two cultures were in furious negotiation. I watched them work on each other, begin to negotiate, and sometimes have to forfeit precious landscapes. I came in search of--was touched-- and at the very conclusion of my part in the experience, realized I had only a momentary window on the world of the refugee. More so, I came away with different perspectives on my own culture and on myself. Over time, although my role has changed, contact with the community has remained constant.

For the Lao, the experience of acculturation and accommodation continues. Lao community members still struggle with the language and with obtaining adequate language training; minimal occupational skills still prevent many Lao men from acquiring jobs in a local economy that is still distressed; family structures continue to change as traditional social interaction, traditional roles and control have to be discarded or modified to accommodate the new culture; health and mental health problems are enormous and for the most part have yet to be addressed; a heavily skewed population with too many young males creates tension and frustration within the community; some alcohol and physical abuse problems have begun to emerge as rejection, failure, and poverty have to be faced; overcrowded homes and diminished welfare grants exacerbate fears of being evicted, of not having enough food, of getting sick; abandonment or disillusionment on the part of most sponsors has isolated many refugees from their "American families"; heavy cuts in school and community college programs further isolate those refugees who want and need additional training; lack of internal mechanisms as well as traditional loose-knit community organizations fail to provide strong advocacy for refugee problems from within the refugee community; and burn-out and disillusionment on the part of the committed social service advocates is further decimating the ranks of external support in the greater community.

I have had the luxury of being able to step out of and watch acculturation continue to unfold. As one friend in the Lao community said to me,

> At home I was a man, a person. I had a full life.
> Here I am a refugee--only part of a man. . . only part
> of a life. . .

The results of this experience are not an end. Rather, they are part of the greater continuum which constitutes the personal learning process. As a human being I went out to encounter other human beings. This furthered my efforts to understand myself and the culture from which I originate and the multiple cultures in which I live. While we attempted to clarify who we were and how we perceived things, a greater framework of reference was born of that synthesis. In the field, I was forced to interact and clarify; that method created other responses and reactions. One changes, one is changed through the act of compromising and attempting to understand. Empathy and objectivity are forged into a new tool. One explores, one is explored. The total effect produces information and experiences unique to each fieldworker and the other human beings encountered. In the words of one Lao,

> We do what we can. We look. We listen. We think.
> We try. We are not always so right. We make the
> mistake sometime, but our heart is not wanting to
> hurt. What can I say? Don't you know we Lao are
> just like you in many ways? Yellow or white. . . so
> what! Underneath the skin we are the human being.

Is that not enough to know? All this studying for such a simple answer. . . we all know it if we look to our heart. Sometimes we human beings are pretty stupid!

It would seem, somewhere beyond the antecedents and events that have transpired since 1945 which have contributed to some common history shared by Laotians and Americans, there are lessons to be learned about life and the human condition. Beyond ideologies, beyond the lies of the politicians, beyond the attempt at home to beat criticism of the Southeast Asian War into the ground, beyond the devastation of the land and the people of Laos, beyond the suffering and death in the name of nation and national interest, beyond the refugee camps and the very condition of being a refugee. . . we must raise questions as to the decisions we have made and the underlying motivations that have created these events and situations. We must learn from these experiences and change American policy so that wiser decisions will be made in the future. It would seem in retrospect, that we should have learned something that will be of value as we negotiate the present and prepare for the future. If we cannot and do not apply what there is to be learned to our own lives, to our own cultural structures and the institutions by which they are governed and sustained, then we will have to repeat the harsh lessons and the great human suffering which have characterized American involvement in the Southeast Asian War and the subsequent creation of millions of refugees. We need to open our eyes and hearts, learn from the tragedies of the past, as we face similar decisions related to inhuman conditions we create for peoples in Latin America, in Southeast Asia and indeed, elsewhere on this precious globe we humans find our home.

Notes
PREFACE

1. Philippe Devillers, "The Laotian Conflict in Perspective," in Nina S. Adams and Alfred McCoy, eds., Laos: War and Revolution, (New York: Harper-Colophon Books, 1970), pp. 50-51.
2. United States Department of State, Country Reports on the World Refugee Situation: Report to Congress, (Washington, D.C.: Office of United States Coordinator for Refugee Affairs, 1981), pp. 61-62.
3. Noam Chomsky and Edward S. Herman, After the Cataclysm: Post War Indochina and the Reconstruction of Imperial Ideology: The Political Economy of Human Rights, (Boston: South End Press, 1979), v. 2, pp. 13-17.
4. Khamchong Luanpraseut, "American-Laotian Cross-Cultural Information," in the United States Catholic Conference Newsletter, (New York: United States Catholic Conference, July 1982), v. 1, no. 8, pp. 9-11.
5. United States Department of Health and Human Services, Report to Congress: Refugee Resettlement Program, (Washington, D.C.: Social Security Administration, 1983), pp. 36-38.
6. Interview with a local refugee health service provider; Fieldwork, Eugene, Oregon, 1982.
7. Interview with a local community college teacher of refugees; Fieldwork, Eugene, Oregon, 1982.
8. Noam Chomsky, "The Pathet Lao's Revolutionary Program: Interview with Phao Phimpachanh," in Adams and McCoy, eds., Laos: War and Revolution, p. 444.
9. Interview with a local Laotian community leader; Fieldwork, Eugene, Oregon, 1982.
10. Robert Proudfoot, Annual Lane Community College Refugee Program--Case Management: Report to Oregon Adult and Family Services, (Eugene: Lane Community College, 1982).

258

11. Mark Liff, "Indochinese Refugees: The Newest Americans," in American Education, (Washington, D.C.: United States Department of Education, July 1980), pp. 6-16.
12. Walt Haney, "The Pentagon Papers and United States Involvement in Laos," in Noam Chomsky and Howard Zinn, eds., The Pentagon Papers, Senator Gravel Edition, (Boston: Beacon Press, 1972), p. 269.
13. Peter Martin, "Rerunning the War," in Mother Jones, (San Francisco: Foundation for National Progress, November 1983), pp. 11-17.

Notes
CHAPTER I

A special acknowledgement to Steven R. Swenson, Attorney and Cultural Historian, for his shared knowledge of Southeast Asian history and his editing of this chapter.

1. Senator Thomas J. Dodd, "Speech to Congress," (May, 1962), in Adams and McCoy, Laos: War and Revolution, p. 399.
2. John F. Kennedy, "Statement on Laos," (March 23, 1961, in Adams and McCoy, Laos: War and Revolution, p. 395.
3. Richard M. Nixon, "Statement on U.S. Policy and Activity in Laos," (March 6, 1970), in Adams and McCoy, Laos: War and Revolution, p. 406.
4. Phoumi Vongvichit, Laos and the Victorious Struggle of the Lao People Against U.S. Neo-Colonialism, (Vientiane: Neo Lao Haksat Publications, 1969), p. 60.
5. Noam Chomsky, "Introduction," in Adams and McCoy, Laos: War and Revolution, pp. xv-xxii.
6. Johnathan Mirsky and Steven Scofield, "The United States in Laos," in Edward Friedman and Mark Selden, eds., America's Asia, (New York: Pantheon, 1970).

7. Committee of Concerned Asian Scholars, The Indochina Story: A Fully Documented Account, (New York: Pantheon, 1970), pp. 160-163.

8. Johnathan Mirsky and Steven Scofield, "The U.S. In Laos," in Friedman and Selden, America's Asia, p. 253.

9. Committee of Concerned Asian Scholars, The Indochina Story, p. 162.

10. United States Senate, Senate Foreign Relations Committee Hearings on the Nomination of Richard Helms to be Ambassador to Iran, (Washington, D.C.: Government Printing Office, 1973), p. 41.

11. Phoumi Vongvichit, Laos and the Victorious Struggle of the Lao People, p. 40.

12. Johnathan Mirsky and Steve Scofield, "The United States in Laos," in Friedman and Selden, America's Asia, p. 253-256.

13. Phoumi Vongvichit, Laos and the Victorious Struggle of the Lao People, pp. 44-45.

14. Ibid, p. 57.

15. Ibid, pp. 54-55.

16. Marek Thee, Notes of a Witness: Laos and the Second Indochina War, (New York: Vintage Books, 1973), pp. 40-41.

17. David Wise and Thomas Ross, The Invisible Government, (New York: Random House, 1964), p. 4.

18. J. William Fulbright, The Arrogance of Power, (New York: Knopf, 1966), p. 115.

19. Walt Haney, "The Pentagon Papers and U.S. Involvement in Laos," in Chomsky and Zinn, eds., The Pentagon Papers, p. 251.

20. John Lewallen, "The Reluctant Counterinsurgents: International Voluntary Services in Laos," in Adams and McCoy, Laos: war and Revolution, p. 357.

21. Dan Blackburn, "An Interview with Dr. John A. Hannah, Administrator of U.S.A.I.D.," in Adams and McCoy, Laos: War and Revolution, p. 408.

22. Phoumi Vongvichit, Laos and the Victorious Struggle of the Lao People, pp. 78-81.

260

23. Ibid, pp. 79-80.
24. Marek Thee, Notes of a Witness, p. 35.
25. Ibid, p. 39.
26. Ibid, pp. 38-40.
27. Walt Haney, "The Pentagon Papers and U.S. Involvement in Laos," in Chomsky and Zinn, The Pentagon Papers, p. 235.
28. Fred Branfman, "The President's Secret Army," in Robert C. Borosage and John Marks, eds., The C.I.A. File, (New York: Grossman Publishers, 1976), p. 48.
29. Charles Stevenson, The End of Nowhere: American Policy Towards Laos Since 1954, (Boston: Beacon Press, 1972), p. 20.
30. Walt Haney, "The Pentagon Papers and U.S. Involvement in Laos," in Chomsky and Zonn, The Pentagon Papers, p. 250.
31. Marek Thee, Notes of a Witness, p. 46.
32. Walt Haney, "The Pentagon Papers and U.S. Involvement in Laos," in Chomsky and Zinn, The Pentagon Papers, p. 252.
33. Ibid, p. 257.
34. Ibid, p. 254.
35. Ibid, p. 257.
36. Arthur Dommen, Conflict in Laos: The Politics of Neutralization, (New York: Praeger, 1965), p. 133.
37. Walt Haney, "The Pentagon Papers and U.S. Involvement in Laos," in Chomsky and Zinn, The Pentagon Papers, p. 252.
38. Phoumi Vongvichit, Laos and the Victorious Struggle of the Lao People, p. 47.
39. Committee of Concerned Asian Scholars, The Indochina Story, p. 47.
40. United States Senate, Senate Staff Report for the Committee on U.S. Security Agreements and Commitments abroad, (Washington, D.C.: Government Printing Office, 1971), p.3.
41. Phoumi Vongvichit, Laos and the Victorious Struggle of the Lao People, p. 75.
42. United States House of Representatives, Third Report of the Committee on Government Operations: U.S. Economic

Assistance for Laos Stabilization Programs, Washington, D.C.: Government Printing Office, 1971).
43. David Wise and Thomas Ross, The Invisible Government, p. 151. Arthur Dommen, Conflict in Laos, p. 140.
45. David Wise and Thomas Ross, The Invisible Government, p. 149.
46. Walt Haney, "The Pentagon Papers and U.S. Involvement in Laos," in Chomsky and Zinn, The Pentagon Papers, p. 259.
47. Ibid.
48. David Wise and Thomas Ross, The Invisible Government, p. 151.
49. Ibid.
50. Ibid.
51. Walt Haney, "The Pentagon Papers and U.S. Involvement in Laos," in Chomsky and Zinn, The Pentagon Papers, p. 260.
52. Charles Stevenson, The End of Nowhere, p. 119.
53. Walt Haney, "The Pentagon Papers and U.S., Involvement in Laos," in Chomsky and Zinn, The Pentagon Papers, p. 262.
54. Ibid, p. 263.
55. Ibid, p. 262.
56. Marek Thee, Notes of a Witness, p. 257.
57. Roger Hillsman, To Move a Nation, (New York: Dell Publishing Company, 1967), p. 153.
58. Wilfred Burchett, The Second Indochina War, (New York: International Publishers, 1970), p. 153.
59. Wilfred Burchett, The Second Indochina War, p. 153.
60. Ibid, p. 155.
61. Paul N. McCloskey, Jr., Truth and Untruth: Political Deceit in America, (New York: Simon and Schuster, 1972), pp. 173-75.
62. Ibid, pp. 93-94.
63. Fred Branfman, "Presidential War in Laos, 1964-1970," in Adams and McCoy, Laos: War and Revolution, pp. 216-218.
64. Walt Haney, "The Pentagon Papers and U.S. Involvement in Laos," in Chomsky and Zinn, The Pentagon Papers, p. 270.

262

65. Noam Chomsky and Edward Herman, After the Cataclysm, p. 12.
66. Ibid, p. 122.
67. Paul McCloskey, Truth and Untruth, p. 122.
68. Ibid, p. 123.
69. Ibid, pp. 126-135.
70. Ibid, p. 135.
71. Wilfred Burchett, The Second Indochina War, p. 172.
72. Fred Branfman, Voices From the Plain of Jars: Life Under Airwar, (New York: Harper and Row, 1972), pp. 17-20.
73. Christopher Robbins, Air America, (New York: G.P. Putman's Sons, 1979), pp. 136-137.
74. Fred Branfman, "The President's Secret Army," in Borosage and Marks, The CIA File, p. 56.
75. United States Senate, Senate Staff Report on Security Agreements and Commitments Abroad, p. 1.
76. Ibid, p. 6.
77. United States Senate, Subcommittee on United States Security Agreements and Commitments Abroad Hearings, (Washington, D.C.: Government Printing Office, 1969), p. 552.
78. United States Senate, Subcommittee to Investigate Problems Connected with Refugees and Escapees: War Related Civilian Problems in Indochina, Part II: Laos and Cambodia, (Washington, D.C.: Government Printing Office, 1971), p. 132.
79. Fred Branfman, "The Secret Wars of the C.I.A.," in Howard Frazier, ed., Uncloaking the C.I.A., (New York: Free Press, 1978), p. 93.
80. United States Senate, Subcommittee on United States Security Agreements and Commitments Abroad, p. 540.
81. Christopher Robbins, Air America, p. 236.
82. William E. Colby, Honorable Men: My Life in the CIA, (New York: Simon and Schuster, 1978), pp. 201-202.
83. Christopher Robbins, Air America, p. 237.
84. Ibid, Chapter 9.

85. David Feingold, "Opium and Politics in Laos," in Adams and McCoy, Laos: War and Revolution, p. 339.
86. Christopher Robbins, Air America, p. 191.
87. Ibid.
88. Fred Branfman, "The President's Secret Army," in Borosage and Marks, The C.I.A. File, p. 77.
89. United States Senate, Subcommittee to Investigate War Related Civilian Problems in Indochina, p. 127.
90. Walt Haney, "The Pentagon Papers and U.S. Involvement in Laos," in Chomsky and Herman, The Pentagon Papers, p. 268.
91. Ibid, p. 272.
92. Ibid, p. 277.
93. Fred Branfman, "Beyond the Pentagon Papers: The Pathology of Power," in Chomsky and Zinn, The Pentagon Papers, pp. 303-304.
94. Ibid, p. 303.
95. United States Senate, Subcommittee to Investigate War Related Civilian Problems in Indochina, p. 127.
96. Fred Branfman, "Beyond the Pentagon Papers," in Chomsky and Zinn, The Pentagon Papers, p. 304.
97. Walt Haney, "The Pentagon Papers and U.S. Involvement in Laos," on Chomsky and Zinn, The Pentagon Papers, p. 278.
98. United States Senate, Subcommittee to Investigate War Related Civilian Problems in Indochina, p. 127.
99. Walt Haney, "The Pentagon Papers and U.S. Involvement in Laos," in Chomsky and Zinn, The Pentagon Papers, p. 278.
100. Chou Norindi, "Political Institutions of the Lao People's Democratic Republic," in Martin S. Fox, ed., Contemporary Laos: Studies in the Politics and Society of the Lao People's Democratic Republic, (New York: St. Martin's Press, 1983), pp. 39-61.
101. Fred Branfman, Voices From the Plain of Jars, p. x.
102. Ibid, p. xi.
103. Chanda Nayan, "Economic Changes in Laos, 1975-1980," in Martin Fox, Contemporary Laos, pp. 116-117.

264

104. Noam Chomsky and Edward Herman, After the Cataclysm, p. 119.
105. Ibid, p. 120.
106. Ibid, p. 123.
107. Ibid, p. 124.
108. Ibid, pp. 127-128.
109. Ibid, p. 129.
110. Ibid, p. 130.
111. Ibid, pp. 127-129.
112. Noam Chomsky, "Introduction," in Adams and McCoy, Laos: War and Revolution, p. xxi.
113. Ibid,
114. Bernard J. Van-es-Beeck, "Refugees from Laos, 1975-1979," in Martin Fox, Contemporary Laos, pp. 324-334.
115. Committee for Co-ordination of Services to Displaced Persons in Thailand, The Refugee Services Handbook, (Bangkok, 1982), p. 3.
116. Ibid, pp. 3-4.

Notes
CHAPTER III

1. University of Oregon, Atlas of Oregon, (Eugene: University of Oregon Books, 1976), p. 19.
2. Robert Proudfoot, "Unpublished Census; Laotian Community of Eugene-Springfield," Fieldwork, 1983.
3. Frank LeBar and Adrianne Suddard, Laos: Its People, Its Society, Its Culture, (New Haven: Hraf Press, 1960), p. 18.
4. Keith Putnam, Letter to service providers and refugees, Oregon Department of Human Resources: Adult and Family Services Division, Public Services Building, Salem, Oregon, April 1, 1982.
5. Jaqui Chagnon and Roger Rumph, "Education: The Prerequisite to Change in Laos," in Martin Fox, Contemporary Laos, p. 167.

6. Frank LeBar and Adrianne Suddard, Laos: Its People, Its Society, Its Culture, p. 180.
7. Jamake Highwater, The Primal Mind: Vision and Reality in Indian America, (New York: New American Library, 1982), p. 6.
8. David Kenzie, et al., A Vietnamese Depression Rating Scale: Development and Validation, (Portland: University of Oregon Health Sciences Center, 1981).
9. Paulo Freire, Pedagogy of the Oppressed, (New York: The Seabury Press, 1970), p. 5.
10. Upton Sinclair, The Goosestep: A Study of American Education, (Pasadena: A.M.S. Press, 1923), p. 28.
11. Johnathan Kozol, The Night Is Dark and I Am Far From Home, (Boston: Houghton Mifflin Co., 1980), p. 10.
12. Ibid, pp. 172-174.
13. Ibid, p. 55.

Bibliography

Adams, Nina, and McCoy, Alfred. Laos: War and Revolution. New York: Harper and Row, 1970.
Angell, R. The Family Encounters the Depression. New York: Charles Scribner's Sons, 1936.
Bain, R. "The Validity of Life Histories and Diaries." Journal of Educational Sociology 3 (1929):150-164.
Banks, David, ed. Changing Identities in Southeast Asia. Paris: Mouton, 1976.
Becker, H.S. "The Life History and the Scientific Mosaic." Sociological Work. Chicago, 1976.
_____, and Greer, B. "Participant Observation and Interviewing." Human Organization, (1957):16.
Berger, P., and Luckman, T. The Social Construction of Reality. New York: Doubleday, 1967.
Bernstein, Basil, ed. Primary Socialization, Language, and Education. London: Routledge and K. Paul, 1970.

266

Boas, Franz (Helen Codere, ed.). Kwakiutl Ethnography. Chicago: University of Chicago Press, 1966.

Boggs, Joan, Gallimore, Ronald, & Jordan, Cathie. Culture, Behavior, and Education: A Study of Hawaiian-Americans. Beverly Hills, CA: Sage Publishing Co., 1974.

Borosage, Robert, & Marks, John. The C.I.A. File. New York: Grossman Press, 1976.

Branfman, Fred. Voices from the Plain of Jars: Life Under an Air War. New York: Harper and Row, 1973.

Brislin, Richard, & Van Buren, H. "Can they Come Home Again?" International Education and Cultural Exchange (September 1974):19-24.

Bruyn, Severyn T. "The Methodology of Participant Observation." Educational Patterns and Cultural Configurations: The Anthropology of Education (Roberts, Joan, and Akinsanya, S. K., eds.). New York: David McKay, Inc., (1976):264-274.

Buchanan, Keith. The Southeast Asian World. New York: Taplinger Publishing Co., 1967.

Burchett, Wilfred. The Fugitive War: The United States in Laos and Vietnam. New York: International Publishing Co. 1963.

_____. The Second Indochina War. New York: International Publishing Co., 1970.

Campbell, D. "Qualitative Knowing in Action Research." The Social Contexts of Method (Brenner, M., and Marsh, R.) New York: St. Martins Press, 1978.

Carnoy, Martin. Education as Cultural Imperialism. New York: David McKay, Inc., 1974.

Chagnon, Napolean. The Yanamamo: The Fierce People. New York: Holt, Rheinhart, and Winston, 1968.

Champassak, Sisouk-Na. Storm Over Laos. New York: Praeger, 1961.

Chomsky, Noam. At War with Asia: Essays on Indochina. New York: Vintage Books, 1970.

_____, & Herman, Edward. After the Cataclysm: Postwar Indochina and the Reconstruction of

Imperial Ideology: The Political Economy of Human Rights, v.
2. Boston: South End Press, 1979.
_____. The
Washington Connection and Third World Fascism: The
Political Economy of Human Rights, v. 1. Boston: South End
Press, 1979.
Chomsky, Noam, & Zinn, Howard. The Pentagon Papers,
Senator Gavel Edition, v. 5. Boston: Beacon Press, 1972.
Cohen, Ely. "Parental Factors in Educational Mobility."
Sociology of Education 38(1965:404-425.
Cohen, Yenhudi. "The State System of Schooling and
Cognitive and Motivational Patterns." Social Forces and
Schooling (Shimahara, Nobuo, and Slupuski, Adam, eds.) New
York: David McKay, Inc., 1975.
_____. "The Shaping of Men's Minds: Adaptations
to the Imperatives of Culture." Anthropological Perspectives
on Education (Murray, L., and Diamond, Stanley, eds.) New
York: Basic Books, 1971.
Colby, William. Honorable Men: My Life in the C.I.A. New
York: Simon and Schuster, 1978.
Colclough, Christopher. "Basic Education: Samson or Delilah?"
Convergence 9 (1976):48-63.
Coles, R. Privileged Ones. Boston: Little, Brown, and Co.,
1977.
Committee for Co-ordination of Services to Displaced Persons.
Handbook: Refugee Services in Thailand. Bangkok: CCSDP
Resource Center, 1982.
Committee of Concerned Asian Scholars. The Indochina Story:
A Fully Documented Account. New York: Pantheon, 1970.
Coolidge, Harold, J., & Roosevelt, Theodore. Three
Kingdoms of Indochina. New York: Crowell Press, 1933.
Coppa, Frank, and Curran, Thomas. The Immigrant Heritage of
the United States of America. boston: Twayne Publishers,
1929.
Cushing, Frank. "My Adventures in Zurri." Century Illustrated
Monthly Magazine 25:2, (December, 1882):206.

Decornoy, Jacques. "Laos: The Forgotten War." Bulletin of Concerned Asian Scholars. New York: 1970.

Denzin, K. The Research Act. New York: McGraw Hill, 1978.

Diamond, Stanley. Primitive Views of the World. New York: Columbia University Press, 1960.

Dollard, John. Caste and Class in a Southern Town. New York: Doubleday and Co., 1957.

Dommen, Arthur J. Conflict in Laos: The Politics of Neutralization. New York: Praeger, 1965.

Douglas, John. Investigative Social Research. Beverly Hills, CA: Sage Publishing Co., 1976.

DuVignaud, Jean. Change at Shebika: Report from a North African Village. Austin: University of Texas Press, 1970.

Edgerton, Robert. Methods and Styles in the Study of Culture. San Francisco: Chandler and Sharpe, 1974.

Ellsberg, Daniel. Papers on the War. Beverly Hills, CA: Sage Publishing Co., 1972.

Frazier, Howard. Uncloaking the C.I.A. Houston: Free Press, 1978.

Freilich, Morris. Marginal Natives at Work: Anthropologists in the Field. Cambridge, MA; Shenkman Publishing Co., 1977.

Freire, Paulo. "By Learning they Can Teach." Convergence, 6:1 (1973):78-84.

_____. Cultural Action for Freedom. Cambridge, MA: Harvard Educational Review and Center for the Study of Development and Social Change (Monograph Series no. 1), 1970.

_____. Pedagogy of the Oppressed. New York: Herder and Herder, 1976.,

_____. The Political Literacy Process: A n Introduction. Geneva: 1970.

_____. "To the Co-ordinator of a Cultural Circle." Convergence 4:1 (1971):61-62.

269

Friedman, Edward, and Seldon, Mark. America's Asia: Dissenting Essays on Asian-American Relations. New York; Vintage Press, 1971.

Fulbright, William J. The Arrogance of Power. New York: Knopf Publishers,1966.

Gamio, Manual. The Life Story of the Mexican Immigrant. New York: Dover Publications, 1971.

Geertz, Clifford. "From the Native's Point of View: On the Nature of Anthropological Understanding." Interpretative Social Science (Rabinow, P., and Sullivan, W., eds.) Berkeley: University of California Press, 1979.

Georges, R., & Jones, J. People Studying People: The Human Element in Fieldwork. Berkeley: University of California Press, 1980.

Glazier, Nathan, & Moynihan, Patrick. Beyond the Melting Pot: The Negros, Jews, Puerto Ricans, Italians, and Irish in New York City. Cambridge, MA: Massachusetts Institute of Technology Press, 1963.

Goldstein, Kenneth. A Guide for Fieldworkers in Folklore. Hatboro, PA: Folklore Association, 1964.

Gordon, Milton. Assimilation in American Life: The Role of Race, Religion, and National Origins. New York: Oxford University Press, 1964.

Hall, Edward. The Silent Language. Garden City, NJ: Doubleday and Co., 1959.

_____. The Hidden Dimension. Garden City, NJ: Doubleday and Co., 1966.

Halpern, Joel. Government, Politics, and Social Structure in Laos. New Haven: Yale New Haven Press, 1964.

_____. The Lao Elite: A Study of Tradition and Innovation. Santa Monica, CA: Rand Corporation, 1960.

Handlin, Oscar. The Uprooted. Boston: Little, Brown, and Co., 1951.

Henry, Jules. "Attitude Organization in Elementary School Classrooms." Schooling in the Cultural Context: Anthropological Studies of Education (Roberts, J., and

270

Akinsanya, S. K., eds.) New York: David McKay, Inc., 1976:169-182.

Henry Jules. Culture Against Man. New York: Random House, 1963.

_____. Jules Henry on Education. New York: Vintage Books, 1972.

Hersh, Seymour. Chemical and Biological Warfare. Indianapolis: Bobbs-Merrill, 1968.

Higham, John. Send them to Me: Jews and Other Immigrants in Urban America. New York: Atheneum, 1975.

_____. Strangers in the Land. New York: Atheneum, 1963.

Highwater, Jamake. The Primal Mind: Vision and Reality in Indian America. New York: New American Library, 1982.

Hillsman, Roger. To Move a Nation. New York: Dell Publishing Co., 1967.

Honigman, J. "The Personal Approach in Cultural Anthropological Research." Current Anthropology 17:2, (1976):243-261.

Hraba, Joseph. American Ethnicity. Illinois: Peacock Publishers, 1979.

Hymes, Dell. "Qualitative Research Methodologies in Education: A Linguistic Perspective." Anthropology and Education Quarterly 3:3, (August, 1977), 165-176.

_____. "What is Ethnography?" Sociolinguistics Working Paper #45. Austin: Southwest Educational Development Laboratory, 1978.

Jones, M. A. American Immigration. Chicago: University of Chicago Press, 1960.

Kaplan, Abraham. The Conduct of Inquiry: Methodology for Behavioral Science. San Francisco: Chandler Publishing Co., 1964.

Kimball, Solon T. Culture and the Educative Process. New York: Teacher's College Press, 1974.

Kenzie, David, et al. A Vietnamese Depression Rating Scale: Development and Validation. Portland, OR: University of Oregon Health Sciences Center, 1981.

Kozol, Jonathan. Death at an Early Age. New York: Bantham Books, 1967.

_____. The Night Is Dark and I Am Far From Home. New York: Bantham Books, 1976.

Kraus, Michael. Immigration: The American Mosaic. Princeton, NJ: Van Nostrand and Co., 1966.

Langer, Paul, and Zasloff, Joseph. Revolution in Laos: The North Vietnamese and the Pathet Lao. Santa Monica, CA: Rand Corporation, 1969.

"Laos: The Labyrinthine War." Far Eastern Economic Review. April 16, 1970.

"Laos Rides Out the Storms." Southeast Asia Chronicle. June, 1980:1-32.

Lasch, Christopher. The Culture of Narcissism: American Life in an Age of Diminishing Expectations. New York: W. W.

Lebar, Frank, & Suddard, Adrianne. Laos: Its People, Its Society, Its Culture. New Haven: Hraf Press, 1960.

Liff, Mark. "Indochinese Refugees: The Newest Americans." American Education, July, 1980.

Lipsit, Seymour. "The Biography of a Research Project." Sociologists at Work: Essays on the Craft of Social Research (Hammond, Phillip, ed.) New York: Basic Books, 1964.

Lofland, John. Analyzing Social Settings: A Guide to Qualitative Observation and Analysis. Belmont, CA: Wadsworth Publishing Co., 1971.

Lowie, Robert. Robert H. Lowie Ethnologist: A Personal Record. Berkeley: University of California Press, 1959.

Luangprasuet, Khamchong. "American Cross-Cultural Information." United States Catholic Conference Newsletter, 1:8, (July, 1982).

Malinowski, Bronislaw. The Sexual Lives of Savages in Northwestern Melanesia: An Ethnographic Account of Courtship, Marriage, and Family Life Among the Natives of

272

the Trobriand Islands. New York: New Guinea Eugenics Publishing Co., 1929.

McCloskey, Paul. Truth and Untruth: Political Deceit in America. New York: Simon and Schuster, 1972.

Marin, Peter. "Rerunning the War." Mother Jones, 8:9, (November, 1983):11-29.

Mausemann, Vandra. "Anthropological Approaches." Comparative Education Review, (October, 1976):368-380.

Mead, Margaret. Coming of Age in Samoa. New York: W. Morrow and Co., 1928.

_____. An Anthropologist at Work: Writings of Ruth Benedict. Boston: Houghton Mifflin Co., 1959.

Melville, J., and Herskovits, Frances. Dahomean Narrative: A Cross-Cultural Narrative. Illinois: Northwestern University Press, 1958.

Ogbu, John. The Next Generation: An Ethnography of Education in an Urban Neighborhood. Berkeley: University of California Press, 1974.

Olson, Bonnie. "Women on the Nicaraguan Front." Northwest Passage, December 16, 1980.

Pelto, P., and Gretel, H. Anthropological Research: The Structure of Inquiry. New York: Cambridge University Press, 1978.

Proudfoot, Robert. "Unpublished Census: Laotian Community of Eugene-Springfield, Oregon." Fieldwork, 1983.

_____. Annual Lane Community College Refugee Program - Case Management: Report to Oregon Adult and Families Services. Eugene: Lane Community College, 1982.

Pullen, James, and Ryan, Rosemary. Labor Force Participation Among Newly Arrived Southeast Asian Refugees in the Portland Area. Portland: Portland State University Press, 1982.

Putnam, Keith. "Letter to Service Providers and Refugees." Salem, OR: Adult and Family Services Division, 1982.

Rabinow, Paul. Reflections on Fieldwork on Morocco. Berkeley: University of California Press, 1977.

Radin, P. The World of Primitive Man. New York: H. Shuman and Co., 1953.

Riis, Jacob. Battle With the Slum. New York: Charles Scribner and Sons, 1902.

_____. Children of the Poor. New York: Charles Scribner and Sons, 1892.

_____. How the Other Half Lives. New York: Charles Scribner and Sons, 1890.

Robbins, Christopher. Air America. New York: G. Putnam and Sons, 1971.

Rohner, Ronald. The Ethnography of Franz Boas: Letters and Diaries of Franz Boas Written on the Northwest Coast from 1886-1931. Chicago: University of Chicago Press, 1967.

Samarin, William. Field Linguistics: A Guide to Linguistic Fieldwork. New York: Holt, Rheinhart, and Winston, 1967.

Schusky, Ernest L. Manual for Kinship Analysis. New York: Holt, Rinehart, and Winston, 1965.

Sherman, Charles E. "Rationale for the Use of Ethnography in the study of Educational Problems." Center on Education, Development, and Research Quarterly 14:1, (Spring, 1981).

Shimara, Nobuo. "Cultural Evolution: Technology as a Converging Force." Social Forces and Schooling, (1975):15-48.

Sinclair, Upton. The Goosestep: A Study of American Education. Pasadena, CA: A.M.S. Press, 1923.

Solomon, Barbara. Ancestors and Immigrants. Boston: Harvard University Press, 1956.

Southeast Asia Chronicle. "Laos Rides Out the Storms." 73 (June, 1980).

Spaulding, Seth. The World's Students in the United States: A Review and Evaluation of Research on Foreign Students. New York: Praeger, 1976.

Spindler, George D. "Village or City?: Identity, Choice, and Cultural Change." Schooling in Cultural Context. New York: David McKay, Inc., 1976:114-129.

274

_____. Being an Anthropologist: Fieldwork in Eleven Cultures. New York: Holt, Rheinhart, and Winston, 1970.

Spradley, James, and McCurdy, David. The Cultural Experience: Ethnography in a Complex Society. Chicago: Chicago Science research Association, 1972.

Spradley, James. The Ethnographic Interview. New York: Holt, Rheinhart, and Winston, 1979.

_____. Participant Observation. New York: Holt, Rheinhart, and Winston, 1980.

Stanley, M. "Literacy: The Crisis of Conventional Wisdom." Convergence 6:1, (1974).

Stevenson, Charles. The End of Nowhere: American Policy Towards Laos Since 1954. Boston: Beacon Press, 1972.

Stuart-Fox, Martin, ed. Contemporary Laos. New York: St. Martins Press, 1984.

Taylor, Philip. The Distant Magnet: European Immigration to the United States of America. New York: Harper and Row, 1971.

Thee, Marek. Notes of a Witness: Laos and the Second Indochina War. New York: Vintage Press, 1973.

Toye, Hugh. Buffer State or Battle Ground? New York, 1968.

United States Department of Health and Human Services. Report to Congress: Refugee Resettlement Program. Washington, D.C.: Social Security Administration, 1983.

United States Department of State. Laos Fact Sheet; Mutual Security in Action. Washington, D.C.: Government Printing Office, 1959.

United States House of Representatives, Committee of Foreign Affairs. Mutual Security Program in Laos: Hearings Before the Subcommittee on the Far East and Pacific. (85th Congress, 2nd Session, May 7, 8, 1958) Washington, D.C.: Government Printing Office, 1958.

United States Committee for Refugees. 1981 World Refugee Survey. New York: U.S.C.R., 1982.

United States Department of State. Country Reports on the World Refugee Situation: Report to Congress. Washington, D.C.: Office of the Co-ordinator for Refugee Affairs, 1981.

United States House of Representatives. Third Report of the Committee on Government Operations: U.S. Economic Assistance for Laos: Stabilization Programs, 1971. Washington, D.C.: Government Printing Office, 1971.

United States Senate. Foreign Relations Committee Hearings on the Nomination of Richard Helms to be Ambassador to Iran. washington, D.C.: Government Printing Office, 1973.

United States Senate. Staff Report for the Subcommittee on U.S. Security Agreements and Commitments Abroad. Washington, D.C.: Government Printing Office, 1971.

United States Senate. Subcommittee on U.S. Security Agreements and Commitments Abroad Hearings (October 20, 21, 22, 28, 1971) Washington, D.C.: Government Printing Office, 1971.

United States Senate. Subcommittee on the U.S. Security Agreements and Commitments Abroad Hearings: Activities of U.S.A.I.D. in Laos (April, 1972). Washington, D.C.: Government Printing Office, 1972.

United States Senate. Subcommittee to Investigate Problems connected with Refugees and Escapees: War Related Civilian Problems in Indochina, Part II: Laos and Cambodia. (April, 1971) Washington, D.C.: Government Printing Office, 1971.

University of Oregon, Atlas of Oregon. Eugene: University of Oregon Books, 1976.

Vongvichit, Phoumi. Laos and the Victorious Struggle of the Lao People Against U.S. Neo-Colonialism. Vientiane: Neo Lao Haksat Publications, 1960.

Whiteside, Thomas. Defoliation. New York: Ballantine Books, 1970.

Whyte, W. F. "Interviewing in Field Research." Human Organization Research (Adams, R. H., and Preiss, J., eds.) Homewood, IL: Dorsey Press, 1960.

276

Wise, David, and Ross, Thomas. The Invisible Government. New York: Random House, 1964.

Wolcott, Harry. "Criteria for an Ethnographic Approach to Research in Schools." Human Organization 34 (1975):111-127.

_____. "Teachers v. Technocrats: An Educational Innovation in Anthropological Perspective. Eugene, OR: Center for Educational Policy and Management, 1977.

Wolf, R. L. Strategies for Conducting Naturalistic Evaluation in Socio-Educational Settings: The Naturalistic Interview. Michigan: Western Michigan University Evaluation Center, 1979.

Ziegler, S. "School for Life: The Experience of Italian Immigrants in Canadian Schools." Human Organization 38:3, (1980).